WOMEN WHO WORK

WOMEN
WHO
WORK
(aint Me!)

Rewriting the Rules for Success

IVANKA TRUMP

Portfolio / Penguin

PORTFOLIO / PENGUIN
An imprint of Penguin Random House LLC
375 Hudson Street
New York, New York 10014
penguin.com

Hand-lettered illustrations by Viv Jordan

Library of Congress Cataloging-in-Publication Data
Names: Trump, Ivanka, 1981– author.
Title: Women who work : rewriting the rules for success / Ivanka Trump.
Description: New York, NY : Portfolio, [2017]
Identifiers: LCCN 2016049443 | ISBN 9780735211322 (hardcover) |
ISBN 9780735211339 (e-book) | ISBN 9780735216785 (international edition)
Subjects: LCSH: Women—Vocational guidance. | Career development. |
Work-life balance. | Success in business. | Success.
Classification: LCC HF5382.6 .T78 2017 | DDC 650.1082—dc23
LC record available at https://lccn.loc.gov/2016049443

Printed in the United States of America
1   3   5   7   9   10   8   6   4   2

Designed by Amy Hill and Cassandra Garruzzo

While the author has made every effort to provide accurate telephone numbers, Internet
addresses, and other contact information at the time of publication, neither the publisher
nor the author assumes any responsibility for errors or for changes that occur after
publication. Further, publisher does not have any control over and does not assume any
responsibility for author or third-party Web sites or their content.

To Jared, Arabella, Joseph, and Theodore,

*for your unconditional love and unending support.
Thank you for pushing me to be a better wife, mother,
and advocate for women everywhere.*

*To the women who've contributed their voices to
this conversation,*

this book is for you.

Contents

Preface

At the time I was writing this book, my father was running for president of the United States. My manuscript was completed before we knew the results of the election. As I write this preface, my father's inauguration is only days away. These last nineteen months have been an amazing journey—and it's just getting started.

Inspiring and empowering women who work—at all aspects of their lives—has been my mission throughout my entire career. Today, I have the opportunity to take that work to new heights and advocate for change on a far greater scale than I'd ever imagined.

Over the last year and a half, I've had the honor of traveling across our country, meeting the men and women of our great nation and listening to their hopes and dreams, their challenges and concerns. I have grown tremendously as a person, and the experience has been life changing.

In these weeks following the election, I have been grateful for the overwhelming amount of outreach I've received from people across America who have shared their stories and offered to extend their ideas and expertise in the areas I am deeply passionate about, including the education and economic empowerment of women and girls; leveling the playing field for female entrepreneurs and job creators; and advancing the potential of women in our economy.

When my father takes office as our nation's forty-fifth president, I will take a formal leave of absence from both The Trump Organization and my apparel and accessories brand. On paper, this separation is straightforward, but emotionally, this was not an easy decision for me to make. I have known since I was a child that I wanted to be a developer and an entrepreneur. It is difficult to step away from businesses that I have worked hard to build and that I believe in so fully, but the potential to improve the lives of countless women and girls has caused me to fundamentally consider where my work will do the greatest good.

I recognize the privilege and responsibility I have to use my voice to make positive impact where I can. I am committed to working harder than ever to help unleash the full power of women and girls to accelerate the pace of progress both in our country and around the world—and I look forward to furthering the cause together.

IVANKA

DEFINE SUCCESS ON YOUR OWN TERMS, **ACHIEVE** IT BY your OWN RULES & **BUILD** A LIFE YOU'RE PROUD to LIVE.

ANNE SWEENEY

Women Who Work

Rewriting the Rules for Success

W arm scarf wrapped tightly around my neck, I carried everything I needed on my back. Around mile three of the eighthour hike through Patagonia, I paused to take in the incredible view that stretched before me: crystal blue water below, snowcovered peaks dotting the horizon. I felt calm and grateful that bright, frosty morning, a contrast to the uneasiness I felt in New York, which had prompted this life-changing journey.

I had just decided to leave the Brooklyn-based real estate company Forest City Ratner, my first employer and professional home of the previous twelve months, to take the leap and join our family business. I had always intended to work at another firm for a while, to gather experience from a different perspective, and then to join my father and brother at The Trump Organization. But as the day approached, my mind swam with questions prompted by the unknown. I knew from working at Forest City that I loved real estate and had the potential to excel. What I didn't know was what working with my family would be like. Could I thrive in an environment where there were such high expectations, tied to the most personal of relationships? Was this unequivocally what I wanted to be doing? What would happen if I performed poorly? Or what would happen if, in spite of excelling, there wasn't great professional chemistry?

I knew that family businesses, in general, tend to have binary outcomes. They either work incredibly well or are a total disaster. A meager 12 percent survive into the third generation, and I knew of some family ventures that had caused irreparable damage among parents, siblings, and grandparents. While I never questioned my passion for real estate or my love for my family, I was wrestling with whether the timing and the decision to combine them were right for me.

Women in real estate development were (and sadly still are) somewhat rare; perhaps some of my reservations stemmed from the fact that outside of my family's business, I'd only ever known of a handful of women at the highest ranks in their industries. The one who mattered most to me, of course, was and still is the most capable woman I know— my mother.

When I was eight or nine, I would sometimes accompany her on construction site visits to the iconic Plaza Hotel in New York. As the top executive in charge of its redevelopment, she would meticulously inspect each inch of the prior day's work—impeccably dressed, in full makeup and four-inch high heels—while I would run the hallways and explore the hotel. For me, it was great fun, but for my mother, it was all business. She had extraordinarily high expectations, not just for others but for herself, and people rose to the occasion. It was my mother, unapologetically feminine in a male industry, who first embodied and defined for me what it meant to be a multidimensional woman—a woman who works at all aspects of her life.

A world-class athlete (she was a member of the Czech Olympic ski team), she had three children in seven years *and* oversaw design and operations for many other significant real estate projects in addition to the Plaza. She ate breakfast with my brothers and me every morning, managed our schedules with careful attention to detail ("To keep your kids out of trouble, keep them busy," she loves to tell me now), and orchestrated her own schedule to maximize spending time with us. A fashion icon, the consummate hostess, and a lifelong entrepreneur, my mother is today "Glamma" to my kids and one of my greatest sources of support. By example, she taught me to define success on my own terms, to set my own priorities, and to be true to my values.

Now, as a wife, mother, and businesswoman myself, I understand that it wasn't nearly as easy for my mother as she made it look. Twenty-five years ago, it was an unspoken sign of weakness to admit you had passions or interests outside of work, especially if you were a woman. This was a critical time historically, when women were fighting for a place at the table. My brothers and I were lucky, as our mother was one of the few who were able to mix work and family. Most women weren't comfortable even discussing their marriages or their kids on the job. If she was employed outside the home, a woman was expected, like her male counterparts, to put work first, above all else. If she had children, or wanted children, she was told she *could* "have it all," but was never clearly shown how. As a result, some women backed away from demanding their fair share of opportunities and accolades, unclear how best to navigate their personal and professional dreams and ambitions.

I've often reflected upon that trip to Patagonia, as it captured a moment in time that was truly pivotal in shaping the rest of my life. As much as I wrestled then with the decision to join my family at The Trump Organization, it turns out that that soul-searching journey led me right where I belonged. Today, I'm an executive vice president at The Trump Organization, cofounder of Trump Hotels and Scion, and founder of my own eponymous fashion brand. Undeniably, one factor in my success has been the doors that my family's name and my privileged upbringing have opened. I'm deeply grateful for all the opportunities afforded to me, but they alone didn't guarantee my success. Curiosity, passion, hard work, and perseverance have enabled me to prove my value to myself and others beyond my surname. I don't take lightly the fact that I'm fortunate, and I try to give back in kind. My grandfather always told me, "To whom much is given, much is expected." I consider the position I'm in to be a great responsibility and one I intend to use wisely.

While we have made a lot of progress since my mother's generation, many of the realities these women faced are still a concern for us today. Too often, for reasons like a lack of flexibility or poor support at home and/or at work, women are talking themselves out of great opportunities. This is a crucial issue. Forty-seven percent of the U.S. workforce is made up of women; 70 percent of all mothers support ourselves or contribute financially to our family's bottom line; and 40 percent of American households have female primary breadwinners—yet we still say "working woman" as if she were an anomaly. We *never* say "working man." Typically, when the conversation turns to women and work, there's often still an ingrained negativity, a "you versus me" or an "us versus them" mentality. Instead of the conversation feeling inclusive and supportive of all women and their choices around life and work, the dialogue is often reduced to an outdated, one-dimensional expectation of what a "working woman" should do, how she should act, and what she should look like.

The time to change the narrative around women and work once and for all is long overdue; in fact, it's become my life's mission. The good news is that, for the first time in history, modern professional women, like you and me, are openly embracing the fact that our lives are multidimensional. We're owning who we are, endeavoring to become the best versions of ourselves inside and outside the office, and surrounding ourselves with people who support these goals. We're aspiring to do work that we love, work that inspires us, *and* we're pursuing our passions and unabashedly making them priorities. We're training for marathons and learning to code. We're planning adventures with our kids and weekend getaways with our friends. We are defining what it means to be a modern woman who works—for ourselves and our families, for the companies at which we're employed, for our culture at large, and for the generations to come.

Whether you are the founder of your own company or a stay-at-home mom, an assistant in a large corporation or a part-time freelancer working from home, I believe that, when it comes to women and work, there isn't one "right" answer. We are all trying to figure out how to create meaningful lives for ourselves and our families. What that looks like, and how to achieve it, is different for each and every one of us.

So why write a book about it? Because despite the many advancements women have made, we've still got a long way to go. Because I'm inspired to provide solutions that educate and empower women to be their best selves, both personally and professionally. Because I want my daughter's generation to think about work differently. Because I'm committed to inspiring women to redefine success according to what is important to each and every one of you—and encouraging you to design a life that honors your individual passions and priorities in a way only *you* can.

Like you, I'm a woman who works—at every aspect of my life.

WE ARE WOMEN WHO WORK—AT SEIZING OPPORTUNITIES

> The size of your dreams must always exceed your current capacity to achieve them. If your dreams do not scare you, they are not big enough.
>
> **—Ellen Johnson Sirleaf, president of Liberia**

For years, fashion brands portrayed the working woman as a one-dimensional, suit-clad caricature, striding down Fifth Avenue, briefcase in hand, a stern expression on her face. As a twenty-five-year-old woman, I found this image passé and completely unrelatable. A female ad executive would never have perpetuated such a dated stereotype; it seemed more likely that these campaigns were created by seventy-year-old men looking to sell women's work wear. The women I knew—my friends, my mentors, the women I worked with at The Trump Organization—weren't cold, stoic caricatures focused solely on their careers. They were smart and feminine; they had lives and passions outside of the office, and an interest in expressing their personalities through their fashion choices while still being appropriately dressed for work.

In fact, I had already taken a first step toward reimagining the options available to modern, self-purchasing women when in 2007 I launched my fine jewelry collection. I had been at The Trump Organization for about two years when I met a potential partner in real estate who had long-standing ties to the jewelry industry. Although I passed on the real estate deal this man showed me, we realized we shared a mutual interest: to create an alternative to the historically male-centric fine jewelry retail experience. Women were interested in buying jewelry for themselves—and were no longer waiting for a man to do it for them.

After launching the collection, I soon realized that beyond jewelry, there was an enormous disconnect between how professional women looked, how we lived, how we spent our time and sought to express ourselves, and the apparel and accessories that were available to us.

WE ARE WOMEN WHO WORK—AT GROWING BUSINESSES

After starting my fashion brand, it was exciting to see women on the street wearing my heels or carrying handbags from my collection. I was really proud of the fact that my collections captured a femininity and a sense of fashion that working women hadn't been able to express even just a decade before. My company was not just meeting the lifestyle needs of today's modern professional woman with versatile, well-designed products; it was *celebrating* those needs, at a price point she could afford.

My business was growing quickly, so I needed to assemble a top-notch team to help my company realize its full potential. I interviewed an exhaustive list of candidates, remarkable women who hailed from some of the best-known and most successful brands in the fashion and luxury goods industries. After assembling my team, we spent a lot of time together working to carefully formulate our brand's mission and clarify the ideals for which we wanted to be known: passion, optimism, and determination.

The more I spoke with people about our brand *and* our corporate culture, the more I realized that no one in the fashion or media industries was *engaging* our generation in a meaningful way, addressing our professional goals, ambitions, and aspirations.

WE ARE WOMEN WHO WORK—AT EMPOWERING ONE ANOTHER

Women leaders are moving toward being exactly who they are, at work, at home and in the world, without shame or regret. And this is a classic example of how to model success to others—by being happy with who we are internally, and showing that to the outside world.

—Elizabeth Cronise McLaughlin, executive coach
and founder of The Gaia Project for Women's Leadership

The Women Who Work initiative evolved very organically, from my personal experience, and from observing the women around me—my team, my friends, all the women I knew, who were working hard at their careers, their relationships, their families, and their passions outside of the office. We knew it was important that we communicate the right message, so we did what most businesses traditionally do at this point: we set up meetings with some of the top ad agencies in New York in search of a creative team who could develop some really strong ideas around the concept of "Women Who Work."

During the meetings—without fail—every man in the room (and they were mostly men) told us to drop the word "work" from our mission. They said "work" wasn't aspirational; it wasn't inspiring; it wasn't sexy. One firm suggested "Women Who Do" as an alternative, downplaying the professional tedium associated with "work."

My team and I realized not only did they not get it, but that, as it turned out, we didn't need their "expertise" or validation after all. *We* were the best at conceptualizing the message because we lived it. We knew our audience better than they did because we were members of that demographic—we were mostly millennials, single and married women, with and without kids—and we were *all* passionate about work. We *were* working to create the lives we wanted to live—lives we were proud of and that were uniquely ours—and we believed that there was really nothing more compelling than that.

We thanked the agencies for their time and, despite their recommendations to the contrary, stuck to our beliefs and launched Women Who Work. The rest is history. The message fuels our mission. It informs and inspires every decision our company makes. It's our guiding light.

In November 2014, we launched IvankaTrump.com and made it our goal to bring our brand to life in the digital space, giving millennial working women new content daily, including skill-building how-tos, profiles of industry leaders and rising stars, office-appropriate style stories, and life hacks for simplifying the day-to-day in general. We aimed to make our readers' lives more informed, meaningful, and true to their own individual versions of success. Shortly following the site launch, we unveiled the first #WomenWhoWork campaign, celebrating the different ways in which women are choosing to live—and work at—their lives. #WomenWhoWork became a movement, evolving into an incredible community of talented, curious, ambitious, passionate women, sharing their experiences and insights to move the narrative away from the outdated and ill-informed caricature of how we look, dress, act, work, and view our lives, to a place that's more positive, accurate, and inspiring.

WE ARE WOMEN WHO WORK—AT BEING WIVES, MOTHERS, LEADERS, AND ENTREPRENEURS

If family comes first, work does not come second. Life comes together.

—Anne-Marie Slaughter, president and CEO of New America and author of *Unfinished Business*

I believe that we each get one life and it's up to us to live it to the fullest. This concept is central to our mission. One life isn't just about trying to achieve balance (it doesn't exist!) or managing blended priorities; it's about acknowledging that the priorities that exist *outside* of our job descriptions are just as important to us as the work we do to support ourselves and our families—and just as worthy of our time and attention. Our identities are much more nuanced and complex than any one label could convey, and yet for decades, professional women were referred to only by their job titles; stay-at-home mothers, defined solely by their caregiving duties.

My team and I created the concept of the "extended job title" as an antidote to this oversimplification. An extended job title goes beyond what it says on your business card or who you're caring for at home to recognize more fully who you are as a whole person, and to include what matters most to you—inside and outside your place of employment. Here's a version of mine:

> I am a real estate developer and an entrepreneur. More important, I'm a wife and a mother. I design and build iconic properties all over the world; I have also created and am growing a business that seeks to inspire and empower women in all aspects of their lives. I'm busy teaching my children the value of hard work and the importance of family. I'm working on my cooking skills, planning date nights with my husband, and striving to improve as a runner.

We launched our Women Who Work campaign with a video featuring twelve inspiring women sharing the many things they were working at, both personally and professionally. They expanded their job titles to include the various roles they play that don't make it onto their résumés (sister, wife, friend) and the passions they pursue outside of the office (gardening, boxing, trapezing!), reflecting upon what it meant to each of them to be a "woman who works." My team and I weighed in with videos of our own and invited women everywhere to join the conversation by uploading selfie videos to social media channels, describing their extended job titles with the hashtag #WomenWhoWork.

One of the women featured on my site is Elizabeth Cronise McLaughlin, a respected executive coach and the founder of The Gaia Project for Women's Leadership. McLaughlin left a prestigious Wall Street law firm to start her consulting and coaching business, and she is also the mother of two young children. Of living one life, she says, "As female leaders, many of us have recognized that traditional notions of 'balance' or 'having it all' are impossible, given today's 24/7 work culture. However, as individuals, we are more and more frequently charting unique courses that uplift our values and lead us toward lives we love. . . . The new paradigm of women's leadership sees many of us asking, for the first time, to work in ways that respect the totality of our lives from a holistic level, and thereby to create lives that make us happy in all respects."

So, how to start living life to the fullest? First, you must redefine success. Apart from what society says makes you successful, or what your boss or your partner or even your best friend thinks, what does success mean to *you*?

Let's find out.

REDEFINING SUCCESS: WHAT MATTERS MOST?

> If you do work you love, and the work fulfills you, the rest
> will come.
>
> **—Oprah Winfrey**

It's only natural that, since work looks different to each of us, our goals, dreams, and definitions of success would vary, too.

For me, success means being an involved mother, a loving wife, *and* being incredibly committed to my work. As a result, it also means I go to bed much later and get up much earlier than I did before I had kids! My children are young; my fashion brand is thriving and constantly evolving; my role leading The Trump Organization grows larger and more exciting with each passing day. I'm in a unique place, where my life is both chaotic and amazing, and I wouldn't want it any other way.

Because my definition of a life well lived includes spending the mornings and evenings with my husband and kids, my schedule during the day is laser focused. The first thing I do when I arrive at the office, aside from inhaling a giant cup of coffee, is write down my three to five top priorities for the day, to keep me on task. I maximize my time with colleagues, attend meetings and return calls, visit Trump properties and development sites, do all those things that must be accomplished face-to-face between the hours of eight and six. The rest, I leave for later; I don't respond to e-mails that are not time sensitive during the course of the day. I save anything I can do from home for after my kids have gone to bed.

Technology, the ability to be connected 24/7, allows us to prioritize our families and stay on top of work. But that means work seeps into our home lives as we review presentation notes at the crack of dawn and pore over plans and spreadsheets long after the sun has set. Similarly, our personal lives are with us at the office: A FaceTime conversation with the kids after school. A text from a friend who is coming to town. The reminder that you forgot to reschedule your dentist appointment. The need to figure out what's for dinner—again.

For the modern working woman, this lack of compartmentalization between work and home has fostered greater authenticity, which is particularly important since in today's culture we're always on. As author and speaker Brené Brown writes, "Authenticity is not something we have or don't have. It's a practice—a conscious choice of how we want to live. . . . It's about the choice to show up and be real. The choice to be honest. The choice to let our true selves be seen." We may be wives, girlfriends, or mothers in addition to being employees or executives, but we're not donning different personas for the various roles we play throughout the day.

No one can know what success means to someone else. I know lots of people who are outwardly successful and inwardly miserable—to me, that's not success, but that's the path they've chosen, consciously or not. Success to me means setting goals that feel true to who you are, not trying to live up to the arbitrary bar that society sets for you or what anyone else thinks *should* matter to you. It's about accomplishing as many of your personal and professional goals as you can daily, and feeling fulfilled by your choices at work and at home.

As my mother told me, part of redefining success is knowing that what matters most to you can and will change over time. In a year or five, expect that what's most important to you now (likely other than your family) may be different. While I believe every woman should thoughtfully architect a life she'll love and actively work toward achieving her goals, we must also be flexible, adaptable, and realistic about the fact that our passions, interests, priorities, and relationships shift. Along with cementing the critical skills that are essential for any leader to thrive, in the pages that follow, I'll guide you through a framework for constructing a blueprint for your life that uniquely reflects what matters most to you, and is yours to modify as often as you feel the need.

All women benefit immeasurably by architecting their lives in a way that honors and supports their relationships and pursuits outside of work. Facebook COO and author of *Lean In* Sheryl Sandberg says of women who choose not to have children: "It's not only working parents who are looking for more hours in the day; people without children are also overworked, maybe to an even greater extent. When I was in business school, I attended a Women in Consulting panel. . . . After the [two] married women spoke about how hard it was to balance their lives, the single woman interjected that she was tired of people not taking her need to have a life seriously. She felt that her colleagues were always rushing off to be with their families, leaving her to pick up the slack."

Married mothers aren't the only ones in need of a rewrite to the rules for success. Most women have been characterized at some point or another by a stereotype: "married to her career," "soccer mom," "aspiring superwoman," "harried working mom," and so on. I have been all these things, but I'm not *one* of these things. Rather than be limited by a label, I encourage women, wherever they are in their careers, to prioritize building a life that's true to them and that honors their own individual passions and priorities.

> What is success? For me, success right now . . . is getting out of bed every day bringing 150% to this problem [financial literacy in America] and really trying to solve it, whether it takes five years or fifteen years or three decades. I don't know, but it gets my heart and soul every day. And the layering and complexity of having a great husband and daughter and figuring out how I make all that work, it's messy and chaotic, just like everything else, and I absolutely love it.

I think it really comes down to . . . what do you want to accomplish? And what do you want this all to look like? Once you really define that . . . then it's about focusing to make that mess happen.

—Alexa von Tobel, founder and CEO of LearnVest

YOUR MANUAL FOR ARCHITECTING THE LIFE YOU WANT TO LIVE

If you don't see a clear path for what you want, sometimes, you have to make it.

—Mindy Kaling, actress, comedian, and writer

I so respect the writers and thinkers whose books have spurred an essential dialogue on the particular challenges faced by women who work—*Unfinished Business* by Anne-Marie Slaughter, *Overwhelmed* by Brigid Schulte, and *Lean In* by Sheryl Sandberg are just a few. Inspired by these women—and bolstered by conversations I've had, and those happening around me—I've curated my best thinking, as well as that of so many others, in the pages of this book. I've gathered the most important and essential advice that we shared on IvankaTrump.com, plus my favorite books, TED Talks, podcasts, and other resources to help women come together to celebrate how we can achieve success on our own terms, measured by our own individual passions and priorities.

Ultimately, my hope for this book is that it will help our generation change the narrative around women and work, and embolden you to become a more enlightened leader who creates the life you want to live. It evolves my personal mission and that of the brand I've built into a new worldview—a one-life mentality—to aid you in navigating the different challenges and opportunities you face now, and in the years to come.

Organized around the arc of a woman's career—from identifying your passions early on to leading yourself, your team, and/or your company with purpose—each chapter will empower you to create the life you want to live:

Chapter One: Dream Big asks, What gets you out of bed in the morning? What lights you up? It delves into how and why it's essential to find your passion and tap it as inspiration in creating a life you love. Pinpointing your passions, prioritizing your goals, and uncovering your purpose, wherever you are in your career, will help you draft a road map for your life. Whenever you're feeling stuck, unsure, or conflicted about a situation, whether it's personal or professional, the passion framework presented in this chapter will help to guide your inner compass and either keep you on track or point you in an entirely new direction.

Chapter Two: Make Your Mark helps you to put your passions to work *at* work, by distinguishing yourself in your company and your industry through the three foundational spheres—communicating, connecting, and networking. From learning how to become a better listener to presenting like a pro in a public forum, connecting authentically with your team to bonding with your boss, fostering in-person relationships to inspiring a sponsor, maximizing these critical skills is essential to becoming a world-class leader.

Chapter Three: Stake Your Claim represents a turning point in your career. You've established yourself as a leader. Now it's time to step up to build and manage a top-notch team whose exceptional talents and multidimensional lives inspire you to lead laterally, versus top down. In this chapter, you'll also learn to set yourself apart as a master of negotiation—an essential skill in positively influencing the bigger picture of women and work—as well as to take charge of your own career by ramping up your professional development to break through the glass ceiling.

As you ascend the career ladder, the demands placed upon you will grow, and managing your life (your time, aspirations, and passions) becomes critical. **Chapter Four: Work Smarter, Not Harder** centers on prioritizing what matters most to you and guides you to thoughtfully allocate your time so you can live your life deliberately. The value of rest, the importance of creating mental space, and the brain-boosting benefit of hobbies are explored, as are the concepts of connecting with and centering yourself so that you learn to maximize your efficiency and boost your productivity, leaving time for what you really love to do.

Chapter Five: Tip the Scale centers on letting go of work/life balance by seizing memorable moments instead. When you're living one life, it's less about the pursuit of balance and more about seizing meaningful moments to ensure that your personal priorities are aligned with your professional goals. This chapter explores the importance of your partner and family and the need to prioritize work and family according to *your* values. Essential rules to support this include setting boundaries and being present, asking for flexibility, working remotely, creating memorable rituals, and crafting a family mission statement, among others.

Along with specific best practices that I've employed at my company, such as flexible work schedules, **Chapter Six: Lead with Purpose** enlists you to join the Women Who Work movement wherever you are in your life and help change the conversation yourself. The chapter shows how to foster environments that allow multidimensional women (and men) to thrive, developing a more positive and inclusive workplace while still creating high-performance expectations and a results-oriented culture.

This book includes my perspective and reflections on how to lead thoughtfully and well, knowing that our words and our actions affect not just those around us but also generations to come—those who will inhabit the corporations and build the businesses of tomorrow. It offers a hopeful, more authentic alternative to the way work has worked previously, one that is aligned with the ways in which modern women really live. And it suggests a framework to encourage you to determine what success means to you at various points in your life, and how that knowledge should inform your life's choices so that you may write and rewrite your own rules for success.

PASSION

COMES FROM *feeling* LIKE YOU ARE A *part* OF SOMETHING THAT YOU *believe* IN, SOMETHING *bigger* THAN *yourself*.

SIMON SINEK

CHAPTER ONE

Dream Big

Identify Your Passions to Create a Life You'll Love

Passion to me, and to many of the women I know, is our purpose, our reason for being. It's what infuses our lives with meaning, what keeps us engaged until after midnight and motivates us to get out of bed before sunrise. Passion is what makes us feel most alive.

My greatest passion is being a wife and a mother to my three children. I'm the first person they see in the morning, and the last to give kisses at night. Making sure I have uninterrupted time with my family before and after work during the week, and again on weekends, is a huge priority for me. My husband and I strive to keep Saturday and Sunday as unscheduled as possible; those two days are much less structured, so we're able to be totally focused on the kids and each other and more spontaneous with family time.

I'm also deeply passionate about being an entrepreneur, about identifying and seizing new opportunities. I love disrupting established industries, like hospitality and fashion, with a fresh vision, and bringing that perspective to businesses, like real estate, that I have loved for as long as I can remember. After years of hard work conceiving, planning, and developing a project, you can see, touch, and experience the tangible results of your efforts. Founding the Trump Hotels brand, growing its global footprint, and launching our newest venture, Scion, enable me to blend the best of what I love about the business.

I'm passionate about inspiring a community of women to come together and support one another's personal and professional choices, about providing empowerment through IvankaTrump.com and Women Who Work, and changing the conversation around work and women—to free us from dated stereotypes to pursue our passions so that we may all create the lives we want to live.

When it comes to business, whatever it is I'm doing, I'm incredibly dedicated to creating solutions for modern women who are living full, multidimensional lives.

My father has always said, if you love what you do, and work really, really hard, you will succeed. This is a fundamental principle of creating and perpetuating a culture of success, and also a guiding light for me personally.

I also believe that passion, combined with perseverance, is a great equalizer, more important than education or experience in achieving your version of success. I know plenty of brilliant people with immense potential who fell short of expectations (theirs and others'!) because their competition was more inspired to succeed. There are countless examples of industry legends who triumphed over their more seasoned or well-educated peers due to their single-mindedness, self-motivation, and enterprising nature. As Grammy Award–winning musician and Oscar-nominated actor Will Smith says, "I've never really viewed myself as particularly talented. Where I excel is ridiculous, sickening work ethic. . . . The only thing that I see that is distinctly different about me is: I'm not afraid to die on a treadmill. I will not be outworked, period. You might have more talent than me, you might be smarter than me, you might be sexier than me. You might be all of those things. You got it on me in nine categories. But if we get on the treadmill together, there's two things: You're getting off first, or I'm going to die. It's really that simple." Anyone who knows me knows that I will outwork anyone. No matter where you went to school, your diploma will take you only so far. If you are laser focused and fiercely devoted to your purpose, you are far more likely to succeed.

Passion has driven my career and is an important quality I look for in prospective employees, the first part of a trifecta that also includes a deep commitment to hard work and unflagging perseverance in the face of challenge. People who are enthusiastic, diligent, and committed to excellence almost always become highly successful; conversely, it's hard to be truly great at what you do if you aren't genuinely passionate about it.

PASSION EQUALS HAPPINESS

> The biggest mistake people make in life is not trying to make a living at doing what they most enjoy.
>
> —Malcolm Forbes, publisher of *Forbes* magazine

When we're passionate about something, we are engaged, fulfilled, *happy*—and, contrary to what our parents and their parents were taught, happiness begets success. "What we spend our time and mental energy focusing on can indeed become our reality," Shawn Achor, author of *The Happiness Advantage*, says. "New research in psychology and neuroscience shows that . . . we become more successful *when* we are happier and more positive."

People used to think that if they worked hard enough, they'd become successful; once they were successful, *then* they'd be happy. In fact, the opposite is true: when we are happy—when our mind-set and our mood are positive—we are smarter, more motivated, and more inclined to succeed. For example, as Achor notes, research shows that doctors in a positive mood made accurate diagnoses 19 percent more quickly; students who felt happier prior to taking math achievement tests far outperformed their neutral peers. Even optimistic salespeople outsold their pessimistic colleagues by 56 percent. Prior generations were told that happiness was a luxury worth delaying in favor of hard work; our generation intuitively understands that happiness begets success; we are committed to working hard and taking more risks (like venturing out on our own or joining a start-up rather than an established firm) so that we can enjoy our lives now—*and* later.

"It's really about following your gut and your heart and taking it to the next level. All I can attribute my success to, to date, is just working really hard at what I love, and continuing to push myself to ask questions and to be better at what I do every day," says Rachel Blumenthal, CEO and founder of Cricket's Circle and Rockets of Awesome. I believe that redefining success includes wanting to lead a good life today, not at some unnamed point in the future—to be both happy and thus successful.

"One of the biggest drivers of success is the belief that our behavior matters; that we have control over our future . . . [F]eeling that we are in control, that we are masters of our own fate at work and at home, is one of the strongest drivers of both well-being and performance," comments Shawn Achor. While there's plenty you *can't* control in your life, knowing what you love and what you're good at can help you create a life that prioritizes what makes you tick, helping you to succeed and feel more satisfied overall. Whether that means putting aside your nonurgent work after hours to have an adventure with your partner or getting away for a girls' weekend with friends, spending more quality time with your kids or learning to cook, having interests outside of your industry or profession matters greatly to your health and feelings of well-being. These passions and aspirations are just as important as your professional goals in redefining success according to what matters most to you; the key is to figure out how to prioritize them.

The elusive state of "being happy" has been reflected upon and debated by humankind for millennia; according to Achor, scientists define it as "pleasure combined with deeper feelings of meaning and purpose." The Greek philosopher Aristotle used the term *eudaimonia*, which translates to "human flourishing." *Women Who Work* not only embraces but celebrates the fact that work takes many forms. What inspires you may be very different from what motivates me; what's most important is that each of us becomes the best version of ourselves in the ways that honor our many and varied facets.

> Recognize the way that you want to compose your life. Don't accept anything else. You're going to have to work anyway, right? We're all working hard. So, we might as well work hard for something that is joyful and enriching . . . there's no "get-out-of-work-free" card.
>
> I'll tell you the thing that gets me up in the morning. What gets me up in the morning is I feel I have a meaningful

contribution to make to this world and that fires me up. That makes me feel alive. And being a mom . . . and recognizing this is an incredible privilege. I get to shape these little human beings and send them out into the world and I am not going to take that for granted for a second.

—**Dr. Nadine Burke Harris, CEO and founder of the Center for Youth Wellness**

Prioritize Your Passions by Being Proactive

Many think that happiness is to be found outside ourselves . . . but actually, happiness is something that comes from within.

—**The Dalai Lama**

Stephen Covey, the best-selling business author, often emphasizes the enormous value of being proactive. To a certain extent, we all know what "being proactive" means: it's the opposite of reactive. On one level, it means taking the initiative, creating opportunities that interest you, rather than sending out a résumé and waiting for the phone to ring. That *is* being proactive, but Covey takes it much further, espousing the value of proactivity in our lives at large and in every decision we make, from the slightest comment to the grandest gesture.

"Your life doesn't just 'happen,'" Covey argues. "Whether you know it or not, it is carefully designed by you. The choices, after all, are yours. You choose happiness. You choose sadness. You choose decisiveness. You choose ambivalence. You choose success. You choose failure. You choose courage. You choose fear. Just remember that every moment, every situation, provides a new choice. And in doing so, it gives you a perfect opportunity to do things differently to produce more positive results." *You choose.* When it comes to creating the life you want to live, consciously or not, you choose the kind of work you do, the character of the people who surround you, the type of organization to which you will or won't devote yourself, the sort of responses you have, positive or negative, effective or ineffective, to the challenges (big and small) life throws at you. You choose your words and your behaviors, even when you aren't thinking about them—what you say, how you say it, how you act.

Optimistic, proactive people speak positively of themselves and their capabilities—*I can, I plan to, I trust*. The opposite—negative people—are swayed by the external and are frequently victims of circumstance. You can spot them pretty easily by the language they choose—*I can't, I won't, I'm worried, the problem is*. Proactive people are passionate and productive; they focus their energies on the things they can influence and improve: their families, their health, their work. These issues are within their scope of command, and they attend to them because they are important to their lives.

My husband, Jared, is by far one of the most positive, proactive, and solution-oriented people I've ever met. He's incredibly pragmatic, always cool in the face of adversity; he finds it unproductive to focus on the problem (versus the solution) or to react emotionally. He's my greatest teacher in this regard, the calm, soothing voice of reason that guides me to focus on what matters most, even in moments of crisis or chaos, when I naturally tend to be a bit more emotional. When I have a lot of different stressors coming at me, he'll say, "Just take one thing at a time. Slow down and focus on what you have the ability to control. Focus on solutions."

Occasionally when I'm particularly stressed and can no longer see the forest for the trees, I recall a scene from the movie *Bridge of Spies*. The lawyer, James Donovan (played by Tom Hanks), is talking to his client, who's just been sentenced to life in prison. Donovan, slightly exasperated by his client's calm in the wake of devastating news, says, "Do you never worry?" The accused man reflects, then pragmatically asks, "Would it help?" Reactive people tend to dwell on counterproductive emotions, like worry and fear, and focus their energies on things they can't control— bad weather, a canceled flight, a sick babysitter. Reactive people fret to no avail, expending precious time and resources ineffectively.

You'll never be able to proactively devote your time to what really matters to you if you can't stop negatively overreacting to your daily obligations and demands. In Chapter Four, I'll share how consciously choosing where to place your time and energies—versus simply responding to everything life throws your way—is an essential skill for every leader to learn. For now, if it turns out you're more like me than Jared, here's an exercise, adapted from *The Happiness Advantage*, that might help you to develop a more positive mind-set.

See the Good in the Everyday

Make a daily list of the good things in your job, career, and life. Really, do it. According to Shawn Achor, there are "over a decade of empirical studies that have proven the profound effect it has on the way our brains are wired." Simply writing down "three good things" that happened that day focuses your brain to "scan the last 24 hours for potential positives," be they small or large. Doing so even five minutes a day eventually rewires the brain to look for positive growth opportunities while forcing typical irritations and frustrations out of your immediate field of vision.

One study found that people who did this every day for a week were happier and less depressed at the one-month, three-month, and six-month marks than those who did not. Remarkably, even after they stopped, they remained happier and showed higher levels of optimism. Best of all, Achor notes, these positives need not be "profound or complex, only specific . . . the delicious take-out Thai food you had for dinner, your child's bear hug at the end of a long day, or the well-deserved acknowledgment from your boss at work" can make an enormous difference in how you see your life and the world.

Achor also recounts an anecdote about two gentlemen he met on break during one of his talks. "One glanced up at the sky and said, 'It's nice that it's sunny today.' The other said, 'I wish it wasn't so hot today.'" While both things were true, according to Achor, each man was only able to focus on *his* perception of the weather—the first, a positive reaction, the second, negative.

Our subjective perceptions inform our reality, and our attitudes influence our mind-set and actions. Becoming aware of and owning your reactions and responses is an integral step toward discovering who you are, and realizing your potential.

Begin with the End in Mind

> If you carefully consider [how you want to be remembered], you
> will find *your* definition of success. It may be very different from
> the definition you thought you had in mind. Perhaps fame,
> achievement, money or some of the other things we strive for
> are not even part of [it].
>
> **—Stephen Covey, author of *The 7 Habits of Highly Effective People***

While your retirement is likely many decades away, looking at your life
and career from a point far into the future can bring clarity to your personal definition of success as you eliminate the noise of your daily life.
Psychologists and life coaches frequently encourage this exercise as a
way to gain a more objective perspective on what you really value, and
to identify the steps necessary to embark upon a more fulfilling path.

Close your eyes and conjure a scenario that creates a positive looking-
back point for you. I like the image of celebrating a milestone birthday. I'm
standing at the end of a long table, adorned with beautiful bouquets of
blush-colored peonies, and seated on both sides are the people who've mattered most to me in my life: my husband and my children; my parents and
my siblings; college friends and high school classmates; colleagues from The
Trump Organization and my own company, to name just a few. In reflecting upon my marriage and motherhood, my long career as a developer and
entrepreneur, what would I say? What would others say about me?

The specifics matter less than the exercise of realizing that all the
decisions you make, however small, lead here.

What's your scenario? Who's sitting at your table? What do you
hope to have accomplished? How have you impacted your community
or the world at large? Think of this day from the vantage point of your
current career. Do you like what you're doing and what you're working
toward? Is there an industry you'd rather be in? A position you'd rather
hold? Would you rather be working for yourself? What about family,
friends, and personal accomplishments? Do you hope to be married
and have children? To have visited every continent? To have mastered

a foreign language? What is it that you'll wish you'd done that you haven't?

Long term, we aren't remembered for how late we stayed at the office, how many buildings we developed or deals we closed. As important as those things may seem right now, we just aren't. We're remembered for the impact we made on our communities, the time we spent with others, the memories we shared, how well we loved our family and friends. As the oft-repeated adage goes, "[People] may forget what you said, but they will never forget how you made them feel." Or, as David Brooks, political and cultural commentator for the *New York Times*, says, "Eulogies aren't résumés. They describe the person's care, wisdom, truthfulness and courage. They describe the million little moral judgments that emanate from that inner region," underscoring the value of creating an extended job title, redefining success, and architecting your life according to what *you* value.

Should you live for your eulogy or your résumé? It can be challenging to keep those principles and passions that are most important to us top of mind; it can be even harder to incorporate our virtues and values into our daily lives. We are *so busy*, all the time, it's easy to simply react, from hour to day to week, answering e-mails, putting out fires, crossing things off our to-do lists without proactively considering how and where we're spending our time. We all know someone who was driven to earn another professional degree, a bigger title, or a higher salary, only to realize that her ambition had blinded her to what was truly most important.

The bottom line is, we spend far less time and energy on what matters most to us than we do on the minutiae of our day-to-day lives. Creating a framework that marries our passion and values with our habits can help.

> To begin with an end in mind means to start with a clear understanding of your destination. It means to know where you are going so that you better understand where you are now and so that the steps you take are always in the right direction.
>
> —Stephen Covey

Find Your True North

Have you ever wondered why some people seem to be lucky? . . . When we take ownership of our careers, we get lucky. People who take responsibility feel they can shape their destiny. They feel in control, and that gives them the confidence and commitment to pursue their passions, even when the odds of winning are not great. Also, when things go badly or the feedback is negative, it won't knock you down, because you know you have the power to create a better outcome tomorrow.

—Joanna Barsh and Susie Cranston,
authors of *How Remarkable Women Lead*

In his book *The Secrets of Happy Families*, author Bruce Feiler—a fellow admirer of Stephen Covey's—recounts how, in his role as a corporate consultant, Covey often asked his clients to "write a one-sentence answer to the question 'What is this organization's essential mission or purpose and what is its main strategy to accomplish that?'" Ours, at my brand, for example, is to inspire and empower women to create the lives they want to live. Everyone at our company knows this; it's core to our DNA.

If you had to come up with one sentence to describe your core values/personal mission/manifesto, what would it be? Simon Sinek, author and master of asking "why," writes, "A clear sense of WHY sets expectations." As Feiler notes, author and management consultant Jim Collins says, "One thing we know about life is it's going to hit you in random and unexpected ways—some good, some bad. . . . If you don't have your own frame, you'll be whipsawed by life. If you do, you're more likely to succeed."

In addition to a one-liner, writing a personal mission statement is an incredibly valuable way to begin with the end in mind. Because you are writing it yourself, about yourself, it is unique, both in what you decide to reflect upon and in how you craft it. To be truly valuable, however, it must contain ruminations on what you want to be (what Covey would call "your character") and what you want to do ("your contributions and achievements"), and include the principles upon which you believe your life is based.

How you write it is up to you, but typically you want a mission statement to be short enough to memorize. A bulleted list or a paragraph is the most common form. Statements can be commanding ("do not fear failure") or aspirational ("I will seek peace"); they should reflect timeless and enduring principles, not things that could or should change next week. Your mission statement will become the standard by which you evaluate major, life-changing decisions, the basis for making daily choices in the midst of situations that affect your life. It should reflect your truth, empowering you with clarity, strengthening you to adapt when life throws curveballs your way, and providing a constant reminder of who you are and what you value.

While I would strongly advocate creating a mission statement wherever you are in your career so that you can consciously carve out a path going forward that honors your passions and priorities, remember that what matters most to you will likely change over time. The core of your mission statement—your foundational values—probably won't, but your relationships (other than your family) and your interests might. Your mission statement is the blueprint for architecting a life you love; it is your true north that will keep you on task through time.

> We are more in need of a vision or destination and a compass
> (a set of principles or directions) and less in need of a road map.
> We often don't know what the terrain ahead will be like or what
> we need to go through it; much will depend on our judgment at
> the time. But an inner compass will always give us direction.
>
> —Stephen Covey

The revered psychiatrist Viktor Frankl said that happiness "cannot be pursued; it must ensue." That's really what identifying your passions, determining what's most important to you, and architecting a life you'll love is all about. And yet, as valuable as it can be to actively explore your potential, sometimes the opposite—doing less, not more—is equally useful. The spiritual teacher Ram Dass observed, "The quieter you become, the more you can hear." In fact, the process of writing a mission statement can be meditative in its own right, as it requires deep thought, soul-searching, and careful consideration before committing anything to the page.

Although it might seem like writing a personal mission statement is just adding another project or assignment to your already full plate, I cannot overemphasize the dividends it will pay. By investing in this process, you will feel more organized, more grounded, more cognizant about what matters to you in the big picture, and clearer about how to honor that in your day to day. "Writing or reviewing a mission statement changes you because it forces you to think through your priorities deeply, carefully, and to align your behavior with your beliefs. . . . You have a sense of mission about what you're trying to do and you are excited about it," writes Covey.

Start the journey of creating a personal mission statement by breaking the process up into smaller steps. Try drafting an extended job title (like my team and I did in launching the #WomenWhoWork campaign in 2014) that goes beyond what you do or who you care for to capture your *aspirations*. As I've said, the extended job title is an antidote to the oversimplification of referring to women solely by what it says on their business cards ("EVP Development & Acquisitions") or for whom they care ("Arabella, Joseph, and Theodore's mom").

Write your extended job title from a future perspective, encompassing specific professional and personal dreams or intentions. Include career, relationships, family, hobbies, avocations (like volunteer work), travel, and so forth. Keep it handy—print it on nice paper, laminate it, and display it on your desk at home or on your bedside table. (The framework I share later in this chapter will help you reflect on it when you're in need of clarity or redirection.) It won't capture your values in quite the same way as a detailed mission statement, but it will keep your thinking on track and your goals fresh when life throws distractions in your direction.

Finally, you might think about your mission from a personal branding perspective. Tina Wells is the CEO of Buzz Marketing Group, which she founded twenty years ago when she was just sixteen, and includes an impressive roster of clients like Microsoft, Sony Music, and Johnson & Johnson. She's also a blogger, the author of a best-selling tween fiction series, and an expert on personal branding. "I really became interested in the idea of personal branding in 2008," says Wells. "After the financial crisis, millennials were—and still are—underemployed. It has never been more important to stand out and create a career that's true to you. The key is making employers aware of who you are and what you stand for."

According to Wells, building your personal brand really means defining what you're passionate about and determining how to make a living off of it. "The happiest people I know are the ones who have figured out what they love and how to make money doing it," she says. "They've built careers that are true to their personal brands."

"Your personal brand statement not only says what you do, it also says what you're passionate about," she adds. To create one for yourself, write this sentence and fill in the blanks: "I'm passionate about ____, and this is what I do with that passion: ____." For example, Wells says, "I'm passionate about pop culture—everything I've done in my career centers around it. I don't limit myself to doing one thing (running a marketing company). Instead, I'm able to translate my passion into many seemingly unrelated things, like writing my best-selling young adult book series, *Mackenzie Blue*, while still building a career that aligns with my personal brand."

Likewise, for me, when it comes to my fashion brand, I am more than the founder of a company that sells apparel and accessories; I'm an entrepreneur who is devoted to creating solutions to problems and who has made it my life's work to inspire and empower women in every aspect of their lives.

Identify Your Passions—Then Develop Them over Time

> Whatever your dreams are, start taking them very, very seriously.
>
> —Barbara Sher, author of *Wishcraft*

Your mission statement is meant to codify what's truly valuable to you; the next step is to identify exactly what you are good at, in order to dream bigger and achieve your goals. The framework I present later in this chapter guides you to honor these passions, reflect upon them throughout your life as needed, and deepen them over time.

Angela Duckworth, psychologist and author of *Grit: The Power of Passion and Perseverance*, believes that "what we eventually accomplish may depend more on our passion and perseverance than on our innate talent." She maintains that most people don't serendipitously uncover their passions; they dabble in a number of things they think they might like, and they don't usually become passionate about something until they've started getting good at it and have received praise from others.

If we think, for example, that we aren't good at writing, then no amount of effort or exposure to literature is going to change that. If, however, the opposite is true—if we believe, as Duckworth does, that anyone can become a gifted writer over time—well, that requires expending far more time and commitment than talent: taking classes, journaling, reading, and seeking and receiving feedback. "Our vanity, our self-love, promotes the cult of the genius," said Nietzsche. "For if we think of genius as something magical, we are not obliged to compare ourselves and find ourselves lacking."

If we maintain that our passions are discovered through introspection alone, we are both blameless and helpless if they escape notice. Duckworth, instead, suggests that passions are fostered—we create them ourselves, through discovery, development, and a lifetime of deepening. Most people spend years "exploring several different interests, and the one that eventually came to occupy all of their waking (and some sleeping) thoughts wasn't recognizably their life's destiny on first acquaintance," she writes.

Of course, you need to start by figuring out what you generally like and dislike, but genuine interests aren't always discovered through soul-searching; they emerge through repeated interactions with the outside world. Discovery is unpredictable and nonlinear; you can't really know in advance what will move you and what won't, so you need to expose yourself to lots of different things. "One of the huge mistakes people make is that they try to force an interest on themselves," says Jeff Bezos, founder and CEO of Amazon. True interests become passions when they develop and deepen over time and are supported by other people—colleagues, mentors, managers—through positive reinforcement.

Discovering your passions, now and in the future, is within your control and within your grasp; it is not something intangible that you were blessed with (or not). It's about working hard to excel at something, rather than relying solely on our inborn gifts to clue us in to what will truly make us happy. In fostering a passion, Duckworth recommends the following:

✓ EXPLORE YOUR INTERESTS: Ask yourself what you like to think about. What matters most to you? How do you enjoy spending your time? What can't you stand doing?

✓ DEVELOP AND EXERCISE YOUR INTERESTS: Once you have a general direction, an inkling of what you enjoy, go out into the world and do something with it. Experiment, try, learn. Find ways to trigger your interest repeatedly. Be patient. This takes time. "Enthusiasm is common," says Duckworth. "Endurance is rare."

✓ DEEPEN YOUR INTERESTS OVER TIME: Keep asking questions, dig, find other people who share your passions, especially a mentor (see Chapter Two). Committing yourself to fostering a passion will enhance your knowledge, expertise, confidence, and curiosity until you feel you can truly call that passion your own. "There are no shortcuts to excellence," Duckworth says. "It all takes time—longer than most people imagine. It's doing what you love, but not just falling in love—*staying* in love."

Gather Wisdom from Others

There's also great value in identifying your strengths from the perspective of others who may know you better than you know yourself. "Before you can leverage your strengths, you need to figure out what they are," says Wharton professor and best-selling author Adam Grant. "People take self-assessments, but they are flawed by our self-perceptions. Sometimes what we think about ourselves just isn't true." Grant recommends asking others and assessing their feedback, based on the heavily researched Reflected Best Self Exercise:

1. CHOOSE YOUR SOURCES AND SEEK FEEDBACK: Pick ten to twelve people who know you well, from both your personal and professional life, and various capacities. Have a conversation in advance of this exercise so they can prepare; tell them you're going to ask them to write a story or narrative about a time when you were at your best.

2. MAKE SURE THE STORIES INCLUDE SPECIFICS: While it's nice to hear that you're "kind" or "inventive," examples that remind you of when you stole the talent show in eighth grade or nailed a presentation at your sales conference provide clearer feedback than statements that purely list qualities.

3. IDENTIFY PATTERNS AND PAINT YOUR SELF-PORTRAIT: Make a list of common themes in the feedback, including the examples that best typify what those themes suggest about your strengths. Then draft a short character sketch that describes who you are when you're at your best.

4. PUT YOUR STRENGTHS INTO ACTION: Create a step-by-step plan of how and when you'll capitalize on these strengths. Identifying your strengths isn't enough; it's in the planning process where people who mapped out ways to adjust their jobs to incorporate these strengths were happier and more productive over the next six months.

Recall What You Were Passionate About as a Kid

Some of us are lucky enough to remember what we loved to do as children and are blessed to have parlayed those passions into professions;

my good friend and photographer Abbey Drucker is one. "I can close my eyes and remember that moment as a little girl," she recounts of a spontaneous third-grade photo session that cast a vision for her future career in photography. "Fast forward to sixth grade, I lined up my girlfriends in their swimsuits alongside a pool. I didn't realize it at the time, but I was creating a fashion shoot."

At sixteen, Drucker made the decision to go all-in on her dreams of becoming a photographer. She quit sports to focus on her portfolio, then dedicated herself to applying to art schools; at eighteen, she moved to New York City. Beyond being incredibly talented, her persistence has paid off: she's traveled the world on photography assignments and her roster of clients includes *Vogue*, *Allure*, and Capitol Records. She's collaborated with some of Hollywood's biggest names, from Emma Stone to Steve Buscemi; she's also shot me and done some of my favorite brand campaigns. "I wake up every day and I feel thankful to do what I love for a living," she adds.

As a little girl, I spent hours playing with Erector sets, Tonka trucks, and Legos, anything to do with digging or building. I remember crawling around in the dirt, scooping and moving small mounds of earth, pretending to prepare the land for development. When I was a bit older, I would often shadow my father on construction sites as he oversaw projects under development. I would leave sleepovers early on Sunday mornings to join him on these site visits.

Long before graduating from Wharton, I had committed to the idea of being a developer. I had majored in real estate, also studying finance and art history, a combination I felt would prepare me well. By spring of my senior year, I had accepted the position at Forest City Ratner; I couldn't wait to get through my last exams, graduate, and get to work.

Early one morning during finals, the phone rang. I'd been up late studying and had been asleep for only a little while but I answered, groggy, knowing that no one would call a college student at 8 A.M. unless it was really important.

It was Anna Wintour, the editor in chief of *Vogue*. Anna is someone I have always admired; we met when I'd done modeling as a teenager. I spent the first thirty seconds of the conversation trying to shake off my haze and concentrate on what she was saying: She'd heard I was graduating soon. She knew I liked fashion. She wanted to offer me a job at *Vogue*.

I was completely taken off guard, but awake enough by now to be extremely flattered and honored. I knew working with Anna at *Vogue* could positively influence my career in a big way. (What I didn't know then was that I would eventually start my own fashion brand—and that the experience would have been all the more relevant.)

But I'd already given my word to Forest City. I just wasn't willing to delay my dream of becoming a builder. Though I was enormously grateful for the opportunity, I graciously declined, and shared with Anna my plans to work at Forest City prior to joining my father and brother at The Trump Organization. I remember confiding to her that real estate was my passion. To this day, she has been a friend and supporter.

I immediately called my dad. I told him Anna Wintour had just offered me a job. "I think you should consider it, Ivanka," he surprisingly replied. "Working at *Vogue* sounds very exciting. Anna's the best in the business. You could learn a lot from her." I was shocked that he would encourage me to consider anything other than real estate; for so long, it was all we discussed. I was unnerved by the conversation and started to wonder if my father didn't want me to eventually join the family business. I worried that he doubted my abilities as a developer.

On the day of my graduation, I grilled him on his response. He said he didn't doubt me, he only wanted me to carefully consider the job at *Vogue* to be sure that I was, in fact, serious about real estate. My father wanted me to choose real estate *for me*, not for him. He wanted to make sure it was *my* passion—and that I didn't have blinders on to other incredible opportunities for personal and professional growth.

My parents both believe that if you commit yourself fully to something you love, you can accomplish great things—but if you don't feel genuine passion for what you do, you'll always lose to someone who does.

The call from Anna Wintour, and the clear decision to decline a very coveted first job, helped confirm for me that real estate was, in fact, my true passion. This remains true to this day, but I've also added some others!

PASSION BEGETS SUCCESS

After joining The Trump Organization in 2005, I was excited to immerse myself in every aspect of the business; I needed to accumulate experiences in order to figure out both what I was good at and what I really enjoyed. I discovered early on that I had an intuitive understanding of marketing as well as an eye for design and a strong aesthetic point of view. But the aspect of the business that I discovered I love the most is negotiation and deal making.

I've since spearheaded some of our company's most high-profile acquisitions, such as the $200 million conversion of the historic Old Post Office (now Trump International Washington, D.C.) and the $250 million renovation of the iconic Doral Golf Resort in Miami (now Trump National Doral).

The Old Post Office is a national landmark, the second-tallest structure in the nation's capital (after the Washington Monument). When it was built in the 1890s, its grandeur was meant to signal to the rest of the country that Pennsylvania Avenue was America's Main Street. The building has been long admired by residents of and visitors to our nation's capital as well as architectural enthusiasts around the globe, and you didn't have to be a visionary to see its potential, despite the fact that time had taken its toll. In March 2011, when the federal government announced it was seeking private sector partners, the Old Post Office became the most sought-after redevelopment opportunity in the country. My father and I fought hard against the largest hotel companies and developers in the world to win the deal.

Beginning in April 2011, my brother Eric and I joined dozens of architects, investors, and developers in a walk-through of the building. It needed tons of work, of course, but its raw beauty, architectural significance, and enormous potential were perfectly apparent to all. With its intricately carved stone edifice and granite façade; nine-story glass skylight atrium and soaring ceilings; and extraordinary millwork on stately wood doors, original moldings, and marble wainscoting, you simply could not rebuild this iconic historical structure today.

The U.S. government's General Services Administration–led bidding process was long and complex, and I was involved in every aspect of it, from selecting the construction company and dozens of architectural firms and contractors to negotiating each component of the acquisition. I traveled by train almost weekly for eight months to study the building, gather intel on other hotels in the city, and meet with contractors and engineers. We submitted a proposal that was two hundred pages long and took months of work by our team to assemble. I met with historic preservation officials and went through the lengthy governmental review process with dozens of agencies to ensure that we would be able to preserve the historic aspects of the building while allowing it to function as a twenty-first-century luxury hotel.

After this exhaustive evaluation process, we were ultimately awarded the deal in early 2012 by the U.S. government, based on criteria that included our vision for the property, the strength and experience of our development team, our company's financial wherewithal, and our plan to bring vibrancy to Pennsylvania Avenue. I also believe that my long-term personal commitment to the property made a substantial impact in the bidding process. I can envision Arabella overseeing this hotel someday (if she so chooses!), and I shared that with the selection committee. This makes the Trump DC incredibly important not just in our portfolio but also to our family.

If the Old Post Office was rare for its architectural beauty and prime location, the Doral Golf Resort and Spa was appealing in its scale and prestige—eight hundred acres in the heart of Miami, containing four championship golf courses (including the famed Blue Monster), more than six hundred guest rooms, and a hundred thousand square feet of meeting space.

The acquisition process was complex, in part because the property was in bankruptcy. I was pregnant with Arabella throughout the early negotiations. Then, in my ninth month, the sellers called to tell me they were accepting a higher offer from a different bidder. Unwilling to match, I thought the deal was dead.

Just a few days after I gave birth, the seller called again to say that they would do the deal at our price—but that meant my having to fly with my father from New York to Miami to complete the due diligence on the property before signing a contract. Five days later, the deal was done and the contract had been signed. We paid $150 million for the resort—the land alone is worth $1 billion. We also invested more than $250 million to renovate the entire resort, bringing it back to its storied glamour—and then some.

Winning a deal is exciting, but I always joke that that's when the real work begins! My father, brother Eric, and I created a plan for a phased renovation, which was complex in that we were redoing every aspect of this enormous property—from the ballrooms to the restaurants, the pools to the golf courses—while staying open and operational. And when you obsess over the details like I do, renovating 643 guest rooms is no small feat. In the end, we reenvisioned the entire massive resort, Trump National Doral, with a lot of love and care, and after years of hard work, I could not be more proud of the end result.

In addition to development and acquisitions, I personally oversee the design and creative vision for each Trump Hotels property; my role enables me to blend several of my passions, as we add luxury hotels to our portfolio, from Waikiki to Vancouver, Panama to Chicago. In 2016, we launched Scion, a four-star lifestyle brand. Whereas Trump Hotels stands for five-star luxury, Scion targets a new customer in search of connection, so the hotels are centered on community and innovation. Scion hotels offer energized social experiences and shared work spaces designed to bring people together to exchange ideas and create.

Alongside my brothers, I also actively oversee The Trump Organization's residential and commercial real estate portfolio, from deal evaluation and predevelopment planning and financing to design, construction, sales, and marketing. We're in charge of making sure that The Trump Organization's world-renowned physical and operational standards are met and adhered to. I'm involved in every decision large and small, from the acquisition phase to determining the interior design direction for residences and hotel suites. I have a big job and a ton of responsibility— and yet I love what I do, every day. I feel grateful that I get to work with my amazing father and brothers, and that we are partners in this incredible adventure. My father's advice to my younger self has proven true—when you're passionate and you work hard, you can achieve great things.

> Do work you love. Think about what you're good at. What do you do where the time flies by? That's your passion. Ask yourself how you can turn that into a business. That's what's going to make you happy. Not everyone is built to be an entrepreneur, but if you are, there is no better thing than to wake up and work on something you own, that you built, that you love. That's when it becomes a life instead of a job.

> **—Angela Benton, founder and CEO of NewME Accelerator**

LIVE AND WORK WITH PURPOSE

> Life is a verb, not a noun.

> **—Charlotte Perkins Gilman, sociologist and author of _Human Work_**

By this point, you've no doubt devoted lots of thought to what you care most about, what your passions are, and how you must prioritize them to architect a life you will love. You've created a personal mission statement that reflects who and what matter most to you. By laying your foundation in this way, you have cultivated a kind of inner compass, whose clarity and strength will guide you through the highs and lows of both your professional and your personal life.

What Matters Most to You Right Now? Modifying Your Life's Blueprint

How do you review and refresh your passions and priorities as your life progresses and evolves? Use this flexible framework, which encapsulates everything you've learned in this chapter, to discover, develop, and deepen your passions wherever you are in your career path, and as a guide for the rest of your life:

1. **START BY ANSWERING THE SAME QUESTIONS YOU HAVE ANSWERED BEFORE:** What do you do that feels as natural as breathing? What makes you feel most productive and at ease? When do the hours disappear like minutes?

2. **EVALUATE YOUR ANSWERS.** Do they reflect your current priorities, both professional and personal? If not . . .

3. **ENVISION THE DINNER SCENARIO YOU IMAGINED EARLIER.** Who is at your table? How would they describe you? Do these sentiments align with your current priorities? Or have those priorities changed? The goal here is to objectively define, in the absence of daily distractions, what matters most to you in the bigger picture right now—then compare that with how you are spending your time day to day.

4. **RETURN TO YOUR PERSONAL MISSION STATEMENT.** Your values are likely the same, but have your circumstances changed? Are your goals, wishes, and dreams the same? Consider how your mission applies to these new life circumstances.

5. **IF YOUR CORE VALUES HAVE CHANGED**—it's not common, but it can happen—edit or rewrite your personal mission statement to capture what's new or different.

6. **REPEAT AS NEEDED** throughout your career and life.

Whatever you do, do not underestimate the importance of identifying your passions and determining the right career, job, or industry accordingly at various points in your path. From my own observations, I can attest that choosing blindly or not assessing a major career move against both your personal and professional passions will be much more difficult, and potentially far less satisfying, down the road. I have friends who weren't in love with their company or industry, but they stayed far longer than they should have, sometimes out of inertia, sometimes because they didn't have a plan B. "It's just for now," they'd say, the expectation being that they'd do whatever it was that they settled for in the short term until . . . when? Until they didn't have bills to pay?

We often don't realize that while we're waiting for our lives to begin, they already have—and they're made up of all the decisions we make, big and small, conscious or not. The temporary job in the company that's not a great fit leads to a promotion (who wouldn't want that?), which affords a better apartment (and higher expenses); a new job in the same industry that you don't love pays more, but begins to pigeonhole you somewhere you didn't intend to stay long term. When we don't consciously choose to build our careers according to our values and interests, we can end up letting life choose for us.

Honor yourself by exploring the kind of life you deserve. Question and consider everything, but know that when you are truly passionate about something, you'll feel it in your heart and gut. You'll know you're doing work that matters and marries well with your interests and strengths because you won't be able to wait to get back to it. And there will be no question as to when you've landed upon your purpose, because it will feel like home.

> Purpose is what drives you. It's the source of your inspiration and the compass that guides your way to making a difference, and at the same time, to the deepest level of happiness. And that's the real deal. . . . When you have purpose in life, you're making a difference for the people around you.
>
> —Joanna Barsh and Susie Cranston

Open Yourself Up to Possibility

> If you're being given a number of takes [while making a film], trust that the thing you were trying to do—you kind of did it. Why not try something else? You could take that idea and [apply it] to life.
>
> —Cynthia Nixon, actor and director

I always tell people one of the absolute best things you can do to discover your passions is experiment in as many areas as possible that you *think* you're interested in, whether or not you're sure. Lynda Gratton and Andrew Scott of London Business School have described the advent of an "explorer phase," in which "people in their twenties keep their options open and experiment with different roles and skills to better understand what they are good at and what they enjoy." These so-called explorers build networks based on new experiences and take risks they wouldn't as easily be able to take later, as it's a time in life when there are potentially few restrictions and even fewer repercussions. There's less downside financially, particularly since people at this age are likely not yet caring for their own family and haven't yet committed to an industry, a specific job, or a particular organization.

But what if you're not in your early twenties, and you *do* have considerable financial obligations, such as student debt? How can you develop your curiosity over the course of the rest of your life, even if just for personal fulfillment? Or maybe even parlay it into a career change?

I personally love the word "curious." I identify with it quite a bit because I am deeply curious, and that's how I develop my interest in the things that ultimately turn into passions for me. For one thing, you have to read, which can trigger lots of interests and ideas. I consume a tremendous amount of information: books, newspapers, trade publications, magazines (that start as pleasure reading but become work related as I'm always tearing out pages and sending them to my team). TED Talks and podcasts are another way I diversify my own information bias and expose myself to bite-sized, snackable bits of information on topics—like, say, neuroscience—that I'm never going to read a whole book on but are mind expanding and may trigger an idea.

Another way to foster your curiosity is to talk to people. I interact with people all day long and I'm constantly probing and vigilant, wanting to see things from a different point of view. I drive my teams crazy by asking third parties to weigh in on our business plans and big-picture initiatives. I don't go to people looking for them to affirm my perspective, though; instead, I ask what they think to get *their* perspective and broaden mine. You can learn so much from the opinions of others and it literally costs you nothing.

When I had the idea for my brand, I realized I was going to have a much steeper learning curve in fashion than I did in real estate, which I had been exposed to my whole life. So I was proactive and met with people in the industry who had created or worked at companies I respected—Tory Burch, Ralph Lauren, Michael Kors, and Calvin Klein, of the established players; Warby Parker, Reformation, and Everlane, of the new guard, to name a few. I sought out their wisdom and experience in trying to understand a business that I had never planned on entering, and peppered them with questions about design, product, teams, business models, and infrastructure.

If, like me, you're looking to get into a different industry, you're probably not going to just throw caution to the wind and spontaneously quit your job. Contrary to popular myths, most people don't successfully start their businesses that way (see Chapter Six for lots more on entrepreneurship). When you find that you're interested in something, you're going to want to network, make connections (more on both later), meet people, and explore your options. You'll do your research. And you'll learn to become more open to possibility. Most women's lives, past their early twenties, look more like a tree than a road. Your path will no longer be straight, from point A to point B, but clustered, like branches, each representing rich and varied experiences.

Reshma Saujani's story provides a great example. She's now the founder and CEO of Girls Who Code, a national nonprofit that is arming girls with computing skills, but it was during a run for Congress that Saujani became inspired to create the organization. In visiting local schools, she personally witnessed the gender gap in computing classes and set out to do something about it. Launched in 2012, Girls Who Code has reached tens of thousands of girls in every state—90 percent of whom say they intend to study computer science in college.

Before engineer Debbie Sterling founded GoldieBlox, the toy company dedicated to inspiring the next generation of female engineers, she was a marketing director at a jewelry company and a consultant for organizations such as Microsoft and the New York Knicks. It was only when Sterling spent six months at a grassroots nonprofit in rural India that she became inspired to create a mission-driven company, leading her to discover her true passion.

Heed your heart's desires and search your soul, then find opportunities in which you can test out your interests and ideas—take a class, join a workshop, consider a side job after hours. Then do it again, and likely again. Only over time, and with practice, do we start to truly develop the passions that can change our lives. Expose yourself to new ideas and novel ways of thinking. Talk to people, and not just those you *always* talk to. Hollywood producer Brian Grazer makes an effort to meet someone new every two weeks and really get to know them, in order to expand his view of the world and ensure he isn't developing blind spots. For me, 2016 was a real eye-opener! Having talked to people on both sides of the political aisle during my father's campaign for the presidency, I learned firsthand the importance of gathering and considering disparate viewpoints. It's very easy in life and in business to think you have a diverse community of people and perspectives in your inner circle, but more often than not, it's more like an echo chamber.

If you're curious, driven to experiment and try new things, seek out people in those areas you're interested in. Get to know them. Look for their advice—you can never go wrong asking people how they got to where they are. If nothing else, it's flattering, and it makes people like you more for having sought their sage counsel.

> Dream bigger. Think about the thing that you would be most pumped to accomplish and then double it. Set your goals higher because the truth is, this goal here? You may not get there. Maybe you get halfway there. Maybe you get a quarter of the way there. You have to believe in yourself because if not, who else is going to believe in you? But if you at least start with a much bigger vision or goal and have that in the back of your head, you're going to go further. Dream bigger and believe in yourself because no one else is going to dream for you.
>
> —Alexa von Tobel

Develop Your Passions over the Course of Your Life

> You need passion. You need to be absolutely passionate about
> what you believe in. If you don't feel passionate about anything,
> chances are you haven't discovered what you're really good at
> yet. Keep looking.
>
> —Chris Guillebeau, entrepreneur and author of
> *The Art of Non-Conformity*

No matter what point you're at in your career, it's a perfect time to discover what you love to do. Have you topped out in your company? Learned everything you could and are looking for a new challenge? Are you recently unemployed and in search of a fresh start? Or maybe your career is humming along, and as a leader you feel fulfilled—but as a person, you're hungry to experience new things.

Perhaps you've just had a baby and you are contemplating those professional passions that will fit best with your new responsibilities, or, at the other end of that continuum, maybe your last child has just gone off to kindergarten—or to college—and you'll suddenly have that much more time to devote to other things that you care about. All the tools and techniques in this chapter are meant to be used throughout your life, at any and all times, as a means of creating a blueprint for what matters to you most right now.

Discovering new passions throughout your life provides a great opportunity to build upon your experiences in other industries. In my case, I never planned to tackle the fashion industry; I was really just pursuing entrepreneurial opportunities I couldn't resist. When you're a student, both in work and in life; when you are curious, open-minded, hardworking, and optimistic in everything you do, opportunities sometimes present themselves that you otherwise might not have noticed or seized.

Umber Ahmad, master baker and creator of Mah-Ze-Dahr in New York City, is an inspiration to anyone looking to capitalize on a passion and start anew in a completely different field. After ten years in investment banking and private equity, Ahmad left Wall Street to cofound an investment company, Specialized Capital Management, where she identified her true calling—helping businesses grow. She develops a marketing presence for her clients, helping them to become competitive brands and expand internationally. It wasn't until she worked with celebrated chef Tom Colicchio that she even considered turning her baking—a private avocation—into something more. "I boldly brought Tom Colicchio my food. He asked me what I wanted to do with it, and I thought he meant how I wanted to pack up the leftovers," she said.

But Colicchio saw something special, beyond leftovers. "I told him I wanted to do for myself what I'd been doing for other people. I wanted to build a brand," says Ahmad. Since then, she's set up shop online at mahzedahrbakery.com, her treats are available through JetBlue Airways, and she's opened a store on Greenwich Avenue in New York City.

Ahmad applies everything she learned in her previous careers to running Mah-Ze-Dahr: "It's critical to bring your experience with you . . . even if it seems totally irrelevant. You didn't spend your whole career developing a skill just to leave it at the door. You don't need to reinvent the wheel, but you can reinvent your energy. For me, I'm no longer a banker, but I am still quite skilled at business development, financial management, leadership, et cetera, all of which made building the Mah-Ze-Dahr brand and launching the business that much more successful."

She recommends making a list of those things you know and do well; it will give you an advantage in your new field that others don't have. And because you are forging your own path, you can make your own rules. Ahmad jokes that she "doesn't look like a traditional pastry chef." Nor did she follow the industry standard of starting out with a bricks-and-mortar store. For her, it was more cost effective—and less risky—to start selling online, build a following, and then branch out with her store in New York.

Ahmad—who still thinks like a banker more than a baker—recommends looking five years out and asking, "Where do I want to be, and how am I going to get there?" While that may seem contrary to "dreaming big," she maintains that the only way to get there is to plan ahead.

And she adds, "It might be hard, but that's OK. If you're following your passion, you'll be happy every day. Maybe not all day, every day. But every day."

Pursuing your passion doesn't always mean going out on your own; not everyone aspires to become an entrepreneur. Finding the right company to devote yourself to can be just as rewarding as starting your own.

Michelle Kohanzo, now managing director of the Land of Nod, is a prime example of someone who has dedicated herself wholeheartedly to an industry and to a company she believes in. Kohanzo began her retail career as a salesclerk at The Limited, while planning to become a middle-school teacher; much to her surprise, she loved every aspect of the business. Soon, she moved to Crate & Barrel's catalog division, and then, in 1999, to the Land of Nod. "My daughter was eight months old and I was ready for a new challenge," Kohanzo told writer Jenna Fain of The Everygirl. "I loved the idea of working for a start-up and I was also insane about the brand, so it was a perfect fit. I was the tenth employee and started answering customer calls. In the old days we all did a bit of everything. We packed boxes, checked in merchandise, wrapped gifts, whatever needed to be done. It was fun and very casual. It took about three months for me to get promoted to Customer Service Manager and from there I have played nearly every role in the company. I launched and managed our Web site, opened all of our stores, managed logistics, managed marketing, managed IT, and most recently ran our merchandising department. With each move I learned more and more about the business and as my career grew, so did the company. The Land of Nod is truly my passion and I have been so lucky to be a part of the company's growth and success over the years. It's really an honor and a dream come true to lead the company."

How did Kohanzo find fulfillment while climbing the corporate ladder? She asserts, "My mentor gave me some great advice early in my career and it really sums up my approach. He said, 'Don't strategize your career. Go where the company needs you and you'll be successful.' . . . Having found my passion, I would say, don't settle—keep looking. There is nothing more rewarding than loving what you do every day. . . . It's not all about your salary and your title. At the end of the day, the most important thing is that you love the people you work with and you're passionate about what you do. Nothing else matters."

YOU ARE A WOMAN WHO WORKS—AT PRIORITIZING HER PASSIONS

As a woman who works, you choose proactively how to spend your time. You know what's most important to you, how to plot a plan for success, beginning with the end in mind and establishing your true north. As such, your life's blueprint reflects your foundational values, and what matters most to you right now.

For me, living a life according to my passions is really about the journey; there's no definitive road map or final destination. My ideas of success and my personal and professional goals are constantly evolving, but my compass is clear. As long as I'm passionate about my work, I'm confident that I will continue to challenge myself and pursue excellence in every venture.

The next step for you in achieving excellence—and architecting a life you'll love—is to make your mark at your company and your industry, the topic of Chapter Two.

> Don't ask yourself what the world needs; ask yourself what makes you come alive. And then go and do that. Because what the world needs is people who have come alive.
>
> **—Dr. Howard Thurman, theologian and author**

THE MOST
COURAGEOUS
ACT IS STILL
TO THINK
FOR YOURSELF.
ALOUD.

COCO CHANEL

CHAPTER TWO

Make Your Mark

Become a World-Class Communicator, Colleague, and Networker

A s you now know, to find fulfillment in your career and attain the greatest satisfaction in your life, you must devote yourself to your passions. But to achieve the greatest impact as a leader means making sure you know the fundamentals and acquire the skills to make your mark at your company and in your industry. Making your mark means upping the ante and distinguishing yourself as top class in everything you do—communicating and connecting with your team, boss, and clients; creating a solid network of meaningful contacts; working with a mentor; and establishing a reputation that will precede you wherever you decide to go from here.

As a woman who works, you're not just making a living, you're making a difference, by creating a life you love and inspiring others to do the same.

COMMUNICATION: THE CORNERSTONE OF SUCCESS

> You can have brilliant ideas, but if you can't get them across,
> your ideas won't get you anywhere.
>
> —Lee Iacocca, American automobile executive

In person or on the phone, one-on-one or in a large group setting, you are a woman who works at communicating. Perhaps you're a natural storyteller (or not); maybe you'd rather take the stairs than make small talk with the company president in the elevator. Or you're *great* face-to-face, but your verbal ease doesn't translate to speaking in front of a large group.

Regardless of your bent, clear communication is pivotal to your success; even the best of us can always get better. Being able to communicate effectively and convincingly is crucial; it can make the difference not just between success and failure, but between being good at what you do and being great. And it's not just what you say, but how your message is received by others—intentions don't always equal impact. Just as perception is sometimes more important than reality, what you mean often matters less than what's heard. Taking extra care to consider how your intention might be interpreted is essential to excellent communication.

Master the Art of Conversation

At a time when we text more than talk, it's easy to forget that communication is not just a means of relaying information but also a way of engaging with others socially. In fact, research shows that whether you participate in lighthearted banter or deeper, more meaningful discussions, talking makes even the most introverted among us feel happier. According to journalist David Roberts, the act of conversing plays a significant role in a whole range of social, commercial, and professional settings as "it weaves and reweaves the social fabric, enacting and reinforcing social roles." The purpose of speaking, therefore, is not just to impart knowledge but, as Roberts says, "to *do* something: reassure, acknowledge, nurture, enjoin, reject, dominate, encourage."

Whether meeting with a new colleague or a potentially important business contact, you need the conversational skills not only to get off on the right foot with someone new but also to make a strong, positive impression.

One of the best ways to master communication?

Ask questions and listen well.

As for me, all I know is that I know nothing.

—Socrates

No matter what level you're at in an organization, knowing when and how to ask questions is a key component of effective leadership, as is learning to become a better listener. When faced with uncertainty, even now, I do exhaustive research and I speak with everyone I know who has an educated view on the topic at hand. Asking intelligent questions of the right people is the best way to learn, grow, and avoid mistakes. By the right people, I mean know the difference between what's appropriate to ask your peers and what you should be asking your boss; and don't ask anything you can learn by doing your own research. When someone asks me "How many people work at your company?" or "How many properties is The Trump Organization developing?" it simply tells me that they aren't being resourceful and didn't do their homework. Don't ask something that can easily be found online.

Early on in my career, I worried that asking questions would expose my inexperience. The reality is that I *was* inexperienced, and everyone knew it! No one expects a twenty-two-year-old who's new to the job to know everything. It took me a long time to realize that. I still ask plenty of questions when I need to; when my family acquired the Doral Resort in 2012, I was spearheading the negotiations, but my father was instrumental. His experience proved invaluable to me as we hammered out each facet of the deal. I constantly want to be growing and evolving as an entrepreneur, so I seek out creative, smart, inspiring people; try to absorb as much as possible from them; and apply what I learn to my own career and areas of interest.

Asking questions means not just knowing who to ask but *how* to ask—and then listening and learning from those answers. Drawing people out is a great way to start a conversation. Most people love to talk about themselves and their experiences, and for good reason—research shows that it stimulates the same pleasure centers of the brain that are triggered by eating good food and falling in love. "When you ask a 'what' question, chances are you will get a simple answer," advises psychiatrist and my good friend Dr. Samantha Boardman. "When you ask a 'why' question, you explore a person's underlying motivation. Every question you ask has the potential to narrow or expand the dialogue."

Listening is a critical skill for your career, whatever stage you're at. As the Dalai Lama said, "When you talk, you are only repeating what you already know. But if you listen, you may learn something new." You can ask intelligent questions all day long, but if you're not listening—really listening and processing the information someone is sharing—you can't learn.

As a generation, we've stopped listening. We tend to rush to speak first or make our own point without truly hearing what the other party has to say. We have two ears and one mouth—use them in that proportion!

Sharpen Your Listening Skills

Whether you're looking to learn from a colleague or are hoping to shine in an interview, effective listening involves hearing what the other person is saying and also paying attention to their nonverbal communication cues. Here are three key dos and don'ts to take to heart, from Dr. Boardman:

FOCUS ON WHAT YOU MIGHT DISCOVER: Adopting an open mind-set can help to squelch any impulse you might have to talk out of turn or interrupt someone speaking. As Dr. Boardman says, "Consider reframing the situation. Ask yourself, 'What can I learn from her?'" By keeping an open mind-set, you won't just seem interested—you'll actually *feel* more invested in the conversation.

HEED THE 20-SECOND RULE: Dr. Mark Goulston, author of *Just Listen*, recommends obeying the Traffic Light Rule when deciding when to talk and when to listen: "In the first 20 seconds of talking, your light is green: your listener is liking you, as long as your statement is relevant to the conversation and hopefully in service of the other person. But unless you are an extremely gifted raconteur, people who talk for more than roughly a half minute at a time are boring and often perceived as too chatty. So the light turns yellow for the next 20 seconds—now the risk is increasing that the other person is beginning to lose interest or think you're long-winded. At the 40-second mark, your light is red. Yes, there's an occasional time you want to run that red light and keep talking, but the vast majority of the time, you'd better stop or you're in danger."

LET YOUR BODY SPEAK FOR YOU: "Body language cues like eye contact, sincere nodding, and leaning in communicate interest," says Boardman. "Smile, uncross your arms, pay attention. Nothing kills a pleasant conversation like feeling the other person doesn't care about what you're saying."

Amy Cuddy, author of *Presence*, writes, "When we are feeling powerless . . . we make ourselves smaller. We shorten, slouch, collapse, and we restrict our body language. . . . Carrying yourself in a powerful way directs your feelings, thoughts, behaviors and body to feel powerful and be present (and even perform better)."

When you can admit that you don't know something without feeling inadequate or embarrassed, you become free, and more open to gaining wisdom or knowledge from another. Many of us think we already know what another person is going to say. Why ask a question at all if you already know the answer? Admitting that we don't know something and that we want to learn more sparks our curiosity, and maybe the discovery of new passions, both of which are essential to succeeding in your role.

Elevate Your Meetings

If you had to identify, in one word, the reason why the human race has not achieved, and never will achieve, its full potential, that word would be "meetings."

—Dave Barry, columnist and author of *Dave Barry Turns Fifty*

Few of us would naturally link curiosity, passion, and the art of conversation with meetings—arguably one of the most dreaded facets of organizational life, second only to public speaking (up next!). Most meetings deserve the bad rap they get for that very reason—rather than be seen as an opportunity for discovery and learning, they feel like an imposition, an unwelcome disruption to getting our "real work" done. That's because meetings are typically too long, off point, and often entirely unnecessary.

When given the opportunity to lead a meeting, you'll need to know how to inspire the group as well as make the gathering less onerous, more efficient, and ideally more insightful. Executive coach Jim Kochalka has worked with my brothers and me for years, and he's been instrumental in helping us improve our efficiency and that of our organization. More recently, he's coached my brand team, and has been particularly effective in guiding us to lead more productive meetings. Here are six of his tried-and-true rules:

✓ INVITE THE RIGHT PEOPLE: "Carefully consider who you ask to join—invite only those people who are truly necessary to accomplishing the meeting's purpose. Not only will doing so keep the meeting focused and short, it'll also keep things on task by avoiding having too many cooks in the kitchen. Think of it this way: If you've got eight people in a two-hour meeting, that's like using sixteen hours of paid time to discuss a given topic," says Kochalka. As you invite each person, ask yourself whether the meeting is worth that expenditure of resources.

✓ DEFINE THE MEETING'S PURPOSE: "Meetings are typically held to inform, discuss, or decide. If the intent of your meeting is only to inform, and not to discuss the information or make a decision about it, it may be more efficient to simply send the information via e-mail or present it on a conference call," he adds. Leading and participating effectively in meetings require discipline. Circulate an agenda in advance and then stick to it. I like to provide (and receive) materials twenty-four to forty-eight hours in advance so that everyone has ample time to read and digest the content. This way you can discuss the issues at hand from an educated perspective rather than just inform everyone present about them. Don't share ideas that are off topic; hold them for the right time or follow up later to stay on track.

✓ BE REALISTIC IN YOUR TIMING: When planning for your meeting, consider how much time each item will realistically take to discuss. Jim Kochalka observes that people often underestimate this, which is why meetings often run over. I deliberately overestimate time in my calendar to ensure that my day's schedule doesn't get derailed when meetings invariably start late or run long.

✓ KNOW YOUR ACRONYMS: "Everyone should honor two simple acronyms in any meeting: WAIT ('Why am I talking?') and ELMO ('Enough, let's move on'). WAIT eliminates unnecessary distractions and tangents, because it forces people to ask themselves if what they want to say is really necessary and will help achieve the goal of the meeting. ELMO prevents that phenomenon we're all familiar with, in which the team gets stuck on one topic and the meeting runs an hour over before you even know it."

✓ CHOOSE THE RIGHT MEDIUM: "The most effective way to present information in a meeting depends on how much you want people to focus on what is directly in front of them versus how much they need to see the bigger picture. If you distribute a twenty-page deck, they'll simply skim through it. The advantage of a screen is that you can capture attention more easily since everyone is looking at the same material; the disadvantage is that you can't refer back to the slide. A great combination is a screen and then whiteboard for real-time comments," advises Kochalka. Similarly, decide beforehand whether an in-person meeting is preferable to a conference call. Large groups on a call can be inefficient as people tend to get distracted (answering e-mails, for example) and not fully listen. If you really need a group's undivided attention, hold the meeting in person.

✓ ID THOSE ACTION STEPS: "Don't leave the room without determining who's going to do what, by when. Meetings frequently hit sticking points where topics are taken 'offline' but actually simply die in the room, so disciplined follow-up is important." Often meetings run over and people scramble to return to their desks. Assign someone to recoup deliverables postmeeting before it breaks up.

Transitioning from a Small to a Large Audience: Public Speaking

Be sincere; be brief; be seated.

—Franklin D. Roosevelt

Public speaking. The mere phrase is enough to strike terror into the hearts of many; in fact, delivering a speech in front of an audience is the number one fear in America, followed only by death. This isn't a recent phenomenon, either. Celebrated writers Mark Twain and Dale Carnegie—talented, charismatic, successful raconteurs, to whom, it would seem, speaking in front of others would come easily—have been credited with quotes that belie a shared anxiety: "There are only two types of speakers in the world. 1. The nervous and 2. Liars," said Twain. Quipped Carnegie: "There are always three speeches for every one you actually give. The one you practiced, the one you gave, and the one you *wish* you gave."

Researchers trace the sweaty-palmed, heart-racing reactions we have to public speaking back to the primitive fight-or-flight response buried deep in our limbic brains; in our cave-dwelling days, a lone human, separate from the group, was a prime target for a predator. Though there are obviously no woolly mammoths cornering us at a client meeting, that primordial threat of being separated, isolated, on the spot, and alone translates into a modern fear of criticism, rejection, and not measuring up.

I've done plenty of public speaking throughout my career, but the pinnacle came last year when I had the honor of introducing my father as the Republican nominee for president of the United States at the Republican National Convention. I was speaking live to tens of millions of people on an occasion of unparalleled importance for our country and my family. To say I was nervous would be an understatement! True to form, it was my husband who talked me off the ledge and gave me the confidence to push through. He reminded me to take one step at a time, and helped me focus on my goal so that I wasn't overwhelmed by the enormity of the opportunity.

I realized, in those days leading up to the convention, that public speaking, particularly in such a challenging forum—where I would be addressing both a live audience in a packed arena and viewers at home—is equal parts substance and presentation. The speech has to be well written and thoughtful, of course, but good content with a lukewarm execution gets lost. A great delivery amplifies your message and makes it more memorable, and ultimately more impactful.

When I was preparing to speak at the RNC, there were a few strategies I employed that will likely prove useful to anyone getting ready to deliver prepared remarks in front of a group, whether it's forty people or forty million viewers!

✓ VISIT THE STAGE OR VENUE BEFOREHAND: Standing where you will actually be presenting, get a sense of the room. The goal is to eliminate uncertainty and gain familiarity. You can prepare yourself by knowing how long the walk is from the entrance to your spot, and visualize where you're going to present as you practice. Find out if you have a podium to stand behind and, if so, whether it's wood or glass (you wouldn't want to put a big binder on a glass podium, for example). If you're going to be holding a microphone in your hand, without a podium, you'd better have that speech down cold as you won't be able to discreetly refer to note cards.

✓ STAND UP WHEN YOU'RE PRACTICING: Time yourself as you say your speech aloud. It always takes a lot longer to get through a speech or presentation than you think it will. Practice speaking aloud as you would when presenting—seek to modulate your tone, speed up and slow down, and punctuate certain words for emphasis.

✓ PRACTICE IN FRONT OF PEOPLE: Classic studies by the late Stanford psychologist Robert Zajonc demonstrated that the mere presence of other people raises our awareness. If you practice alone, you won't have a chance to adjust to that factor. When practicing for the RNC, I lined my kids up on the couch and made them listen to me countless times! Rehearse over and over again, out loud. If you keep stumbling on the same sentence or word, change it.

✓ USE YOUR BODY: Once in front of your audience, plant your feet for balance and confidence. Consultant John Paul Engel, who began his speaking career on Capitol Hill delivering briefs on employment numbers and economic data, says that over the years he's learned that using some of the same body language cues you use in conversation—but in a more exaggerated way—can be useful in reinforcing key points. Moving when you're transitioning to a new message, stepping forward and bending slightly toward the audience as if you were telling them a secret when delivering an important point, or raising three fingers when you have three points to make are some examples.

✓ GET IN THE ZONE: "The single most important thing a great presenter does is carve out a quiet space before stepping onto that stage or platform," says Joan Detz, author of *How to Write and Give a Speech*. Clearing your head and rehearsing mentally result in laser focus and positive energy.

✓ RENAME YOUR ANXIETY "EXCITEMENT": Adam Grant warns, "Don't try to calm down. Not only do people who try to relax (and succeed) before speaking show a lack of persuasiveness and confidence during their speech, one of the hardest things to do is to relax on command, which, in turn, can make you more anxious. Instead of saying, 'I am calm,' or 'I'm nervous, scared and anxious,' repeating 'I am excited!' can actually help you feel less afraid and more enthusiastic about tackling the challenge at hand."

✓ CHECK THE NEWS: Be aware before you speak of anything that might be relevant to your presentation. There may be something timely that you'll want to either include or eliminate from your content.

✓ PRACTICE, PRACTICE, PRACTICE: There are no shortcuts if you want to nail your delivery and maximize your message's resonance.

All these tips aside, probably the most reassuring thing I do in moments of high stress is to remind myself of what matters most and express gratitude. If I bomb totally, my kids won't look at me any differently. I ask myself, "Will I be less in the eyes of my husband?" No. If anything, he may love me a bit more—because he'll know I need it! Do the best you can. If you fail, and it does happen occasionally, keep perspective and ask yourself: "In the eyes of those who are most important to me, what's the real consequence?"

> The goal is to provide inspiring information that moves people to action.
>
> **—Guy Kawasaki, author of** *Enchantment*

CONNECTION: THE KEY TO SATISFACTION AT WORK

> I define connection as the energy that exists between people when they feel seen, heard, and valued; when they can give and receive without judgment; and when they derive sustenance and strength from the relationship.
>
> **—Brené Brown, speaker and author of** *Daring Greatly*

When you're focused on simply finding or doing a job in order to make ends meet, the concept of satisfaction at work might seem irrelevant, even precious—but similar to passion, connecting with a career, a cause, and our colleagues is an essential component to success. For women who work, it's not just about climbing a ladder but about best utilizing our many talents to find meaning in our lives. Work provides us with a sense of purpose; a vehicle for creative self-expression; the opportunity to contribute to a mission that matters to us and to others. As Adam Grant puts it, "Meaning-making . . . [provides] a chance for us to reveal who we are through what we do."

When we align ourselves with a purpose, a project, and a team that reflect our interests and values, we are more productive and more likely to achieve great things. Research shows that "people with strong networks and mentors enjoy more promotions, higher pay, and greater work satisfaction." In particular, studies show that female leaders benefit from professional development and active career support. And when they lead, they often achieve higher team performance because of their ability to connect.

Sadly, according to a 2013 Gallup report, only 30 percent of American employees feel engaged at work—worldwide, across 142 countries, that figure drops to 13 percent.

Your boss, coworkers, team members, and mentors have an enormous amount of influence on how you feel about your work and how largely you succeed. As Matthew Kelly, author of *The Rhythm of Life*, says, "The people we surround ourselves with either raise or lower our standards. They either help us to become the best version of ourselves or encourage us to become lesser versions of ourselves. . . . No man becomes great on his own. No woman becomes great on her own. . . . We all need people in our lives who raise our standards, remind us of our essential purpose, and challenge us to become the-best-version-of-ourselves."

You are a woman who works at connecting—with your team, your boss, even yourself. Embracing your authenticity, being a supportive coworker, and going a step further to connect with your boss personally can help foster professional relationships that will lead to greater satisfaction and bigger rewards for you *and* your team.

Be Authentic to Create Connection

> There are two ways of spreading light: to be the candle or the mirror that reflects it.
>
> —Edith Wharton

"Authenticity [is] the new currency in business—it matters that much," explains executive coach Elizabeth Cronise McLaughlin. Authenticity means being yourself, and being comfortable being yourself. Your goal is to get to a place where you can be the same person, all the time, in every area of life.

If you're following your passions, both at work and on your own time, you are far more likely to be comfortable extending yourself to others in a genuine way than if you feel confused or conflicted. It's exhausting to don one persona at the office and another at home. If you're struggling with feeling comfortable in your own skin or in your current role, McLaughlin recommends hiring a coach, finding a mentor (see page 69), or seeing a therapist to explore strategies to help you feel better. Being yourself isn't just important to your performance—it's important to every aspect of your well-being.

Authenticity is fundamentally about trust. When we are authentic—when we are honest and genuine in our interactions—others know they can rely on us to show up and to keep our word; they can also depend upon us to speak the truth, even at challenging professional moments.

That said, in an era of oversharing, it's important to note that being authentic doesn't mean candidly sharing every thought that comes to mind, wearing your emotions on your sleeve at the office, or using authenticity as an excuse to be unprofessional ("I am who I am!"). Part of growing into your role as a leader means using discretion where necessary; it's naïve to think that acting inappropriately (under the guise of being authentic) won't affect your boss's or your team's perception of you, or your ultimate success.

I like the concept of marrying authenticity—being forthright with ourselves and others about what matters most—with sincerity, which is about aspiring to become a better leader, friend, wife, and mother. "When we're focused not just on who we are, but who we sincerely want to be, we'll push ourselves to become our ideal selves," says Adam Grant. "We won't be looking to make our existing selves more transparent. We'll be trying to become a higher version of ourselves."

BE A TEAM PLAYER

> Building relationships is part of your day job. It's not just about
> advancing; it's about maintaining your well-being and that of
> your teams. Connectedness . . . addresses a deep human need.
> A leader with strong connections to colleagues and team
> members can share her sense of meaning and mission—inspiring
> others to make extraordinary commitment to the work, too.
>
> **—Joanna Barsh and Susie Cranston**

Cultivating authenticity is essential to creating strong bonds with your coworkers, but it's just the beginning. In order for people to learn that they can trust you, they have to get to know you, which best happens organically, over time, and with genuine, sincere effort. The ability to work well on a team can truly make (or break) your career; strong team players are able to do more and make a bigger impact on their companies, so it's a skill well worth developing.

How can you ensure that you're giving your team your best and your all?

Know that there's room for everyone to rise: It's only natural to feel competitive with some members of your team, but the key to a happy, functional workplace is to remember that you and your colleagues are on the same side, working toward the same goals. In fact, "more women than ever before are refusing to compete with other women in the workplace, opting instead to lift them up at work in concrete, change-making ways," shares McLaughlin. "Look around your workplace and ask yourself: am I supporting the women I work with, women on my team and women who could use my mentorship? If not, it's time to act. The truth of women's leadership is that, in fact, there is plenty of room for all of us at the top, and when one of us succeeds, we all win."

In meetings, really listen to what your colleagues have to say: Don't rush to communicate your own ideas. Support their thoughts; don't be quick to shoot them down or contradict them. Whether you agree or disagree with what they have to say, be considerate in your responses.

Don't gossip: While it's sometimes easy to get caught up in "who said what about whom," especially if the people around you are doing it, focus instead on making a difference. Keep things positive and professional. After all, "Gossip inevitably blows back on the person circulating it, most often in the form of performance reviews that question the focus of the employee on the true task at hand: their work," says McLaughlin. "Place your attention on your performance and your productivity, and leave the water cooler gossip to others."

Lead by example: In my experience, there is no better way to prove you're a team player than to show your team that you wouldn't ask them to do anything you wouldn't do yourself. Leading by example doesn't just mean doing the right thing at a high level; it means you're in the trenches with everyone else, doing what needs to be done, even—or especially—when it's hard. Model for your team that everyone does the tough stuff, and when you face it head-on, it's not as overwhelming. Pick up that project that has no ownership or never seems to get completed. Take on the more onerous tasks that others avoid. Demonstrate that you're a self-starter who isn't just checking the box on a task, but going the distance to do the job well. Let your team see that you're willing to take on more than everyone else. For every employee who runs from a fire—or makes a negative impression by looking to avoid tough or mundane tasks—there's an opportunity for someone else to make a positive impression by unflinchingly embracing things that may be undesirable, but necessary.

I've done this throughout my career, and I always notice someone on my team who does the same. It's not only a great strategy for establishing your value, it's a habit that will set you up well for continued future success.

> We don't accomplish anything in this world alone. Whatever happens is the result of the whole tapestry of one's life—all the weavings of individual threads from one to another that create something.
>
> **—Sandra Day O'Connor, Supreme Court justice**

Bond with Your Boss

Now that you're forging authentic relationships with your coworkers, how do you best connect with your boss? A positive working relationship with a supervisor is often built on the right amount of self-disclosure. In my experience, people just starting in the workforce are either reluctant to talk about themselves or end up going too far in the other direction and sharing too much too soon. How do you know what to say, and just how personal to get?

Take a cue from those around you. When your boss shares something that was pivotal early in her career, that's an opportunity for you to respond in kind. Connecting her story with something personal from your background or experience creates a natural bond. Look for these cues and, if they aren't obvious, ask questions. Inquire about her previous career history; ask her how she got to where she is today. Before you know it, you've planted the seeds for a personal relationship and given her the opportunity to see you as someone with broader experiences to bring to the team.

Even though you likely spend plenty of time together day to day at meetings, on calls, and discussing projects, make it a priority to get out of the office every few months to catch up and break bread—away from the phones, e-mails, and frequent interruptions. Spending even an hour together can really help you bond on a more personal level. Establishing this connection also makes it easier to be forthcoming about your thoughts and feelings about your relationship, your role on the team, your career aspirations at the company and at large.

Think you deserve a promotion? Hoping for more than a cost-of-living raise? (You'll learn everything I know about negotiating on pages 91–104.) Broaching these topics in a setting that's warmer and more casual than her office will take the pressure off you both; continuing the dialogue in a more formal way at review time will alleviate the need to try to cover everything in one sitting. And sharing your thoughts a few months prior to your annual performance appraisal will give your boss the opportunity to pay closer attention to what you're working on, providing you both with more proof that you're deserving of advancement.

CAPITALIZE ON YOUR CONNECTION: WORKING THROUGH OFFICE CONFLICT

> Never argue with a fool; onlookers may not be able to tell the difference.
>
> —Mark Twain

Sometimes, despite our best efforts, conflict arises in the office. Not getting along with your boss, coworker, or team can be very stressful, in part because most of us spend more time at work than anywhere else, and also because we are hardwired to want to work well with others. When we're at odds, awkwardness and bad feelings can impede our productivity, erode goodwill, and possibly lead to being fired.

The first thing to do, says Elizabeth Cronise McLaughlin, is to evaluate your own role in the situation and own it. "This is often the hardest step in resolving conflict, because it involves taking a long look at the dynamic and figuring out the part of it for which we bear responsibility. If you made a mistake at work that upset your boss, you need to own up to it and apologize. If you're in constant conflict with a coworker because you're secretly envious of her success, you need to own that, too." And if you're repeatedly butting heads with a member of your team because she doesn't seem to understand your instructions, stop to reconsider the effectiveness of your own communication. "Candid, objective self-evaluation in any conflict is the most important step to resolving that conflict now and down the road."

Next, consider how you'd like a difficult conversation to go, from start to finish. This isn't a script to follow. McLaughlin asks her clients to write down "how they want to enter the conversation emotionally, how they want the conversation to flow, and how they want all parties to feel when the conversation is over." Keep the goal of the conversation in mind. This exercise will ground you for when you do have the actual conversation, and ensure that things stay on track.

When you meet, communicate your desire to resolve the conflict. Begin with an apology. This step can be tough, says McLaughlin, "but you stand a much better chance of resolving any conflict in your work-place if you begin the conversation . . . by owning what's yours, apologizing for your part in the dynamic, and clearly expressing your desire to move forward."

McLaughlin recommends Marshall Rosenberg's nonviolent communication strategy, which involves using "I" language about your own behavior, aligning your observations with your needs and values, and then asking for the buy-in of the other party to resolve the conflict. Saying to your coworker, "When I hear you interrupt me in meetings, it really upsets me," puts the onus on *your* observation, feelings, and reaction, not the other person's behavior, and invites her empathy and assistance. Compared with the more confrontational approach of saying, "You always interrupt me" or "You make me mad," this strategy is much more likely to result in resolution. Also, avoid categorical statements that put the other person on the defensive, i.e., "You never," "You always," and so on.

"Keep in mind that a lack of effective communication is often at the root of conflict," McLaughlin adds. "The more clearly you can express your desire to end the conflict and effectively explore solutions to it with the other person involved," the more likely you are to resolve the conflict for good.

NETWORKING: WHOM TO KNOW, WHAT TO SAY, AND HOW TO BE A VALUABLE CONTACT

It's not what you know but who you know that makes the difference.

—Anonymous

The ability to network well is an important asset to your career and a natural outgrowth of developing strong communication skills and relationships. Now that you've learned to communicate more effectively in the office, it's essential to apply those skills to connecting in your company and industry. You are a woman who works at networking—which doesn't come easily to everyone, but *can* be taught. In person at events, or one-on-one with a mentor, your network is one of your greatest resources—a fount of information, wisdom, experience, and opportunity.

> People influence people. Nothing influences people more than a recommendation from a trusted friend.

> —Mark Zuckerberg

Foster In-Person Relationships

We touched very briefly upon networking when we explored how to develop your curiosity, and validate and experiment with your passions without quitting your day job. Typically, the most common hurdle in networking is that you don't know who to approach *and* you feel sheepish about the fact that the overture seems, well, transactional. I completely agree that it's not always easy to extend yourself to a perfect stranger, especially when it might seem like you're doing so only for your own personal benefit.

So my response is—*don't*. Socially or professionally, whether I'm at a party or an industry conference, I always prefer forming a strong bond with one new person I can connect with over collecting a stack of business cards from a bunch of people I've spoken to only briefly. As my friend Tony Hsieh, the CEO of Zappos, has said, "Focus on just building relationships and getting to know people as just people, regardless of their position in the business world. . . . If you are able to figure out how to be truly interested in someone you meet, with the goal of building up a friendship instead of trying to get something out of that person, the funny thing is that almost always, something happens later on down the line that ends up benefiting either your business or yourself personally."

Try reframing the concept as a relational experience rather than a transactional one: networking is genuinely wanting to learn something from someone versus trying to "get" something out of them. Building relationships by showing an interest in *what* another person knows, not *whom* they know—which amounts to an exchange of insight and wisdom—is much more meaningful and far less of an ask. It also shows that you value the person not just for what they can "do" for you but for what they can teach you.

I find the best way to broaden your network is to make genuine connections with people across all industries, or, as Adam Grant recommends, through "weak ties," a term originally introduced by sociologist Mark Granovetter in 1973. Typically, we rely on what Grant calls our "strong ties"—those people we know well and truly trust. Yet Granovetter's research revealed that people were 58 percent more likely to find a new job opportunity through acquaintances than good friends.

"Strong ties tend to give us redundant knowledge," says Grant, building on Granovetter's work. If everyone you know knows the same people and/or are from your same industry, they're likely thinking about things in the same way you are. Weak ties are effective because those people work in different industries or travel in social circles unfamiliar to you. In this case, the goal is to engage with people who aren't carbon copies of the people you work with every day. I've had a lot of deals come to fruition through relationships I've made in totally unrelated fields—I first met Tony Hsieh in Washington, D.C., in 2009 at a White House roundtable event to discuss the future of the economy. Jared and I were honored to be included at such a prestigious gathering of the country's top young business leaders. Tony and I crossed paths again some time later, when he appeared on an episode of *The Celebrity Apprentice*. Now, our relationship has come full circle, as his company sells my collection online. Opportunities come from strange and unexpected places; it's not always the obvious course that pans out.

Another incredible source of contacts is what Grant calls "dormant ties," comprised of the people you used to know, from your childhood, college, or earlier jobs. A study showed that when hundreds of executives were asked to seek advice from dormant ties on a major work project, they gleaned more useful information from them than from current contacts. The reason? Your formative bonds with these people remain strong, and, in the time since you've been in touch, they have lived fascinating lives, complete with new relationships and experiences. If, in your former life, you treated them well, they'll remember that and will usually respond in kind.

Develop your network because you genuinely like people, respect them, and want to get to know them. Whether you're reaching out for career reasons or to cultivate a new passion, when the relationship itself is the reward, the fact that this person is a "valuable contact" becomes an added bonus.

The more diverse your contacts are, the more likely you'll derive both personal and business benefits down the road. My husband once remarked that by using your lit candle to light another, your candle doesn't burn any less bright. I love to think about this when fostering connections. In my experience, those who have the best networks are often the people who are the most giving. They don't connect people for their own benefit, but because they see a mutual interest and legitimately want to make a difference for others.

My favorite personal example of this is how Jared and I have introduced seven couples who've gotten married. Seven! (We joke that our hidden talent is matchmaking, but that we don't give guarantees. So far, so good, no divorces!) We see how our friends' strengths, passions, and personalities align, and we love helping the people we care about find happiness.

FIND A MENTOR

Colleagues are a wonderful thing—but mentors, that's where the real work gets done.

—Junot Díaz, author of *The Brief Wondrous Life of Oscar Wao*

In making your mark, you are communicating thoughtfully and strategically; you're asking smart questions, becoming a better listener, running meetings in a more enlightened manner, and delivering your presentations with confidence and poise. Your team respects you; your boss says she couldn't live without you. You're broadening and deepening your network to include people you've really gotten to know and care about.

Now what?

You're full of ambition and big ideas; you have clear goals, but you need guidance. What you really need is a mentor—someone who can advise you on your short- and long-term objectives, connect you with people in your industry, and troubleshoot challenges with you as they arise.

Recall that I created IvankaTrump.com and #WomenWhoWork to encourage and facilitate a new form of mentorship between and among my extensive network and the many young women who were reaching out to me for professional guidance. My mission is to empower and inspire women and this was a scalable way to do that. It's so important to have someone experienced in your corner, available to give advice, sharpen your skills, and offer a different point of view.

Angie Chang is a vice president at Hackbright Academy, where she helps women build their skills and provides them with mentors, pointing them toward careers in tech. She also founded Bay Area Girl Geek Dinners and founded Women 2.0, two organizations geared toward connecting women in the tech industry. Chang is passionate about creating a network of women who teach each other and build each other up in their careers. Here are a few of her best tips for standing out in a crowd and finding the person who's right for you:

Talk to everyone: "Make your presence known to potential mentors by attending happy hours, talks, and conferences focused on your industry or the industry you're interested in. Formulate an opinion about the current state of the industry and where it is going, and test out your hypotheses at cocktail parties. Sharing your thoughts, experiences, and new ideas to attract and find a like-minded potential mentor is a crucial first step."

Create a personal board of advisers: "Imagine you are creating a board of three to five advisers to guide you through various things you're working at—everything from a skill that will further your career to a newfound hobby. Having a group of mentors, as opposed to just one, will make you more well-rounded."

Identify a good fit: Your ideal mentor "should be accomplished, of course, but there's more to it. A good mentor is someone who is able to see your potential and is willing to develop it. A mentor doesn't have to be the CEO or a VP. Some of the best mentors are one level ahead of the mentee."

Take it slow: You wouldn't ask a guy to be your boyfriend on the first date; nor should you aggressively pursue a mentor. You have to gradually build the relationship before you ask someone to commit. "To build rapport, be unfailing. Don't flake on meetings and be extremely responsive and proactive." Once you establish the mentorship, initiate a standing appointment. "Fulfill your obligations, show that you do your research, and make sure you demonstrate to your mentor that you are learning and growing" because of her advice.

Show that you have a vision for your future: "A mentor wants to see that you have a general direction—you know where you want to go and you have specific goals" to get there. You aren't expected to have every little detail figured out, but a mentor needs you to have an endgame in mind so that she knows how to help you.

Listen and execute: "As a mentor, there's nothing more frustrating than a mentee who doesn't take your advice. Listen to your mentor," show that you're taking her suggestions, and demonstrate how you're using her advice. "Give regular updates about what you're specifically doing" to implement her ideas.

Manage the relationship: Take the initiative and manage up. "You have more to gain from the connection, and your mentor's time tends to be more valuable than yours. It's your responsibility to check in with your mentor regularly with updates on what you've been doing to research your short- and long-term goals."

While it can be hard to ask for help, particularly from someone you may not know well, who you do know is busy and accomplished, mentoring is a reciprocal relationship. You bring a fresh perspective to an industry she knows well; you may even be able to supplement her skill set in those areas where she's lacking. Also, most successful people agree to mentor someone because they care to have a positive influence on the next generation of leaders. Having an accomplished mentee is a reward in its own right. When you succeed, your mentor does, too.

INSPIRE A CAREER SPONSOR

While a mentor can be key to your success, a sponsor—someone who advocates on your behalf behind the scenes and helps to build your reputation—is also incredibly important, and entirely different.

"A sponsor is often a senior-level person who has recognized your worth and contributions and advocates on your behalf without you knowing about it," explains career coach Pamela Weinberg. Meaning, you often don't realize you have a sponsor, until certain doors have been opened. "They may put your name in for a promotion or assignment, and can boost your workplace reputation, supporting you in situations where you're not present to represent your interests."

So if you don't know who your sponsor is, how do you go about securing one? "Seek out senior leaders who are not only respected in your workplace, but who also have the authority to advocate for you and get things done," advises Elizabeth Cronise McLaughlin. "Your best sponsors will be those who garner admiration and influence such that others will follow their recommendations."

Weinberg suggests building relationships with executives at your company by doing such things as volunteering when charitable opportunities come up, joining the company running group, or getting involved in other after-hours activities. "Doing so allows key people to get to know you in a variety of settings," she explains. If you've identified someone who could be a potential sponsor, McLaughlin suggests simply swinging by her office and saying, "I'd love an opportunity to work with you on your next project. Would you be willing to keep me in mind?" When she does, ensure you do your best possible work.

Adam Grant notes that the best way to cultivate a sponsorship situation is to find out what leaders' major priorities are, and offer to contribute. "You can ask them what their biggest challenges are, if they have any projects where they could use extra help, and if they know anyone else who's doing work that's up your alley." He suggests saying something like, "I'm looking for opportunities to develop my skills in these three areas—are you involved in anything that might be relevant, and are there other people you'd recommend contacting?"

If you show senior members of your company what you bring to the table, they'll take notice. "Proving your value is fundamentally about making yourself indispensable to senior leadership," says McLaughlin. "This means not only doing your best work within your assigned responsibilities, but also being a creative problem-solver. I recommend that my clients imagine that they were in charge of their company or team, and consider what they might do to generate new business, fix an ongoing issue, or create a dynamic new offering." Proposing solutions and new lines of revenue and becoming a go-to thought leader within your company is a surefire way to show you matter.

If you want higher-ups at your company to notice and endorse you when opportunities arise, be a person who runs toward the fire and embraces those tasks that never seem to get completed. Take the initiative and get results.

YOU ARE A WOMAN WHO WORKS— AT MAKING HER MARK

One of the best ways to discover your worth, cultivate your confidence, and make your mark is to surround yourself with people who clearly see your value—on your team, in your industry, within your network, and in the whole of your life. Forging an authentic community of women who cheer your successes, learn from your failures, and support you all the same is key to ascending to the next level of your career and staking your claim. My father always says, if you're going to be thinking anyway, you may as well be thinking *big*. From deals and acquisitions at The Trump Organization to launching and growing my own company, I approach my professional aspirations with an eye toward accomplishing something even greater tomorrow.

Work hard, stay humble, and challenge yourself in every aspect of your life. Seek feedback on your work from your community, peers, and superiors. Criticism may be hard to hear, but in the end, it will make you better. Be confident enough to ask questions. The whole of your career will benefit if you take these critical steps now, and on a daily basis, to set yourself up to make your mark—then stake your claim—in your company, your industry, and your life.

THE MAGIC WORKS
THROUGH YOU. NOT
BESIDE YOU.
NOT AROUND YOU.
Not for you. Through You.
CHOOSE your STAGE,
Do Your Dance,
STAKE YOUR CLAIM.

MIKE DOOLEY

#ITWISEWORDS

CHAPTER THREE

Stake Your Claim

Maximize Your Influence at Work

I f you're like me and you're excited by the idea of maximizing your influence, taking on new challenges, and inspiring others, you're ready to stake your claim. Staking your claim represents a turning point in your career: you've achieved a certain level of success, and you're going to be deepening your professional skills, advancing to a more senior leadership role, and making the greatest impact where you are—or thinking about where you're going next.

Simply put, staking your claim means declaring something your own. Early in our country's history, as new territories were acquired or opened—particularly during the gold rush—a citizen could literally put a stake in the ground and call the land theirs. The land itself, and everything on it, legally became that person's property.

In business today, staking your claim means owning your experience, developing your expertise, and using both to carve out a successful niche for yourself. It's earning a reputation based on excellent performance and impeccable integrity; committing yourself 100 percent to hiring and leading a top-notch team of people who share your passions and values; knowing your worth and negotiating promotions and raises; or leaving your current situation to pursue your dream job.

You are a woman who works at managing your team and your career. In staking your claim, you'll be augmenting those foundational spheres of success you developed in Chapter Two—communication, connection, and networking—with the more elevated power bases of leadership, negotiation, and professional development.

Opportunities multiply as they are seized.

—Sun Tzu

MANAGING A TEAM: LEARNING AND LEADING

We are what we repeatedly do. Excellence, therefore, is not an act but a habit.

—Will Durant, author of The Story of Philosophy

At the beginning of my career, I believed that success was an individual pursuit. Since my parents had instilled such a solid work ethic in my brothers and me, I just assumed that that meant taking on as much as I could and doing it all well.

Now I know that success is a team sport. I soon figured out that you can't be an expert at everything, and even if you think you are, you're likely spreading yourself too thin to effectively capitalize on the highest and best use of your skills—those areas where you add unique value.

Construction is a great industry in which to learn lessons about teamwork. You're literally managing hundreds of contractors from different trades, each with his or her own agenda, all of whom must rally around a common goal in order for *you* to succeed. The fact is, a developer is nothing without an incredible team; it doesn't matter how well articulated, grand, or exciting your plans are. The hotel industry is the same. You can build the finest hotel in the world, but if you don't have a stellar management team in place (once you open the doors) to exceed your guest's expectations, she may stay there once but won't return. However extraordinary the property may be, what you've built is completely beside the point if your service isn't exceptional.

The bottom line is, we are happier, more effective, and more productive when surrounded by smart, creative, hardworking people. Shawn Achor tells us why: "When we have a community of people we can count on . . . we multiply our emotional, intellectual, and physical resources. We bounce back from setbacks faster, accomplish more, and feel a greater sense of purpose." Whatever your industry, working with a strong team—whether it's one you inherit, one you hire, or, more likely, some combination of the two—will make *you* more successful.

Starting off on the right foot with your new team is important, and it's up to you to set the tone for how you expect to work. People learn through your actions what you prioritize—for better or worse. I've always believed that a boss has to work harder than anyone else, not just to get the job done but also to send the right message and inspire her team to become their best selves.

Model the behavior you wish to see in those around you. If you want to be able to trust your team—to do excellent work, represent the company appropriately, and act in the team's best interests—your very first priority is to get them to trust *you*, and for that to happen, you must be real and you must be genuine in your concern for them. I've mentioned the power of authenticity before, but when you're in charge of a team, walking the walk, keeping your word, and going to bat for your direct reports is critical. To engender loyalty and goodwill, your team needs to feel like you really care about them, and they won't unless you actually do.

In his TED Talk entitled "Why Good Leaders Make You Feel Safe," Simon Sinek shares the incredibly moving story of Captain William Swenson, who received the Congressional Medal of Honor for selflessly and courageously running into a live-fire situation in Afghanistan in September 2009 in order to usher wounded soldiers to safety and retrieve his fallen comrades. Sinek wondered whether heroes like Captain Swenson exist simply because they are better people, or whether genuine mutuality and respect could be taught and cultivated among leaders like us. He concluded: "What I learned was that it's the environment, and if you get the environment right, every single one of us has the capacity to do these remarkable things, and more importantly, others have that capacity too. I've had the great honor of getting to meet some of these, who we would call heroes, who have put themselves and put their lives at risk to save others, and I asked them, 'Why would you do it? Why did you do it?' And they all say the same thing: 'Because they would have done it for me.'" This deep loyalty seems to stem from a profound bond of trust and cooperation.

Remember that your people are your greatest asset: This is at the heart of learning to lead. The takeaway for business leaders from Captain Swenson's example is that genuine trust and strong cohesiveness emerge among team members when they sincerely feel that their boss or colleagues have their backs and "would do the same" for them, as Sinek explains. It's your job to oversee *people*—not processes or projects, P&Ls, sample designs, deadlines, or logistics. These things all matter—but not nearly as much as the human beings who make all these important functions happen well and on time. Sinek says, "We cannot lead numbers. We cannot lead an organization. We can ONLY lead people." I know a lot of really intelligent people who were great at their jobs but were promoted and became terrible managers. Transitioning from being the one who *does* the work to the one who *oversees* the work can be difficult and often requires you to cultivate a different set of skills. Take your time to get it right, because if you don't, it's hard to regain your team's admiration, loyalty, and respect.

Delegate judiciously: This is another incredibly important lesson for leading. A finance billionaire once told me that to scale a business you have to know how to delegate: "A great employee will do something 80 percent the same way you would do it. The last 20 percent is their personal take on the deliverable. There's a 50 percent chance that your way would be the right way and a 50 percent chance that their way is better. They're not going to do it 100 percent the same way you would, but you have to hope that you hire people who will do things better than you would, who will try things that are smartly conceived. You have to get comfortable with people doing things 80 percent the way you would have done them in order to scale a business." The ability to delegate smartly is critical.

Learning to delegate can be a challenge for the best leaders, especially when you start out small. I have occasional micromanaging tendencies myself, but I know that in order to accomplish big things, I have to trust my people to execute. If you can't rely on someone on your team to do a job well, maybe you haven't hired the right person, or maybe you haven't created appropriate checkpoints throughout the process. Making very clear what it is you want done, allowing people to do it, and checking in periodically are critical to ensuring they arrive at the end goal you have in mind.

In deciding what to delegate, you don't want to send the message to your team that either you're willing to do all the work yourself or that you don't trust them to do it as well as you. So here's a good rule of thumb: If you really *can* do something better than anyone else and it's important to the business, then do it yourself. At the same time, don't do anything that someone else can do better than you. It can be hard to step away, but in order to grow your business and responsibilities, you need to make very smart decisions about how your time is best spent—remember big-picture priorities—and you need your employees to feel a sense of ownership and pride in their contributions.

Be careful not to create fire drills: The worst thing you can do as a manager is elevate everything to a level of urgency or to frequently assign projects that never come to fruition. When people put in a lot of time and effort, often on a tight schedule, it can be really demoralizing if you don't follow up with them and give them feedback on their deliverables.

I have friends in investment banking who will get a call on a Friday night about an urgent report or analysis that needs to be ready by Monday. They spend all weekend working, turn it in on time, then never hear a word about it again. When you start delegating, be mindful not to waste people's time. If a deal or project doesn't materialize, explain to your team why, extol the value of the work they put in, and communicate that it was helpful in your decision-making process.

Know that you can be kind and still be effective: In communicating clear goals to your team, you want to inspire your colleagues, and you want them to feel that you genuinely care about them and their well-being and see them for more than just the value they add to the company. If this is your goal—and it should be—being kind and thoughtful won't be perceived as weakness; rather, it leads to a higher level of collaboration and engagement. That's the incredible value of connection that we explored in Chapter Two.

I expect that my team will accomplish their goals, well and on time, but I can still be gracious in relaying this information. With that said, if you aren't naturally a nice person, it doesn't work to fake it. In my view, there are plenty of brilliant leaders, like Steve Jobs, who weren't known to be particularly warm but were incredibly effective at motivating and inspiring their teams by being doggedly mission driven. Everyone at Apple knew that Jobs would always put the company and the team above himself—not because he was altruistic but because he was fervently devoted to the cause.

An area where typically "kind" managers can falter, especially when they are new leaders, is in offering feedback or constructive criticism to their direct reports, whether in daily discourse, weekly check-ins, or an annual performance review. Either they are fearful of coming off as too soft or not authoritative enough, so they swing too far in the other direction, eroding the warmth and goodwill it takes so long to build; or they want so desperately to be liked that they have a tough time being critical and fail to deliver necessary feedback. This is where well-articulated and quantifiable business goals and expectations are key. If someone isn't living up to predetermined, mutually agreed-upon goals, it's easy to communicate this objectively rather than try to deliver more abstract complaints.

In addition to being honest in your critique of your team member's performance, ask questions in order to understand her motivations. You may find that isolated incidents, or lack of clear direction, resources, or support, have affected her ability to perform. Whatever the reason, you'll both walk away with a clearer sense of what went awry and how it can be remedied, your relationship intact and, often, bolstered.

HIRING TO FORTIFY YOUR WORLD-CLASS TEAM

If you can hire people whose passion intersects with the job, they won't require any supervision at all. They will manage themselves better than anyone could ever manage them. Their fire comes from within, not from without. Their motivation is internal, not external.

—Stephen Covey

At Ivanka Trump, my team and I are striving to create the lives we want to live. Every single person who joins my company knows that we are determined; we embody the mission of the brand and we lead by example. We're respectful; we strive to act graciously always. We're engaged; we're in this together and we trust one another. We're ambitious; we're intellectually curious and always learning and trying to get better. We're motivated; we believe that success is up to us. We're dedicated; we're accountable to one another in achieving our shared goals. And we're optimistic; we see challenges as opportunities. Those are our core values, and I deliberately hire people who embody them.

So how do you build a world-class team? First, you have to find the right people. When hiring, I look for a killer work ethic and the grit to persevere in the face of challenge. I want self-starters, people who are optimistic, dedicated, and really accountable to one another, who work toward achieving shared goals and are motivated to succeed. I like people who aren't shy about describing themselves as "ambitious," and who hold themselves to a higher standard than anyone else—myself included—holds them to.

I also love hiring people who come from other industries. They inevitably bring a unique perspective to the table and rarely think "that's not the way we do it" because they haven't been conditioned to follow an industry blueprint. People who cross over from one field to another are usually very versatile in applying their skills, thinking creatively, and challenging convention. They are experts at opening your eyes to new ways of doing things and can add tremendous value to your team.

I also seek out candidates who are strong where my team and I might not yet be. Elizabeth Cronise McLaughlin echoes that sentiment: "The best leaders are able to identify gaps in their own knowledge, and admit them, so that they can hire others to fill in where they're lacking. Why? Because feigning expertise is a sure-fire way to end up with blind spots in your business. Admit what you don't know, and look to hire others who have expertise you don't have. When you do so, you'll also give others permission to admit what they don't know, and your whole team will be able to benefit by thinking strategically about each other's assets to complete those knowledge gaps."

In aspiring to build a team that supports your strengths and supplements your areas of weakness, it's crucial to self-assess. Refer back to your life's blueprint and reflect upon it, especially if you haven't in a while. Say, "Here are the areas where I'm strong and I'm going to focus the majority of my energy on making them even better." The skills you need to hire for are in those areas where you're weak. Of course, you still require a certain level of proficiency—for example, if you're not a great writer, you can hire someone who's more gifted with words, but you must know enough about the message that you're looking to communicate in order to effectively manage her. If she's not doing an adequate job, you have to be tuned in enough to realize that.

After you know what you're looking for, you're ready to interview. Much like interviewing for a job yourself, interviewing *someone else* can be intimidating. No doubt the person sitting across from you feels she's more justified in being nervous, given that she stands to gain (or lose) an employment opportunity, but I remember going through the process of hiring the first few people on my team at Trump, and it is nerve racking!

Spend some time thinking about the strengths and requisite skill sets that a person needs in order to excel at the role you are looking to fill, and gear the interview specifically toward those things. Write a little cheat sheet of questions about both the candidate's professional and personal history to see if she'd be a good fit. Think about areas that were a source of excitement or concern for you on her résumé. For example, if it looks like she's jumped from job to job in a short period of time, jot down a note to discuss it further.

Ask questions about your candidate's life outside the office. It's a window into who she is as a person. When you ask about interests, hobbies, and passions that aren't work related, you can see what lights her up, and you can also tell, based on that, whether or not her personality and priorities would dovetail nicely with your team and management style. How does the candidate spend her free time? In my organization, I value people who are multidimensional. I like having a team with passions other than work who are curious to learn new things. Rather than worry that it detracts from their job, I know that living one life to the fullest makes my team more dynamic and more fulfilled. Satisfaction beyond the office means they'll bring that positivity and optimism to work.

When you are serious about a potential candidate, request references and call them yourself. Something I do *every single time* I consider hiring someone is request references from *each* place the candidate worked. The true stars typically have them at the ready, and their former bosses and colleagues are happy and willing to speak on their behalf. It's always a huge red flag for me when someone is reluctant or unprepared to provide reference names and numbers.

Again, don't just *ask* for references—call them! I call every single reference personally before I extend a job offer, and I expect my team to do so as well for their own direct reports. It's the best form of feedback, and the most basic thing you can do to assess a candidate outside of a meeting. The cost of hiring the wrong person is simply too great to leave the decision to your gut or chance. As Bradford D. Smart, PhD, author of *Topgrading*, reveals in his book, the cost of mishiring a supervisor is four times her base salary. A sales rep? Six times base. Hiring the wrong mid-manager costs eight times her annual compensation, while a misplaced executive costs the company *twenty-seven times* what she would be paid per year.

You'd be shocked, though, by how many people don't call. I've had friends hire people whom I know well or who have worked for me, and I am certain they've given me as a reference, yet I haven't gotten the call to provide a reference check. Is it because they assume a reference will always say glowing things, so why waste the time? Maybe. But I've received many negative references from people candidates have provided, so maybe not.

It's helpful to know that receiving some negative feedback isn't necessarily a reason not to hire someone. Think of the process as gathering intel about how to ensure your prospective team member will perform at her full potential. You need perspective on who your candidate is from people who've known her longer than you, and in a different capacity, to ensure you're making the right decision for your team. I always ask a reference how she would recommend managing a candidate to be her best self. She can't be weak at the thing I'm hiring her for, but if she isn't as strong in other areas, it may not be a deal breaker. I like to know in advance so that I can surround her with people who can support her appropriately and set her up to succeed. By asking this question, you can learn from references how to maximize the value of a new hire's contribution even before she's set foot in the office.

Also, know that since you're the one asking the questions, you get to guide the conversation. If what you're hearing are all positive generalities, get specific. Ask about a particular situation in which the candidate was challenged or give what Adam Grant calls a "forced choice question," where you ask which of two weaknesses is more likely. For example: "Is Katie more likely to be too detail oriented or not detail oriented enough?" This causes the reference to pause and reflect before answering, versus responding with the first thing that comes to mind. You're more likely to get useful details from a thought-provoking question than general small talk.

Top Hiring Dos and Don'ts

From Deirdre Rosen, senior vice president of Human Resources at The Trump Organization

For eight years, Deirdre Rosen has played an instrumental role in bringing some of the best and brightest talent to The Trump Organization. Starting as the director of Human Resources at Trump New York, she was shortly thereafter tapped to oversee HR for Trump Hotels internationally. In her role as senior vice president of Human Resources, Deirdre added HR for The Trump Organization to her roster of responsibilities. A wife, mother, certified yoga instructor, and barre enthusiast, Deirdre says, "I spend more time with the people I work with than anyone else in my life. I want the people on my team to have something to say. I want to connect with them, learn from their unique perspectives, and push forward with them. I want to see excitement and passion for the purpose of our business and be inspired by them. Some of my most successful hires didn't necessarily have the picture-perfect résumé—heck, I didn't have the picture-perfect résumé when I started in HR—but they had the hunger, drive, and humility to own and learn from mistakes, take advantage of opportunities that stretch their skill set, and just plain work hard to deliver results.

"While there is no silver bullet to finding a perfect hire, below are the best practices that I have adopted and utilize when interviewing candidates."

DO:

1. **HIRE FOR PASSION:** You can teach anyone to do virtually anything. You cannot teach passion. Passion is what you bring to the party.

2. **TAKE YOUR TIME:** Take time to connect. My favorite question to ask toward the end of an interview is "Tell me something about you that is not on your résumé." I have gleaned some of my best intelligence about what makes a candidate come to life by asking her to tell me something interesting about herself. I've heard it all, from "I competed in the Ironman" to "I was a nationally ranked youth oboist" to "I can tap dance." (Full disclosure: this was my answer . . . and I was once asked to prove it, which I did. What this person learned about me was that I am not afraid of a challenge—especially when it involves a triple time step!) It's *all* good stuff. You want to connect with the person who is joining your team, and establishing a rapport from the first encounter is incredibly valuable. It builds loyalty, creates energy, and helps to drive consensus and understanding from the get-go.

3. **MAKE SURE PEOPLE ARE WHO THEY SAY THEY ARE:** Double-check the names provided as references—using Google or LinkedIn—to make sure the references are who they say they are. Do the due diligence.

4. **KNOW THAT EVERY MOMENT COMMUNICATES A MESSAGE:** The interview process should reflect the expectations and

the working environment. Every conversation should communicate to the candidate what it's going to be like when they come to work with you. A chaotic process with multiple fits and starts belies a chaotic work environment. A well-organized process with thoughtful, pleasant, and engaging conversations telegraphs a much different message about the environment. You want to create excitement and buzz about your company—even if the person doesn't get this position, you want them to be eager for another opportunity to join your team.

5. ASK FOR A STORY: I like to ask questions that begin with "Tell me about a time when . . ." For example, Tell me about a time when you had a huge success at work, a time when you felt defeated, a time when you had to build a team from scratch, a time when you had competing priorities from your leader. I'll encourage them to tell me a story and ask follow-up questions to broaden the detail around the situation they are describing, and their role in moving the process forward. Keep in mind, your questions don't need to probe for a negative story; successes are also important to recognize in the interview process. In my experience, the answers to these types of behavior-based interview questions are solid predictors of future behavior. They also reveal opportunities to determine how self-actualized your candidate is—whether they possess the self-awareness to acknowledge growth opportunities as they have been presented with them, and how they view themselves in relation to the team and company.

DON'T:

1. DON'T HIRE PEOPLE WHO REMIND YOU OF YOU: You are already there—why would you want someone who will only reflect your views versus someone who will broaden, enrich, and enliven your perspective?

2. DON'T ASK QUESTIONS THAT ARE ILLEGAL: It seems obvious, but it's worth saying. Asking a candidate how old they are, how many kids they have, or if they are married is most likely

illegal, and most definitely inappropriate—even if you do it with a glint in your eye and start with "I know this isn't an HR-approved question, but . . ." It's also a waste of time. The information you glean from a question like this is not likely to be material to whether this person has the passion and energy to push forward the performance of your team. Hard pass.

3. **DON'T DISREGARD SOMEONE WITH A DIVERSE RÉSUMÉ AS UNFOCUSED OR A "JOB-HOPPER":** While your interviews may reveal one or both of these to be true, by immediately dismissing them, you may miss the opportunity to add a unique viewpoint and experience to your team. At worst, it's a short interview. At best, this person could have the energy, passion, and desire for growth that will perfectly complement your team. This is a "don't" that resonates with me personally, because many years ago, my first HR leader took a chance on my "imperfect" résumé, and here I am today—turns out I was a good bet!

4. **DON'T ASK FOR A LIST OF ATTRIBUTES:** Think: "Give me three words that describe you." Yawn. Anyone can list adjectives. This is not a valid way to predict performance. It is a great way to confirm biases—"Ah, yes! I am also hardworking. . . . This person will be great!"

5. **DON'T EVER SETTLE:** The opportunity cost of a "warm body" is too great. Never settle for "good enough" when *great* might be waiting for you in the next interview.

CULTIVATE THE TALENT ALREADY ON YOUR TEAM

I work hard to identify and foster talent from within; it's one of my father's greatest gifts as a leader, and, by example, one he taught to me. If someone starts out as an administrative assistant but demonstrates sound judgment and an interest in the business, I won't hesitate to give her more responsibility. If she's creative, I might promote her to our marketing team. Before long, a career that at first might have been limited by inexperience morphs into something far more rewarding—both for her and for the company.

In corporations everywhere, there are people who might be in the right organization but whose skills are unidentified and underutilized, their professional passions hidden just beneath the surface. They might lack the platform to showcase their abilities, but possess raw talent. I'm constantly on the lookout for people who are hungry to take on more, because it's worth investing in someone who already knows the organization and demonstrates drive. If it works out, as a manager you receive the loyalty and enthusiasm of a productive, dedicated employee. There's not a lot to lose, and so much to gain—and not just talentwise. According to Matthew Bidwell, a management professor at Wharton, "external hires" get significantly lower performance evaluations for their first two years on the job than do internal workers who are promoted into similar jobs. External hires also have higher exit rates, and they are paid "substantially more"—about 18 percent to 20 percent more. So cultivating the talent you have is good business, too.

Giavona Sullivan started as an assistant on one of The Trump Organization's golf properties and then moved to Florida and worked as a receptionist at the Mar-a-Lago Club in Palm Beach. She was very talented and great with people so soon was promoted to golf membership sales at Trump International. After a couple of years, Gia moved to New York City and began working in our corporate offices, on cross-property golf membership sales. In passing one day, I overheard that she had studied interior design in college, so I decided to give her a small design project as a test. She nailed it, so I assigned her more design work. Finally, I moved her off the golf team and onto the development team, where she proved to be an amazing asset, playing a vital role in major developments such as Trump National Doral, Trump Turnberry, and Trump International Washington, D.C.

Now vice president of Interior Design for the entire company, Gia works a hundred times harder than most people would because she's grateful for the opportunity and she's passionate about what she does. "Most people don't ever get to do something they love and call it their job," Gia wrote in a thank-you e-mail to my brothers and me shortly after her most recent promotion. "The fact that I just so happened to move to NYC and this opportunity came up, and each of you were kind enough—brave enough—to let me give it a try makes me feel especially thankful."

So many stories like this exist at our company, in part because we've created an entrepreneurial culture in which your ability to rise is limited only by your own hunger, drive, passion, and execution.

One of the easiest ways to identify future leaders is to see how respected they are by their peers, how they engage with their immediate team and delegate, and how they see the potential in others, especially when those people don't have a flawless résumé and obvious credentials for the job.

Before you craft the job description for a new hire or call a recruiter, think twice about who might already be employed—or underemployed, or misemployed—by your company. Look beyond the department she works for or even her current job title to consider her potential, and if you're unsure of her background, or whether or not she possesses the right skill set, ask around. Set the stage for an informal interview and get to know her. Sometimes, the passion, experience, and transferable skills that would align perfectly with your team's needs are buried beneath a person's current daily demands. Look for talent in your own organization before searching too far afield. Just be sure that you have the support and buy-in of her direct report before proceeding. Don't poach from colleagues without approaching them first and discussing your interest.

NEGOTIATE EVERYTHING TO WIN

Hard work is nice, but you will never get anywhere in life unless you ask for what you want and are willing to fight for it.

—Sharon Taylor, senior vice president, Human Resources,
Prudential Financial; chair, Prudential Foundation

Learning to negotiate is essential to truly staking your claim—and not just because it's a critical career skill. There's no doubt that strategically hammering out a great deal on behalf of your company or client will inspire your boss's confidence and trust. But the biggest and best reason to negotiate is that doing so can actually help to change the narrative around women and work. Linda Babcock, a professor of economics at Carnegie Mellon University and the coauthor of *Women Don't Ask*, determined that women who negotiated the starting salary for their first job out of school stood to make over $500,000 more by age sixty than those who did not. Moreover, she cites another study that found that women who consistently negotiated their salaries stood to make over $1 million more over their lifetimes than their peers who didn't.

Because your salary, whether at your first job or your tenth, influences how much you make at your next job (and the one after that), negotiating exponentially affects your earning potential over your lifetime. Babcock's research showed that only 7 percent of women negotiate their starting salaries, perhaps because they feel lucky to have simply landed a job, don't feel confident asking for more, or because they don't think they have the leverage to do so.

The fact is, you *can* negotiate your salary—without playing hardball— all the while inspiring other women who work to also advocate for themselves. Adam Grant frequently gets requests for advice on negotiating a job offer. They usually start like this: "I'm in the recruiting process, and I just received an offer from the organization that I want to join. I'd like to sign, but I was hoping for a higher salary. What should I do?"

"According to conventional wisdom," Grant says, "the best way to boost your salary is to get an offer from a competing employer with a higher salary," which can be smart, but some people find distasteful. It can also be a waste of time—both for you and the company with which you're interviewing—if your only purpose in pursuing a second opportunity is to get an offer to use as leverage.

"In many cases," Grant continues, "I've proposed a different strategy. It requires no hardball negotiating and keeps your integrity intact. It's an approach that I used during three years negotiating advertising contracts; since then, I've taught it in my negotiation courses to executives and students, and it proves highly effective.

"The starting point is to approach someone in the organization who you trust, has some influence, and has a vested interest in hiring you." From there, Grant recommends the following four steps:

- ✓ EXPRESS YOUR ENTHUSIASM: Say, "I'm thrilled about the offer. This is my first choice, for reasons X, Y and Z, and I'd love to join the team."

- ✓ EXPLAIN YOUR REQUEST: "I just have a few questions about the terms that I'd like to address before I'll be ready to sign."

- ✓ ESTABLISH YOUR CONTRIBUTION: "I know this position often pays $X, and I believe I can add enough value to the organization to earn it."

- ✓ ASK FOR ADVICE: "I hope it's okay to ask you about this—my relationships with people here are very important to me. I trust you and I'd very much value your recommendations on how to proceed."

"By that point, according to studies conducted by researcher Katie Liljenquist, three things tend to happen," says Grant. "First, you've flattered the contact. Second, you've encouraged your contact to take your perspective. In order to give you advice, the person has to walk in your shoes. With that usually comes a bit of identification and empathy: 'I remember when I was in a situation like that.'"

Now that the contact appreciates your perspective, "you're in for the third response: commitment. In the best-case scenario, the contact will take the initiative to advocate for you directly. Failing that, you'll gain some actionable advice about who to approach and how to make your case, as well as some possible history on precedents for negotiating in your role," adds Grant.

Advice seeking is a powerful way to have influence without authority. If you're worried about seeming manipulative, Grant says, "It doesn't work if it's not authentic. When Liljenquist instructed people to use advice seeking as an influence strategy, their negotiating counterparts saw right through it. It was only effective when people were genuinely interested in learning from the contacts they sought out."

In most situations, this strategy proves just as effective as hardball, and it's much more comfortable to seek advice rather than issue an ultimatum. If it doesn't work, you might have doubts about taking the job, at which point it may make sense to interview elsewhere. Once a comparable offer comes in, says Grant, "It's still not necessary to play hardball. All you need to do is share the terms of the competing offer, and say, 'I'd rather come here. Is there anything you can do to make this an easier decision for me?'"

More often than not, the answer is yes.

> Every time I sat at the negotiating table, my greatest enemy was myself. The words I chose and the strategies I put into play actually undermined my goals. The failure to effectively communicate rested solely on me, every time.
>
> —Mika Brzezinski, cohost of *Morning Joe*
> and author of *Knowing Your Value*

NEGOTIATING FOR A RAISE OR PROMOTION

> Ask for what you want and be prepared to get it.
>
> —Maya Angelou

Beyond negotiating your starting salary, another professional rite of passage is negotiating a raise. Linda Babcock says that women ask for raises and promotions 85 percent less often than their male counterparts, frequently asking for 30 percent less. Often, they don't realize that opportunities exist. "Their perception [is] that their circumstances are more fixed and absolute—less negotiable—than they really are." And when they do ask, unfortunately, there can be negative repercussions. According to Women in the Workplace 2016, a study conducted by Sheryl Sandberg's LeanIn.org and McKinsey & Company, women who ask "are 30 percent more likely than men who negotiate to receive feedback that they are 'intimidating,' 'too aggressive,' or 'bossy' and 67 percent more likely than women who don't negotiate to receive the same negative feedback." A 2011 McKinsey report also noted that men are promoted based on potential, while women are promoted based on past accomplishments.

I remember the first time I approached a boss for an increase in pay, I had to prove my worth to the bottom line in real dollars and cents. I quantified each project that I'd spearheaded and every deal I'd landed over the prior year in order to convince him. It was a valuable lesson to learn, especially at that point in my career. Never assume that your supervisors know the full extent of your contributions. People are busy and preoccupied with achieving their own goals; even the most attentive managers might need you to make your case for a raise or promotion.

Early experiences also taught me the importance of timing when asking for a raise or making bonus-related requests. I wouldn't approach my boss for a raise if I found out from his assistant that he was in a bad mood; I also timed the conversation with when things were looking good for the company and industry in general. Be mindful of what's going on financially in the bigger picture. And know that simply logging your time at a company doesn't automatically qualify you for a raise. The worst way to ask for a raise is to say, "I've been here for two years. . . ." It happens all the time, but it's truly ineffective.

Ask when you feel like you're not being adequately compensated for the job you're doing and the responsibilities you're carrying. Ideally, don't ask around bonus season—your boss is going to be managing multiple people's needs; it doesn't help to add to the stress. Don't ask right before or after you deliver on something big, either—it can feel too opportunistic. Ask during a quiet, unexpected time and allow your boss to focus her attention on your request.

If you're nervous because you think you're bad at hard conversations, realize that it's only a difficult dialogue to have when there's a true discrepancy between what you feel you're entitled to and what your boss feels you deserve. If this exists, you need to know about it regardless. Either your boss doesn't find you as valuable as you believe yourself to be—in which case you should start looking elsewhere—or consider that maybe she's right, and you have significant room for improvement. If she doesn't comprehend the full scope of what you do and therefore doesn't realize that you are being underpaid, give her the benefit of the doubt and the time to make it right.

Here are four more strategies to help you stack the deck in your favor when seeking a raise or a promotion:

- ✓ DO YOUR RESEARCH: Understand your market value and, more important, your value to the company. Be prepared to explain, candidly and concretely, what you feel you're doing that you're not being compensated for. Have confidence in your own worth.

- ✓ ASK TO BE PAID FOR THE JOB YOU'RE ACTUALLY DOING: If your responsibilities have increased but you haven't been recognized since, say, you've taken over for the manager who left several months earlier, approach your new boss and say, "I've been effectively doing this person's job since she departed and I'd like to formally assume her position." Have a conversation. Express that you feel confident you can grow in this role and create value for the organization.

- ✓ PROVE YOUR WORTH: To earn an increase in salary, you need to be increasing your responsibilities and performing at a higher level than when you were hired.

- ✓ DON'T NEGOTIATE IF YOUR BOSS SAYS NO: Typically no means no when it comes to this type of discussion. If your boss says no, you have two choices: you either accept the rationale, think about it, and grow based on the feedback, or you leave. This is a good time to be reflective. Ask why you haven't earned the increase. You may not walk away with a new title or more money, but hopefully you'll learn something that will help you correct your course moving forward.

It is only by being bold that you get anywhere.

—Richard Branson, founder of Virgin Group

NEGOTIATING YOUR SEVERANCE

If you don't ask, the answer's always no.

—Nora Roberts, best-selling author

As challenging as it may seem to negotiate your salary, raise, promotion, or bonus—all positive aspects of your employment—negotiating your severance can be the most difficult of all. There's simply no easy way to handle a layoff, particularly if you didn't see it coming. You'll be feeling a mix of emotions, and asking for a financial package may not even occur to you until the shock wears off. But you should still ask, even if it's not offered or is not an obligation.

While you may not think the company has any reason to agree to it, respected career coach Pamela Weinberg says that it's in their best interest for you to walk away as satisfied as possible. Companies aren't required to offer severance, but check your employment contract and official company policy to find out exactly what you may be entitled to. Even if nothing, it's worth asking.

After you've received the news, give yourself a day or two to process the situation. Don't bring up severance right away. "You'll likely be caught off guard," says Weinberg. "Take some time to calm down and seek professional counsel before going back to your boss with a 'wish list.'" Weinberg recommends having an employment attorney review your severance letter of agreement before you sign it. "Even if you decide not to negotiate your financial package, you may want to negotiate other things, like health insurance and references for your next job," she explains.

Go in with the expectation that you won't get everything you ask for, but you *will* get more than what they originally offered. Weinberg recommends an often-used formula to calculate severance: number of years at the company multiplied by two weeks' pay = severance total. Request back pay for unused vacation days, plus a portion of the bonus you were expected to receive at the end of the year. Request a written letter of recommendation and assurance that it will be upheld if a prospective employer calls for references, and ask for a written agreement that any noncompete clause in your original offer is at this point null and void.

It's a sensitive, emotional time, but avoid saying anything you'll regret. "Remember: relationships matter," warns Weinberg. "Bosses and HR folks are human beings—they'll feel bad about laying you off, especially if your layoff is due to downsizing, as opposed to poor performance." She suggests appealing directly to your boss if you've had a good relationship. She'll be more likely to negotiate your package with you than, for example, an HR person you haven't gotten to know well, who may be having to have the same conversation multiple times, if the layoff is companywide.

Be prepared to be asked to leave immediately, "in which case you'll be escorted to your desk to gather your things," warns life and business coach Gretchen Hydo. It may seem dramatic and even hurtful, but "it's a blessing in disguise," she says. Rather than have to explain the situation to your coworkers, you can leave quietly. "You won't be at your best. You don't want their last impression of you to be teary-eyed and emotional." If you do have the chance to say good-bye, keep it simple. "Don't give details," says Hydo. Even if you stay friends with your former colleagues, resist the temptation to go into detail about your layoff or bad-mouth the company. Also worth noting: even if you're asked to leave immediately, it doesn't mean the opportunity to negotiate your severance has passed.

Know that your manager probably doesn't enjoy the conversation any more than you do—it may not have even been her decision to let you go. "Thank her for all you've learned during your time at the company," Hydo says. "Tell her you'd like to work together in the future. You can even ask for a reference for a future job opportunity."

Once you've left and have had some time to process your change in employment, think about how you'll explain your layoff to prospective employers. "If your company was simply downsized, be straightforward about that," says Hydo. "If you were laid off because you weren't meeting goals or getting along with your coworkers, craft a simple statement that positively acknowledges the circumstances in which you left. For example, if you're asked about it in an interview, say something like, 'My skills weren't a good fit for that role, and I think they'd be much better suited to this particular opportunity,' then give an example to back it up."

Finally, make the most of your time off. "Do some soul-searching," says Hydo. Try to be objective and "ask yourself if your last job was right for you. Consider what you would do if your time, money and skill set weren't an issue." Consult your blueprint; reacquainting yourself with what matters most—and what you really want from your career— will give your job search greater direction and deeper meaning. Hydo adds, "Reach out to headhunters and temp agencies to let them know you're available. Volunteer or take courses to further your knowledge of the industry. This shows initiative and opens the doors of possibility."

BEFORE, DURING, AND AFTER: HOW TO NEGOTIATE ANY SITUATION LIKE A PRO

The need to employ negotiating strategies likely comes into play within your work environment frequently, if not every day—not only as you negotiate your own salary, bonuses, and promotions but also as you field requests for the same from your team, collaborate with your colleagues and supervisors, and negotiate contracts with vendors and freelancers.

My father is renowned for his negotiating skills, so I've been fortunate to learn from the very best. In my deal-making capacity at The Trump Organization, I'm most proud of scoring the storied Old Post Office, now Trump International Washington, D.C., and spearheading the acquisition of the Trump National Doral, as well as initiating many successful partnerships at Trump and in my own business. I negotiate daily on matters big and small. Volumes have been written on the subject of negotiation by many experts; my personal experience has allowed me to create a uniquely tailored approach that I think you'll find useful at any point in your career.

Before the Negotiation

Be prepared: Whether you're negotiating a raise, a contract, or even an apartment rental—do your research. The more you know, the stronger your position. It's tough to argue with someone who can back up her assertions with facts and a rational, knowledgeable argument.

Practice when the stakes are low: When it comes to negotiating, I often hear from women that it makes them nervous. They shy away from difficult conversations because asserting themselves is uncomfortable; they have a hard time taking credit for their accomplishments, knowing their worth, and asking for it. "Negotiating is something you do at least half of your life, yet you never work at it . . . [you must] practice negotiating like you practice a sport," says William Ury, cofounder of the Harvard Negotiation Project and author of the classic negotiation bestseller, *Getting to Yes*. Go into a boutique and try to get a discount. Hang out with a toddler. Call the phone company and threaten to switch providers if they won't give you a deal on your service. It may sound silly, but if you think about negotiation as if it were a sport, you will get better at it with practice. When the stakes are low, hone your skills.

Know what you want: It's the number one rule going into any negotiation, yet most people don't give it the attention it deserves. Set your goals in advance; know what you hope to achieve prior to negotiating. Without a plan, you allow the opposing party to define your goals, instead of the other way around. Elizabeth Cronise McLaughlin says, "Before any challenging conversation or negotiation, I advise all my coaching clients to . . . focus on the emotional responses of all involved. . . . Setting an intention before any negotiation makes you more likely to anticipate a positive response, and also helps to get the negotiation back on track if it deviates from your desired flow. Know your intended outcome, and you'll be more likely to get there."

Consider the other person: If you haven't done business together before, spend some time on Google or ask a colleague with more experience in order to gather some intel as to how the other person thinks before starting the negotiation. Try to imagine what's important to her, and put yourself in her shoes. Think about what matters to her in this deal. Contemplate what she might be unwilling to concede—and why. If you have worked with her before, consult your notes to refresh your memory as to how previous negotiations went.

Turn the tables on yourself: Look at your position from her vantage point and try to identify its weaknesses. "Anticipate the challenges you'll face," says McLaughlin, and think about the counterargument. "A gracious, immediate response to a challenging question is a surefire way to raise confidence in your position, especially when you're face-to-face."

Be honest with yourself: Know that your personality will sometimes clash with the other party and that it's okay to separate yourself from the negotiation if you think your involvement is counterproductive. My brothers and I often assess our counterparts, based on information we gathered in the research phase or prior interactions, and decide who we think would be best suited to spearhead a particular negotiation. You might not be the best person from your team to lead every negotiation. Keep your ego out of it; it's the results that matter. Be gracious, step aside, and let the person most likely to succeed lead the charge.

During the Negotiation

Use body language: Plenty of deals are transacted by phone, but I believe that negotiations should happen in person whenever possible—in which case, your physical presence matters. Make eye contact. Check in with your body and ask: Am I sitting upright? Do I look overeager? Is my posture communicating aggression when that's not helpful, or do I appear meek and intimidated? You may want to lean in slightly to signal your sincerity and interest, but keep your arms close to your body—by your sides, not crossed—to convey confidence.

Don't negotiate by e-mail: It might seem more efficient, but it's a copout that affords the weaker party a strategic advantage, buying her time to craft a strong response to a wobbly position. You also can't press someone as hard in writing as you can live. If the negotiation doesn't warrant an in-person meeting, it's always best to do things by phone.

Make sure you're negotiating with the decision maker: Inexperienced negotiators often don't realize that the person who starts the conversation may not have the authority to close the deal. Then, when the boss takes over, she may not acknowledge important concessions that you've already made. When you begin a negotiation, ask, "Do you have the authority to make a deal, or is there someone else I should be working with?" If the answer is, "Um, let me get my boss," you'll be glad you inquired when you did.

You don't get what you don't ask for: Based on your research, aim high. Then you can make concessions starting from there. You'd be surprised how often you end up close to that aggressive starting point. Contrary to conventional wisdom, be open to proposing monetary ranges. A 2015 study conducted by researchers at Columbia University found that using a "bolstering range" can actually be very effective. According to a March 2015 *Quartz* piece by Max Nisen, a bolstering range "means setting a fairly ambitious number at the bottom range, equivalent to the one you would have used as a single point offer, and then a higher number as the top range." Admittedly, this approach flies in the face of conventional wisdom—that if offered a range, people hear only the high end (or the low end, depending on their interest). Also, the prior thinking doesn't account for the "politeness" factor—that is, research shows, when given a range, employers are less likely to offer less than, for fear of offending the candidate. Do your homework to establish a reasonable range—then use it to your advantage.

Listen more than you speak: When people are nervous, they tend to ramble. Try to get the other party to say more than you by pausing after making a point or asking a question; if you're on the phone, look at your watch for a few seconds to resist the temptation to keep talking. Some of the strongest negotiators I know just sit back and listen. The less they engage, the more likely the other person is to become uncomfortable, start yammering to fill the silence, then slip up and offer information they otherwise would have guarded.

Go for the win: Often, the best negotiations result in a deal that benefits both parties. There are times when you'll want to go for the jugular, but as a general rule you want the other person to feel pleased with the outcome, even if you are the clear victor. Don't be short-sighted. I know people who can't concede a penny, and this mentality costs them valuable future opportunities. You never know when you'll have the chance to work together again.

Be prepared to walk away: Regardless of how high the stakes, you have to be mentally prepared to walk away from a deal. Whether it is a job offer or a rent renewal, you may need to let it be known that you're willing to part ways if you can't agree to terms. I always say, until it's signed, you're not done. Never do a deal that's no longer advantageous simply because you've invested the time and energy. Instead, use what you learn in the negotiation to confirm for yourself whether the relationship is tenable long term. During the course of a transaction—particularly if it's complicated—you'll glean a tremendous amount of information about the people you're dealing with. If it's deeply unpleasant to get through an agreement with them, how will you forge a healthy, productive partnership? Even if you can't actually walk away from a deal—and there are some deals where you genuinely can't—make certain the other party doesn't know it. Either explicitly or subtly, let it be known that you're perfectly willing to let a deal go if you can't make it work. If the other party thinks you're forced by circumstances to complete a transaction, you have no leverage.

After the Negotiation

"Be gracious, no matter the outcome," says Elizabeth Cronise McLaughlin. "Negotiations are moments in our lives when we're called upon to show what we're made of. Taking the high road, even when we don't get an ideal outcome, is important. No negotiation is worth losing one's temper or one's dignity." Plus, the world is small. If you're players in the same industry, you may find yourselves seated at the same table again down the road.

Yes, negotiating is about money and the bottom line, but a lot of times, it's more emotional and complex than just that. Negotiation is paramount to achieving your goals, an essential tool to becoming a woman who works. Or, as William Ury says, "Negotiation is the stuff of life. We think of it as driving us apart, but if you engage in it correctly, it can actually bring us closer together." Becoming a masterful negotiator emboldens us to live our lives unapologetically, and inspire other women—above us, around us, and in generations to come—to band together and advocate for ourselves and one another, personally and professionally.

MOVING ON AND MOVING UP: TAKING CHARGE OF YOUR CAREER

> We keep moving forward, opening new doors, and doing new things, because we're curious and curiosity keeps leading us down new paths.
>
> —Walt Disney

I believe that professional development—managing your career smartly and strategically—is among the most important career skills you can have in staking your claim. You simply will not grow professionally unless you are conscious of where you want to go next, and are willing to apply for promotions and jobs that are a stretch. Staking your claim is as much about being a champion for your own abilities as leading a team or a company, and many women fail to do so at all, or to do so deliberately. Much like taking care of ourselves, professional development is something we must prioritize so that we may become the best version of ourselves and achieve our dreams.

Studies have shown that men apply for jobs that they're only 60 percent qualified for, while women wait until they're sure they're 100 percent qualified before applying. As women who work, we must change this reality. "Growth and comfort don't coexist. That's true for people, for companies, for nations," says Ginni Rometty, president and CEO of IBM.

So how do you know when it's time to move on? How do you

determine whether to stay the course you're on or pursue an enticing new opportunity?

Ask yourself: Am I learning? Am I growing? It's common to lose a little bit of passion when you're grinding it out on a project. But after the deadlines have cooled, if you're truly engaged, your enthusiasm for your job and company should trickle back in. If it's been a number of months and you're still not feeling it, you need to assess whether you're in the right place. Do you love what you're doing? Maybe not every day, but most days? If so, it makes sense to stay put. If not, consult your blueprint and then apply for jobs that stretch your skill set, and for which you might not really be ready. In moving up or moving on, a recruiter—someone who knows the job market inside and out—can be an incredible asset to your career, whether you're actively looking for a job or not. "A recruiter is like any great ally. It's like having someone on the inside who thinks of you first," says Jennifer Lenkowsky, executive recruiter at Russell Tobin.

A recruiter can also be a valuable advocate in breaking through the glass ceiling, which, unfortunately, still exists. It's far better here in America than in much of the world, but we've still got a long way to go. Because industries and companies differ greatly, an excellent recruiter who specializes in your field can help crack it by negotiating on your behalf. "You want someone who's had success placing candidates in the roles you're looking for," Lenkowsky says. She recommends meeting first and asking questions like: What types of jobs do you recruit for? Does my background mimic those of the candidates you've had the most success with? What is the normal time frame for you to find a candidate a job?

Lenkowsky adds, "Ideally, you want no more than three recruiters working for you at any given time. Ultimately, there is a lot of crossover in the agency business, so more than three and you'll probably be spreading yourself too thin and applying against yourself. If a recruiter knows that you're interviewing for a job they're working on with someone else, they'll be more likely to sell up the candidate they're representing instead of you."

While your prior work experience may qualify you for the role, that's not all you should be focusing on as you market yourself for a new job opportunity. Instead, make a point of showing off your communication, social, problem-solving, and leadership skills. Employers value your ability to speak articulately and write clean e-mails, according to a Bloomberg poll in which 70 percent of recruiters said they value communication skills above all else. Results from the study also show that being able to collaborate with a team, work efficiently in groups, and generally get along with your coworkers is incredibly important—surprisingly, even more so than qualities like industry-related experience.

Ensure that the information on your résumé and social media profiles is current and accurate, including dates of employment, titles, and education. "Some unemployed candidates choose to include that they are actively looking for a new opportunity on their social media outlets," says Lenkowsky. "Recruiters will be drawn to a candidate who's aggressively looking for a role, as opposed to a passive one they'll need to entice."

Finally, let your recruiter do her job. The majority of the job-search process should funnel through your recruiter—that includes scheduling interviews, follow-ups, references, and salary negotiations.

If you're actively interviewing for positions, respond immediately to any inquiries that come your way. "I can't tell you how many times candidates have missed out on openings because they didn't get back to me," says Lenkowsky. "If you're going to look for a job, do it 110%! If you're not actively looking for a job, keep in contact with a recruiter you love anyway. I have candidates that I placed twelve years ago who still reach out just to check in and see what the market conditions are," she says. It's good to have a relationship with a recruiter even if you are happy at your job, so that you're top of mind for opportunities that might arise even if you aren't looking.

DIG DEEP

It can be incredibly useful to work with a recruiter to uncover potential new opportunities. But in considering tough, career-altering choices—Should you leave your job? Should you switch careers?—you'll also need to dig deep before making any big decisions. Start by checking in with yourself, advises career consultant and executive coach Maggie Mistal. Become aware of how you feel about your job—pay attention to your levels of passion and motivation, in particular. "The minute you lose interest in doing your job well, that's the time to either recast your role or create your exit strategy," says Mistal. "When a job stops being fun, you stop engaging in it, your quality suffers, and your boss will notice." Then you may have no choice but to move on.

"Before moving on from a job, look for ways to reengage," Mistal suggests. "I worked with a client who was a project manager at a product development company. Her job was to keep the creative team on time and within budget, but she craved doing creative work herself. Rather than quit right off the bat, she offered to help the creative team on a small project or two and asked for advice on classes she could take to develop her creative skills. Over the course of a year, she took on bigger and more creative projects and kept doing her project management role well and, when a position on the creative team opened up, she made the move. She's been a full-time creative for over ten years." Find ways to get whatever it is you're looking for—different work, a higher salary, more responsibility—at your current company, where you've already invested time and energy building relationships and a reputation, before you leave altogether.

If that doesn't work, it's time to consult your blueprint. Have your passions and ambitions changed? Or have they remained constant and it's your job situation that has changed around you? Understanding that—and then what your dream job looks like, or could look like—is essential to making wise career choices. Mistal takes her clients through a series of exercises designed to help you figure that out. "Select and prioritize the top five values that will get you out of bed in the morning and excited for work," she suggests. "Once you have your list of motivators, then you can compare and contrast to determine which job opportunities give you more of what motivates you." When you're fully aware of what you want in a job, you'll be able to trust your own judgment without getting distracted by money, advancement, or other people's opinions. "To put your job satisfaction squarely in your own hands, you've got to know yourself."

If you end up wanting to make a change, start with a soul-search. Again, refer to your blueprint. Reacquaint yourself with who you are—"what you love to do, your unique gifts and talents, what skills you want to utilize, and how you want to make a difference," says Mistal. Then do your research. "See what's out there that aligns with who you are and test out a new career before making a career switch," she advises. "I had a client who was good at seeing the big picture. We looked for ways to use this talent and landed on strategy consulting. To test this career switch, he approached a favorite nonprofit and offered to consult for them for a set period of time. He found that, while he was able to be of service, he didn't enjoy doing the work for someone else—he wanted to develop and implement strategies as a business leader himself. Doing the research in addition to the soul-searching made all the difference in his clarity and confidence moving forward."

Finally, remember that it's never too late to change. Don't put too much pressure on any single decision. You're never too old, experienced, or far into your career to make a change. "No one can pigeonhole you," says Mistal. Granted, it may be less common, but recall Umber Ahmad, who left her Wall Street job to start a luxury baked goods brand. Ahmad says her tenure as a banker prepared her to run a successful food business. "I separated my title ('banker') from my skill set (business development, financial management, leadership, et cetera) and it turned out that my skill set was easily transferable to opening a bakery," she says. In fact, her seemingly unrelated experience proved to be an asset. "Make a list of things you're good at. You'll identify areas of business where you'll be ahead of the game because you'll have skills others in your new field don't have."

> Wake up every day excited to go to work. Find a job that doesn't feel like work but a natural extension of your life and what your priorities are and what you care about. It's so important.
>
> —Lauren Bush Lauren, cofounder and CEO of FEED Projects

RESIGN GRACEFULLY

If you want to achieve greatness, stop asking for permission.

—Eddie Colla, street artist

You've made the decision to move up or move on. If your recruiter has done her job, you may well be looking at a new employment opportunity! Before you pop the champagne, there's one last important step: resign from your current position.

As critical as it is to make a good first impression in landing a job, it's equally essential to leave on a high note. Once you've decided to quit, you must first tell your immediate boss. Face-to-face is always best. In extreme circumstances, a phone call is appropriate (if your boss is on leave or traveling for an extended period of time), but don't resign by e-mail, despite the fact that the company may need notification in writing. It's too easy to misinterpret tone in electronic communications, and you want to be gracious and respectful in giving your notice.

People still submit physical resignation letters when it's required by the company, sometimes as a contractual obligation, and other times to be kept on file by legal or accounting. Regardless of whether it's outlined in your terms of employment, it's a respectful formality. Once you've sat down with your boss and the people you work with, told them of your decision, and expressed appreciation for the opportunity they provided you, then you can submit a simple, straightforward letter.

In terms of how much notice to give, in the early stages of your career, two weeks is standard, but as you move up through the ranks and into management, I personally think that someone in a senior role should offer a month to six weeks' notice. Hasty exits are seldom looked upon well. The only exception is if you are in a position where you have access to secure information or your presence could create a conflict of interest. In that case, sometimes executives are asked to leave immediately.

During your transition period, go above and beyond for your boss and the team you are leaving behind. Don't leave early or take time off.

Also, don't resign immediately after expending all of your vacation days, or take a new position at the end of maternity leave. Be fully present, even though, of course, you're excited to start your new venture.

Regardless of how much notice you're giving, you should always have a strong second-in-command in place long before you go. One of the marks of an effective leader is that she's taken the time and care to train someone other than herself to be able to do a good portion of her job. Lao Tzu said, "A leader is best when people barely know he exists, when his work is done, his aim fulfilled, they will say: we did it ourselves." If you don't already have a replacement for your position, go out of your way to assist your organization in finding and training someone.

Finally, it's crucial not to burn bridges. This should be obvious, but you'd be surprised by the shortsighted decisions people sometimes make. As Warren Buffett says, "It takes 20 years to build a reputation and five minutes to ruin it." It doesn't matter if it's a summer internship or the first, second, third, or fourth position you've held in your career—every professional opportunity provides you with valuable insight, resources, and relationships that are important to preserve. If you stay in the industry, these are the people who will be your advocates and make up your network, the people you will call upon to gain insight, ask questions, and seek guidance. I have worked with people who've decided they want to do something completely different with their lives, and although I have not always wanted them to leave, I was also happy to see them follow their dreams. I have remained a resource to them and an ally when they needed me. You have to be thinking about building a network of people who are genuinely invested in wishing you well and watching you thrive. Future prospective employers will call these people for references, and they're going to be honest in their assessment of you. So try to give as much notice as possible. Of course, sometimes life throws you a curveball and an immediate exit is unavoidable—a spouse is transferred, a family member is sick—but as best you can, think long term and leave gracefully.

YOU ARE A WOMAN WHO WORKS—AT STAKING YOUR CLAIM

I didn't get there by wishing for it or hoping for it or dreaming about it . . . I got there by working for it.

—Estée Lauder

Whether building and managing a world-class team, negotiating like a pro, staging a graceful entrance or exit from an organization, you are a woman who works, and has worked hard, to stake a claim—in your industry, company, and career.

With your leadership experience, negotiating know-how, and professional priorities in place, it's time to reach for the next opportunity, whatever that means to you. Architecting a life you love—a full, multidimensional life—means prioritizing your passions and interests, family and relationships, health and well-being, alongside work that inspires you.

Know your ask, know your worth, know your value. Know that the only way to become the best version of yourself is to honor your many facets and dedicate your life to what you've determined matters. Now that you've achieved the level of success required to stake your claim, it may be time to redefine success as you know it—by working smarter, not harder.

BIT BY BIT...SHE
HAD CLAIMED
HERSELF.
FREEIHG
YOURSELF WAS
ONE THIHG,
CLAIMIHG
OWHERSHIP
OF THAT
FREED SELF
WAS AHOTHER.

toni morrison

CHAPTER FOUR

Work Smarter, Not Harder

Boost Your Productivity to Make Time for What Matters Most

O nce you've staked your claim in your company and industry, you may find yourself at a point in your career when it feels time to redefine success as you know it—by working smarter, not harder. As a woman who works, your professional persona is only part of your story, the preface to a far more complex narrative that includes passions and values that inspire you to pursue a rich life outside of the office, too.

Part of learning to lead, and staking your claim, is realizing that you could spend virtually all of your time focused on the external requirements of your job—those daily demands imposed on you by your clients, your team, even your boss. Except that you shouldn't. This chapter centers on prioritizing what matters most to *you* and offers guidance on how to allocate your time more thoughtfully so you can live your life deliberately. It introduces the concept of proactive planning—the need to spend the majority of your time on nonurgent functions that will truly add value to your business—and shares productivity hacks to simplify and enrich your multidimensional life. The value of rest, the importance of creating mental space, and the brain-boosting benefit of hobbies are explored, as are the concepts of connecting with and centering yourself—so that you learn to maximize your efficiency and boost your productivity by making time for what you really love to do.

Time: The Great Equalizer

> The key is not to prioritize what's on your schedule, but to schedule your priorities.
>
> —Stephen Covey

No matter your age, your background, your education, or your successes, we are all granted 168 hours in a week. My friend real estate tycoon and founder of W Hotels Barry Sternlicht says, "Time is the great equalizer. We all have the same twenty-four-hour day. It's how we use those hours that defines and separates us."

Are you a slave to your time or the master of it? Despite your best intentions, it's easy to be reactive and get caught up in returning calls, attending meetings, answering e-mails, and managing your team, only to realize that it's 6:30 P.M.—and you haven't done a single thing that's of high value or moves you toward accomplishing larger strategic goals all day.

In order to maximize your time, it helps to become conscious of where you're spending it. Productivity expert Laura Vanderkam suggests logging what you do every day for a week. Write it down as often as possible, and in as much detail as you think will be helpful. "Keeping track of our time prevents us from telling ourselves stories that aren't true," Vanderkam explains. "A lot of people think that if they work full time, they have no time for anything else. If you work forty hours a week and sleep eight hours a night, that leaves seventy-two hours for other things. That's a lot of time!" Because I color-code my schedule by business and task (more on that later), I can review the prior month and see exactly where I spent my time. I also review the e-mails in my received and deleted folders to note patterns. If, for example, my construction team is sending me complex questions by e-mail twenty times a day, it would be more effective to set up a face-to-face touch-base meeting with them on a recurring basis to get them the answers they need efficiently.

"People think a lot about what they want to spend less time doing, but it's better to ask what you want to spend *more* time doing," continues Vanderkam. "We can't make more time, but time is highly elastic. It will stretch to accommodate what we choose to put into it." Vanderkam suggests putting your priorities first. "You'll make time for everything else," she adds.

Setting achievable goals is just as important as analyzing what you're spending most of your time on, and allocating that time appropriately. "Often, people set a goal because it sounds good," says Gretchen Hydo. "They want the result, but they don't necessarily want to have to do the work that it takes to get there." Understanding *why* you want to achieve something—cue up your life's blueprint—will help you put a plan into action, stay motivated, and be realistic about just how long things should take. You want to swing for the fences in terms of your aspirations, but be reasonable in estimating the amount of time and work that is required to meet those sky-high objectives. "Make sure that the payoff is relevant to your life and big enough to motivate you," she says. Here are three key strategies for realistic goal setting:

Break big goals into bite-sized nuggets: "Breaking down your goals into actionable steps can help make them seem less overwhelming," says Hydo. "Successful goals are SMART: specific, measurable, attainable, realistic, and timely."

Capitalize on your network: "Surround yourself with people who can walk the journey with you," says Hydo. Rosie Pope, a busy entrepreneur and mom, credits her community of family and friends as instrumental to her success. "As women, we often try to do all of the planning without taking into consideration our partner or team and the role they will play in achieving our goals," she says. "You are not going to be able to do this alone, so building your team—your tribe—will be essential to supporting you on your journey." In addition, involving other people will help you stay on course. "It's easier to stay accountable to others than it is to ourselves," says psychologist Dr. Lauren Hazzouri.

Remember, life is long: When you hit bumps in the road, having your endgame in mind will remind you to look at the big picture and keep moving forward. When Anne Wojcicki's groundbreaking company, 23andMe (a genetic testing and analysis company), received an FDA warning letter, the company was under heavy restrictions for two years. "We have the same mission and goals today that we did when we started," she says of the experience. "The short-term bumps don't matter as much because we're focused on our long-term view."

> Obstacles are those frightful things you see when you take your eyes off your goal.
>
> —Henry Ford, American industrialist

THINK MORE, REACT LESS, AND MASTER YOUR TO-DO LIST

There's an old saying: "If you want to get something done, give it to a busy person." We all know conceptually that time is a finite resource, but not until I began juggling the demands of three kids and multiple jobs did I feel it so acutely. My secrets for staying ahead of the avalanche of demands? Going off the grid once a week, being more proactive—and less reactive—at work, and taking a big-picture approach to work by streamlining processes whenever possible.

Think More, React Less

"The high-minded Greeks called leisure *skole*," recounts Brigid Schulte in *Overwhelmed*. "Like school, they considered it a time for learning and cultivating oneself and one's passions. It is a time not just for play, recreation, and connection with others, but also for meditation, reflection, and deep thought."

From sundown Friday to Saturday night, my family and I observe the Shabbat. During this time, we disconnect completely—no e-mails, no TV, no phone calls, no Internet. We enjoy uninterrupted time together and it's wonderful. In addition to being a sacred part of our religion, we live in such a fast-paced world that it's enormously important to unplug and devote that time to each other. We enjoy long meals together, we read, we take walks in the city, we nap, and just hang out. The break is what enables me to go back to work, full steam, the following Monday—or, more realistically, Saturday night, when I log back on!

I also use my one day of quiet per week to check in with myself—to consider my larger professional goals and strategic initiatives, and to plan for the week ahead. Disconnecting from day-to-day distractions allows me to think big picture and be less reactive to situations that crop up unexpectedly during the week. Bill Gates reportedly did this during his "Think Weeks," when twice a year he would isolate himself from family, friends, and staff and retreat to an undisclosed location with reading material for several days at a time. A caretaker would provide soup and sandwiches twice a day—along with an unending supply of Diet Orange Crush—while Gates would presumably plot Microsoft's future.

On New Year's Day, when we're usually in Florida, I sit down alone with a notebook and headphones to brainstorm a long list of high-level objectives for each of the different businesses that I oversee. I break it out by company and write down big structural, overarching goals that I want to accomplish by the end of the year—not small things that you could easily cross off a to-do list.

I also make a general list of things I want to accomplish personally: meditate more, exercise at least three days a week, finally touch my toes! And I write a list for connecting with each of my kids; I put real thought into coming up with ideas for memorable moments I can create with each of them. Right now, I play with cars with Joseph, on the floor, for twenty minutes each day. Arabella loves books, so I make a note to read at least two per day to her and plan "dates" to the library. With Theodore, I commit to ensuring that I can give him two to three of his bottles each day and rock him to sleep at night.

I also draft a general family list that includes things like how often Jared and I will go on an official date night (every other week!). I know this sounds incredibly formulaic, but committing to these relationship goals with each person in my family, when there aren't other issues that are immediately pressing, allows me to put a plan in place for those times during the year when it *is* more chaotic, I'm not as reflective, but I still want to keep these high-level priorities top of mind. I find that having concrete family goals enables me to schedule the time in advance and makes it more likely that I'll keep my commitments and honor my priorities.

On a more granular level, in determining my activities for the coming week, I have followed Stephen Covey's four-quadrant time management grid for years. In *The 7 Habits of Highly Effective People*, Covey posits that there are four quadrants that encompass work activities, with Quadrant 1 representing matters that are both important and urgent, Quadrant 2 important but not urgent, Quadrant 3 urgent but not important, and Quadrant 4 not urgent or important. Many of us spend the majority of our time in Quadrant 1, where the hottest fires reside: managing crises, negotiating pressing problems, putting out fires, and working on tight deadlines. Quadrant 1 matters are time sensitive and visible. They press upon us, consume much of our time, and demand quick and decisive action.*

So how *do* you define what's important and where to best spend your time? Aren't solving problems and managing crisis situations necessary? Not according to Covey, who says, "Importance . . . has to do with results. If something is important, it contributes to your mission, your values, your high-priority goals. We react to more urgent matters. Important matters that are not urgent require more initiative, more proactivity. We must act to seize opportunity, to make things happen. If we don't . . . have a clear idea of what is important, of the results we desire, we are easily diverted into responding to the urgent."

In contrast to Quadrant 1, Quadrant 2 activities are nonurgent but supremely important: organizational structuring, relationship building, brainstorming new opportunities, short- and long-range planning. Quadrant 2 prioritizes effective personal management: vision, perspective, balance, discipline, and control. Very few crises, if any, creep into the domain

---

* Quadrant 3 activities are urgent but unimportant to your goals and usually involve responding to requests from others. Examples include answering your phone while you're working on an important project or answering e-mail as soon as it pops up. Quadrant 4 includes errands and busywork—activities like paying bills, answering e-mails, and grocery shopping—that are not intense, not urgent, but not enormously impactful to your career or your productivity, either.

of Quadrant 2. When you spend time in Quadrant 2, your effectiveness increases dramatically. You'll clearly see what your highest priorities are and have the courage to say no to less important things, such as attending unproductive meetings that are not essential to achieving your big-picture goals. With Quadrant 2 organizing, daily planning becomes more a function of daily adapting, of prioritizing activities according to those that bring the most value, and of responding to unanticipated events, relationships, and experiences in a meaningful but nonreactive way.

When planning the coming week, look at what's on your schedule or running to-do list. Try to prioritize your activities with Quadrant 2 in mind, and plan to spend most of your time on what directly relates to mid- to long-term goals and priorities. As you consider the list of things to do in total, you may discover that you have been prioritizing or focusing on things you don't want or need to be doing at all. Obviously we need to deal with crises when they arise, but it should be a red flag if we are spending too much time in Quadrant 1. It means we haven't spent enough time in Quadrant 2 building teams, processes, and systems that decrease the amount of fires we need to put out in our personal and professional lives. Inevitably issues and problems will arise; the ideal is to avoid the same issues repeatedly.

Chris Guillebeau, author of *The Art of Non-Conformity*, suggests creating a "to-stop-doing list": a list of "the tasks that drain your energy without contributing to anything worthwhile . . . tasks that bring you down without giving you joy or helping anyone else. Try to come up with at least three to five things that you currently do that drain your time and keep your focus away from more important tasks," he says. Similar to how I prioritize three to five things every morning that *will* add value— bigger goals that I need to significantly move the needle on or projects that I want to complete—when you identify those lesser tasks that take you away from what's most important, you'll see that many of them can be left undone or removed from your weekly activities with few repercussions. Ask yourself: Do these tasks truly create value? What's the worst thing that would happen if I didn't do them? If your boss is making requests that strike you as inefficient, talk to her and propose a solution.

You would be surprised by how open good leaders are to refining processes in order to glean greater productivity and better results.

Your time is limited, so don't waste it living someone else's life.

—Steve Jobs

Master Your To-do List

How we schedule our days is how we spend our lives.

—Gretchen Rubin, author of *The Happiness Project*

Whether it's in a notebook that lies open on your desk or in an app, your to-do list more or less dictates your day. For the sake of your productivity—and your sanity—it helps to get it organized.

I prefer an old-school, analog approach. I know a lot of people like apps, and I've tried many different ones, but I find that I really enjoy writing things down and experience satisfaction from physically crossing them off! Plus, I'm on my phone and computer so much already throughout the day that I don't want another reason to look at a screen.

I have a notebook, a Moleskine, that I love; it's where I jot down miscellaneous things I want to accomplish, so that they're not just floating around in my mind and distracting me from the important tasks at hand. I divide a page in half, listing my daily to-dos on one side and longer-term strategic initiatives on the other. This way, I'm reminded constantly of my high-value, big-picture goals while I'm knocking off the smaller things that I need to get done by day's end.

I've riffed off Ryder Carroll's Bullet Journal, an analog approach to note-taking. I've built an entire system of symbols that denote how timely each item on my to-do list is. The Ryder Carroll system recommends creating a calendar page at the beginning of your notebook for each month, and then daily checklists coded with a box for tasks, a circle for events, and a dot for notes. If an item must move from one day's list to the next, you place an arrow next to it, so you can see what is getting done (boxes checked), and what's not (items moved to the next day's list or stricken if canceled or no longer relevant).

What's especially great about this system is it's intuitive and flexible. Play around with check boxes, bullets, dashes, and other symbols to create your own system, and make a key on the first page of your notebook to denote what each symbol means. Then, when you've completed a week or a month, you can look back to see what activities were accomplished when, and where you've spent the most time.

My digital calendar is color-coded by business and topic—construction, acquisition, design—for similar reasons. When I click on my calendar, I get a visual snapshot of where I'm spending my time and which businesses and areas of each are demanding most of my attention. I like to look at my digital calendar on Friday before I leave the office, to see what's upcoming and to make changes if need be. Did the important meetings get scheduled for the following week? Did I leave myself breathing room for strategic initiatives? Did a meeting sneak onto my calendar that's a notorious waste of time? By looking on Friday, it's not too late to make changes to the coming week.

Prioritize your time so that you're always adding value. As often as possible, be proactive versus reactive, and organize your schedule in a way that aligns with these goals. When you cut down on the number of small choices you make in a day, you conserve your stamina for big decision making, which allows you to feel more in charge of your life and your time. Making time for yourself and for what matters most to you must become your number one goal, not equal to but *before* what you must do for everyone else who relies upon you. Remember: your life's happiness begins with you.

> On a macro level, I've learned when to let things go and have them wait for the next day (or in my case, the next month). On a micro level, automating my life as much as possible—regularly scheduled grocery deliveries, etc.—has been crucial.
>
> **—Eva Chen, head of fashion partnerships at Instagram**

THE IMPORTANCE OF CREATING
MENTAL SPACE: INSPIRE CREATIVITY
AND TAKE BETTER CARE OF *YOU*

> Others inspire us, information feeds us, practice improves our
> performance; but we need quiet time to figure things out, to
> emerge with new discoveries, to unearth the answers.
>
> **—Ester Buchholz, psychologist and author of *The Call of Solitude***

In a world full of distractions, where myriad responsibilities, tasks, people, and priorities compete for our attention, finding time for quiet reflection and deep concentration can be a challenge. But when it comes to cultivating your creativity and connecting with yourself, it's essential to find ways to tune out the noise and turn inward.

Feed Your Imagination

"Even the most left-brain, corporate-minded women among us could benefit from a dash of creativity," says Brit Morin of Brit + Co. Morin is a true digital native who worked at both Apple and Google before turning an eye to her own entrepreneurial efforts. Her Brit + Co Web site blends DIY content with e-commerce, offering everything from recipes and how-tos to online classes pairing expert crafters with a new generation of would-be knitters, printmakers, and calligraphers.

A research report Brit + Co fielded last year on makers and creativity revealed that "77 percent of adults want to be creative but don't know where to start." The biggest impediment? Time.

"According to the study, we're hungry for inspiration and education, but can't find the time to search for it in today's busy (and increasingly virtual) world," she says. "Creativity has verifiable benefits on our health, our happiness, and our productivity, and it has the ability to positively impact and transform our lives. Not only can it help lower your stress levels, but it can also leave you better equipped to tackle tough problems in the workplace."

There's no one better than Morin, "as the founder of a company that champions unlocking creativity at every level," to share these smart ways to boost your creativity and give your brain a break:

- ✓ TAKE A WALK: "Steve Jobs was well known for taking his meetings while walking in the hills behind his house," says Morin. "He believed it was more conducive to creative thinking, and he's not the only one." Research shows that "walking outdoors (or even indoors) boosts your creative inspiration." It's also great for minimizing distractions and encouraging focus. Jared logs miles every Sunday by taking calls on his cell while pacing in circles in the living room or walking outdoors.

- ✓ CLOSE YOUR EYES: "Most of us don't get our recommended eight hours of sleep every night," admits Morin. "A ten-minute power nap may be just the thing to give your brain a creative boost." If you're not a napper, or tend to wake up feeling more sluggish than refreshed, ten minutes of meditation offers the same mind-clearing benefits.

- ✓ LISTEN TO MUSIC: "Studies show that our brains function better after listening to music, but it has to be music we enjoy. Put on your favorite playlist and then let the inspiration flow."

- ✓ READ (SOMETHING UNRELATED TO WORK): "Take a break from staring at your inbox and spend five to ten minutes reading your favorite blog or magazine." (Or book!) "Reading helps us open our minds to new ways of thinking, which is a great way to boost your creativity quickly."

In terms of my own hobbies and interests, once I became a parent, the emphasis shifted from the things I used to love to do solo—like off-the-grid adventure travel—to more family-oriented activities that involve my kids. We love to garden, for example. That's our new thing. Getting our hands dirty happens to have proven emotional and mental health benefits and it helps to connect us all with nature; it also gives me a great way to explain seasons to the kids and encourage healthy eating while having fun in the fresh air.

On the weekends, we hang out in the garden at our country home in New Jersey. Berries are a big hit: strawberries and blueberries; we even have a peach tree and fig bush. A giant sunflower grows out of our little garden bed; that's Arabella's responsibility. So while it's not hiking in Patagonia, it makes me smile and grounds me, literally. Connecting with my kids in a leisurely way on the weekend is a wonderful respite from my harried weekdays.

Highlight on Your Hobbies

The creative ways in which you spend your time outside of the office boast countless mental and emotional benefits. Artistic endeavors facilitate that state of "flow," a concept discovered and coined by the psychologist Mihaly Csikszentmihalyi, in which time disappears and you are completely absorbed by what you're doing. Flow has been shown to reduce stress and provide a heightened sense of happiness and well-being.

You likely already have a list of leisure activities that you enjoy doing. In case you're looking for new ways to strengthen your brain and your body while giving yourself a much-needed fix of fun, here are some popular suggestions:

✓ CALLIGRAPHY: This lost art form may seem precious, but it was considered one of the "six arts" by Confucius and reputedly refines your temperament. Steve Jobs based his first computer typography on the calligraphy skills he learned in college. Why not give it a try and then offer to address your friend's wedding invitations?

✓ COOKING: Who doesn't enjoy great food? I love to cook and I prepare huge meals on the weekend, making Shabbat dinner every Friday night. I gave up cooking for a while when my kids were very young because I felt bad spending so much time in the kitchen when I could have been hanging out with them. But now Arabella and Joseph are old enough to help, so I find recipes that don't require a lot of chopping but do involve things like sifting, pouring, and measuring, so we can enjoy cooking together. We do a lot of baking in our house! Arabella chooses a dessert to accompany the Shabbat meal every week. She looks through beautiful baking books and cookbooks and picks a picture that she likes. Of course, it's usually something impossible, like meringue! But it's really fun for us to be in the kitchen together.

✓ CHESS: Most people think that chess is boring or difficult to learn, but neither is true, and studies have shown that chess will improve your IQ! Thinking strategically exercises both sides of your brain, may help prevent Alzheimer's, heightens creativity, and improves memory.

✓ DANCING: Maybe you get to go dancing more than I do these days, but if not, consider joining a class—ballet, tap, ballroom, or hip-hop. Dancing is good for your brain—it improves memory—as well as your body, providing great cardio and increased coordination and flexibility.

✓ LEARNING A LANGUAGE: Whether you're inspired because you plan to visit a foreign country or just always wanted to speak fluent Italian, learning a new language is a commitment, but well worth it. In addition to providing such health benefits as delaying the onset of dementia, learning a language makes you a more well-rounded global citizen, enhancing your marketability and broadening future opportunities.

See the Value of Self-Care

Part of creating mental space is realizing that *you* are your number one priority—and you need to treat yourself as such. Dr. Lauren Hazzouri says, "Learning to take care of yourself is your most important responsibility," but acknowledges that doesn't come easily to most of us, who are living multidimensional lives. Her recommendation? Treat yourself in the same way you'd treat whoever you know to be your number one priority (Your child? Your partner? Your client? Your best friend?). Hazzouri says, "Start by accepting (and expecting!) for yourself only what you'd accept for your #1." Tempted to clean your house instead of taking an exercise class? Consider whether you'd ask your child/spouse/client/best friend to do that instead.

In the small daily decisions—and the big ones, too—ask, "Would this be okay for X?" If yes, do it. If not, then it's not okay for you, either. Valuing yourself alongside who and what are most important to you is how to become *your* best self. Fulfilling your greatest potential is the key to success and satisfaction in every role of your life.

Get Centered

In the midst of movement and chaos, keep stillness inside of you.

—Deepak Chopra

You can connect with your coworkers, you can connect with your partner, family, and friends—but unless you connect with yourself, it's almost impossible to be a generous colleague or find lasting satisfaction at work and in life. Whether looking inward takes the form of daily rituals that help keep you grounded and open, or deeper reflections on what you hope to achieve in the bigger picture—or ideally, both!—we can all use some help rolling with the stress that crops up day to day and contemplating the hard choices that sometimes accompany creating a life you love.

"Tranquility comes from realizing you have no control over anything except yourself and how you react to things," says holistic nutrition and lifestyle counselor Dorit Jaffe. "Stressing over a situation is actually going to be more harmful to your health than anything." Jaffe works with clients to develop habits and skills for staying clearheaded and calm in the face of stress. As a result, clients sleep better, and they're more relaxed throughout the day. She says the benefits of tranquility are particularly noticeable in the workplace. "You have clearer thoughts," says Jaffe. "You're more diplomatic; you're not on the offensive when you talk to people, and you can work more efficiently with all personality types."

Jaffe recommends the following methods to reconnect with yourself:

Tackle stress first thing in the morning: Jaffe prescribes yoga in the morning to awaken your mind, body, and soul, and to get prepared for the day. "Anything that relaxes you, that relieves stress—walking, running, boxing, or other forms of exercise—is especially helpful." "We know exercise is good for the brain," writes Jessica Hullinger in *Mental Floss*. "It gets blood pumping, facilitates the creation of new connections between brain cells, and encourages the growth of new neurons. It enhances our memory and can reduce anxiety." I try to squeeze in a workout twice during the week (and, ideally, twice more on the weekend) early in the morning, before the kids wake up. Whatever the activity, choose something that you really enjoy doing. "Think of this daily ritual as a treat you're giving yourself," says Jaffe.

Embrace meditation: Jaffe recommends meditation—which, for me, is the best way to start the day. Transcendental Meditation is a practice I picked up several years ago and I couldn't do half of what I do in a day without it. Twenty minutes is ideal for calming the mind, eliminating distractions, and boosting my productivity; more often, even ten minutes, once a day, really helps to clear my head. If you can fit in only five minutes, do it. That's better than nothing! "[Meditation] gives you the clarity to assess the stressors in your life and learn how to cope with them. You can be a problem-solver and think about the situation clearly," says Jaffe. It really changes the way your mind reacts to things, which is beneficial.

Step away for lunch: Lots of people with busy schedules eat at or near their desks. Jaffe counsels, "Take twenty minutes—get up from your desk, don't look at your phone, and just relax. When you're consciously eating and chewing, you'll digest your food better and give your brain the break it needs. You'll come back to your desk with a clearer, more focused mind."

Use breathing exercises: "When you become overwhelmed with a long to-do list, pressure from colleagues, or pressure from yourself, recognize it. . . . Spend one or two minutes breathing deeply without looking at your computer, and then go back to your work. Often, when we're sitting at our desks, we tense up without even realizing it." Work in ninety-minute increments, then take a break. Recenter yourself and relax your body so you can handle your workload efficiently.

Treat yourself: "Get a massage to loosen and care for your body, or have a facial." Scheduling a treat or fun activity—like a weekly dinner with friends—gives you something to look forward to. "Give back to your body and soul, and reward yourself for all that you're doing in your life."

YOU ARE A WOMAN WHO WORKS—SMARTER, NOT HARDER

You are a woman who works smarter, not harder—knowing what you value, boosting your productivity, maximizing your efficiency, and prioritizing time for what (and who) you love. By being mindful of what you want to accomplish professionally—and ensuring that the time you devote to your work is, as often as possible, strategic and high value—you are honoring not only your aspirations as a leader but also the many facets of your personality and roles you play in your life, including (but certainly not limited to!) those of wife and mother. Because having a family matters to so many of us—if not right now, perhaps in your future—the next chapter is devoted to prioritizing your relationship with your partner and children, and finding a work/life rhythm that will enable you to create a life you'll love.

A TRUE BALANCE
BETWEEN WORK AND LIFE
COMES WITH KNOWING
THAT YOUR LIFE
ACTIVITIES ARE
INTEGRATED,
NOT SEPARATED.

MICHAEL THOMAS SUNNARBORG

CHAPTER FIVE

Tip the Scale

Let Go of Balance by Seizing Meaningful Moments

For women who work, living one life isn't about achieving work/life balance (which is a total myth, as you've likely already discovered!) but about nimbly seizing moments as they come and thoughtfully prioritizing your individual goals and passions as you go. For some women, it means making deliberate decisions about who you date and, perhaps, ultimately marry, and deciding when to have a baby (or more than one), if starting a family is among your personal aspirations. Having children will likely require a shift in how you meet your obligations at work. Whether that means staying home while your kids are young (or, if you have a partner, him or her choosing to do so), negotiating for flextime, setting up childcare arrangements, working remotely, or starting your own business (see Chapter Six), prioritizing family also means setting healthy boundaries so that you can maximize your efficiency, boost your productivity, and find a work/life rhythm that's optimal for you. As Dr. Lauren Hazzouri says, "When we learn how to live and become the best version of ourselves, busy doesn't need to feel bad, work doesn't need to lead to overworked, and multitasking doesn't need to make us feel scattered."

For me, family comes first—full stop—despite the fact that I'm obviously very passionate about my career and completely invested in my work. It means getting up at the crack of dawn so that I can prepare for the day before having breakfast with my husband and three children, and leaving the office at six every night to get home in time to give baths and read bedtime stories with my kids. It also means getting back to work, once they are asleep, and cranking until midnight or later.

The life I have set up is consistent with prioritizing my family. And yet I can't possibly do everything or I wouldn't be able to meet all of my professional aspirations and obligations. There are sacrifices, certainly—lack of sleep, less time for friends. I don't do afternoon pickup from school. I don't take Joseph to the sports playgroup in the middle of the day. For some people, that's a compromise they aren't willing to make, and I respect that. Just as success looks different to each of us, so, too, does raising a family, whether it's biological, adoptive, or blended.

I believe having a fulfilling career has made me a better wife and mother. That doesn't mean it's for everyone, and that doesn't mean it's easy. It's hard to say good-bye in the morning, especially during phases of separation anxiety—Joseph cried every morning from sixteen months until two years old when I would leave for the office. It broke my heart each time. But knowing I would fully focus on my family when I got home allowed me to be extremely productive at work. I might spend my day finalizing the acquisition of a new hotel or creating design story-boards with my creative team for our spring collection, but once I'm home, I'm covered in sticky handprints, playing on the floor, and trying (unsuccessfully) to sing my kids to sleep. It's certainly not always glamorous, it's often loud and messy, but I thrive on this particular brand of chaos. It's what works for my family and me.

On the flip side, being a mother also makes me a more effective leader and a better manager. The opportunity cost of not being with my kids elucidates my priorities in great relief, causing me to be tremendously focused. It also highlights the value of preparation and patience, at work and at home. Anyone who's had a toddler—or three!—knows it's nearly impossible to force them to do anything they don't want to. You have to get them on board with the program, persuade them to put on their shoes, convince them to try new foods, entice them to embark (willingly!) on the day's adventures. Being a mother has also made me much more efficient. I think about what I'm accomplishing professionally today and it far exceeds what I was responsible for in the days prior to having children, yet I have much less time in which to do it.

Simply put, being a working mother makes my life fuller and richer, even if more harried and chaotic. As Angela Benton, founder and CEO of the San Francisco–based NewME Accelerator, a company that serves tech start-ups led by underrepresented minorities (women among them) in the industry, says, "It's important to have all these different aspects of life—being a mother, being a businesswoman. . . . Being a mother is great but I love my work, I love what I do. And I get to work with great people, and also help them change their lives. And without one or the other I just don't feel like I would be fulfilled as a human being."

You are a woman who works at every aspect of your life—your career, relationship, family, friendships, hobbies, and passions. Whether or not you are on an official payroll—and whether or not you are a mother—you are no less a part of the women who work community. As entrepreneur and mother of four Rosie Pope says, "When you define yourself less as working outside the home or not . . . you begin to see all of us working, with challenges and joys . . . and you become much more compassionate about the efforts other women are making. . . ." Full time at work, full time at home, or somewhere in between, we all want the same thing: to feel good about the choices we're making and to feel validated—or at least not criticized—by those around us.

Regardless of whether you have children currently, your passions and priorities matter just as much as mine. And yet it's important to recognize the fact that historically and practically, managing a career while raising a family has caused more tension for women than any other single factor. Because I'm a working mother—and because in 2015 nearly two thirds of working women also had children at home—this chapter is largely devoted to these concerns.

In rewriting the rules for success, we are prioritizing our passions and families alongside our work without apology. We are celebrating our multidimensionality. The strategies in this chapter—some contrarian, some surprising, all solution oriented—will empower you to change the world of work for yourself, and for others, for the better.

[Women] somehow wear a zillion hats and work for a number of jobs that we don't necessarily have a title or paycheck for. We are able to juggle work and family and take care of, you know, the silly things like making sure there's ketchup in the refrigerator and serving spoons for dinner.

—**Rachel Blumenthal, CEO and founder of Cricket's Circle and Rockets of Awesome**

PARTNER WITH THE RIGHT PERSON

The most important career decision you're going to make is choosing the right life partner.

—**Anne-Marie Slaughter**

Who you marry, or partner with, has a hugely significant impact on your future success.

Consider this scenario: You're young. You've been dating the same person for a few years. You talk about marriage, maybe having a family. You feel completely supported in your hopes, dreams, ambitions.

Before committing any further, you need to explore your passions and priorities, both personal and professional, and then share them with your partner. What are your deepest personal aspirations? Your most ambitious career goals? Who do you hope to be, and where would you ideally work and live in five or ten years? Dream big but get granular, too.

Similarly, I'd advise you to go deep when exploring your hopes for having a family (or not). Do you want children? If so, how many? When do you expect to start? How and where do you envision raising them? Can you picture yourself at home with them full time? Does your company or industry allow enough flexibility that you could be a hands-on parent and succeed professionally or are there ways that you could transfer your skills to a more entrepreneurial endeavor? Working for a company that values face time over results may prove to be an insurmountable challenge when you've got kids.

Once you find the courage to start these conversations, make a point to continue having them. They're relevant even if you aren't sure about having children. No doubt it's difficult to anticipate what you may want in five or ten years; you could (and may) change your mind about any or all of it, and life will undoubtedly throw some curveballs your way. The point is to become aware of what's in your heart and head and share it with the person you hope to spend your life with—sooner rather than later.

If you suspect that you'll want to continue working after having kids, it's important to discuss this with your partner. Consider Anne-Marie Slaughter's counsel from *Unfinished Business*: "You must be sure that he or she will be an equal partner at home so that you'll have an equal chance to take advantage of opportunities at work."

The good news is, a 2014 study of more than 6,500 Harvard Business School grads over the past few decades found a significant shift in male attitudes—for the better. A third of male millennial HBS grads expect to split childcare responsibilities fifty-fifty with their partners; that's compared with 22 percent of Gen-X men and 16 percent of boomers.

Aside from being more involved in parenting and absorbing more of the responsibilities around the house, a supportive partner contributes to your success in less tangible but incredibly important ways: in acting as a trusted sounding board for your ideas, a sympathetic listener to your frustrations, and a champion of your successes—all of which influence your confidence as a professional exponentially.

I am running a thousand miles a minute—as is Jared—but it works for us because we have each other and mutually put our family first. I wouldn't be able to do half of what I do if I didn't have a husband who cares deeply about me, who celebrates my wins, who has my best interests at heart. If I was married to somebody who, even beneath the surface, didn't approve of my professional ambitions, resented the fact that I work so hard, or was unsupportive of my goals, virtually everything about my home life and work life would be different. "You need someone who adores you at your most powerful," says Elizabeth Cronise McLaughlin. "Nothing can destroy one's focus, ambition, or joy like coming home every night to a partner who cuts us down rather than lifts us up."

> Always strive to give your spouse the very best of yourself, not what's left over after you have given your best to everyone else.
>
> **—Dave Willis, actor, writer, and producer**

Finally, partnering with or marrying the right person is essential if you can foresee wanting to take turns being lead caregiver or breadwinner, a concept writer Hanna Rosin calls "seesaw marriages." Here, McLaughlin shares three ways that this shift in gender roles nationwide is benefiting not just women but the men we love as well:

✓ WE'RE VALUING MEN FOR MORE THAN THEIR SALARIES: "For every woman who's complained about the glass ceiling, there's a man who's been secretly burdened by being valued only by how much he earns. In some homes, men are taking on more of the household and caretaking responsibilities as women take on more high-powered corporate roles," says McLaughlin. In others, many men have become the primary family chef or caregiver for their children. As women, we need to support and embrace this decision for the families who make it.

✓ MEN ARE BECOMING MORE INVOLVED FATHERS: "Stay-at-home dads can be extraordinary parents. Allowing men to more fully assume their nurturing role as fathers," McLaughlin observes, is a great way to shift the balance at home for the entire family, and to provide sons and daughters alike with a new model of what a strong man looks like. It's important to learn to resist the urge to push men aside when they try to step up and be involved fathers.

✓ MORE MEN ARE STEPPING UP AS MENTORS FOR WOMEN IN THE WORKPLACE: "As more women become primary earners, roles are shifting—not just at home, but also at work," says McLaughlin. Male mentors "want to see women rise so that all of us can benefit from a more balanced view of leadership. This evolved vision allows us to have complete home lives and working lives—a view that increases as we see more working moms in power positions."

The best way to make room for both life and career is to make choices deliberately—to set limits and stick to them.

—Sheryl Sandberg, COO of Facebook and author of *Lean In*

WORK AND FAMILY: DECIDING WHICH COMES FIRST AND WHEN, ACCORDING TO *YOUR* VALUES

The richest and fullest lives attempt to achieve an inner balance between three realms: work, love and play.

—Erik Erikson, psychologist

For women who work, the question of whether and when to have children figures prominently. For some, the choice is clear—I have friends who are single or married without children and wouldn't want it any other way. They are committed to their work, and are in loving relationships. They are surrounded by great friends, and are passionate about their hobbies and pursuits outside the office. They have no desire to have children, and they are totally confident in their decision.

Personally, I have always known I wanted to be a mother and have a thriving career—I was married at twenty-seven, had Arabella at twenty-nine, Joseph at thirty-one, and Theodore at thirty-four. Despite knowing I wanted to have a family, the decision of when to start was less clear—as it is for many women. It's also very specifically informed by your personal priorities. What do you hope to achieve before becoming a mother? Are you in the right long-term relationship? How do you envision meeting the needs of your family and your career once you have both? What will your partner's role entail? What will it look like to be a mother and a professional—or to be one at the expense of the other?

Rosie Pope says, "I don't remember making a conscious decision to start a career and a family at exactly the same moment. I do remember knowing I really wanted to be a mom as soon as possible and I also knew that I was going to need to work. At the time, I was twenty-seven. I hadn't known many stay-at-home moms and so it just seemed natural that I would also have a career." Now, as a busy mother, running her multifaceted eponymous brand with her husband, Pope shares her wisdom on how motherhood, career, and partnership come together. "This is what I know now, that I wish I had known then," she says, about having a baby, a career, or both, which may help guide you to make the decisions that are right for you at the optimal time(s) in your life:

If you choose career over baby (at least, for now): Suppose you decide to dive headfirst into your career and wait on the baby front, which many women do. I'm sure you've heard it before, but be sure to consider your biological clock. It can take up to a year for a healthy woman to conceive naturally. Our bodies don't always cooperate at the exact moment we want them to; just because you are ready doesn't mean it will happen immediately. "Keep that in mind when you mark 'Baby no. 1' on your calendar as you approach forty," Pope says. Mother Nature may have other plans. "Anything is possible, just accept that it may not be easy."

If you decide to delay having a baby until later in your career, talk to your doctor about your fertility options and have a backup plan. For example, Pope asks, "What if you get pregnant earlier than anticipated? What if your career does not progress the way you had imagined?" Plans, while necessary and helpful, don't always reflect reality. It doesn't mean you can't achieve your goals, ultimately. It just might not be when and how you had anticipated.

If you choose baby over career (at least, for now): "Occasionally, I meet women who decided to have a baby early on in their career—some right after college," says Pope. "While they often continued to work to support themselves," they generally planned to return to work more fully in the future, once their kids were in grade school. "If you make a choice like this, it's important to consider your finances. Focusing on growing your family first will likely affect you financially unless you have support from a working partner or you've built up your savings" in advance. Discuss this decision early on with your partner to ensure that you're both in agreement and aligned on your expectations.

If you think you may want to return to work later, "stay relevant within your chosen industry or industries . . . by working part time, working from home in some capacity, actively reading, taking a class and/or attending industry conferences in your field. It's fine to go slow. Do a little bit as you're able. It's better than stepping out of the workforce altogether," Pope advises, and it will keep your skills sharp and your network intact if and when you opt to return.

Use your experience to your advantage. If you choose to have a child or children early in your career, and later you decide to return to a traditional corporate setting, be prepared for the fact that you will likely be older than your peers at the same level. Rather than accept it as a disadvantage, consider this: you're wiser, more mature, and may be able to rise more quickly than your younger counterparts. You may also choose to work freelance or start your own business, in which case, your age is less relevant.

Think about your partner, your community, and your extended family, and how they can help you get things done. "Perhaps your partner will work a lot at first and then be able to cut back on work when you dive in."

If you choose both baby and career: If this is your choice, realize that your work, says Pope, "will have to be the same—or better—than other people's, regardless of the time you take off for maternity leave, or the days you need to stay at home when your child is sick." Some people will judge you and think you are less productive than they are because you have to race to get to your daughter's dance recital by six or leave for a parent-teacher conference midday. "Don't let them be right and don't let them get you down. Being a parent gives you an entirely new dimension," with the potential to make you better at what you do.

Learn to be totally in the moment: "Work hard to focus on the here and now. You'll be tempted to feel, when you are at work, that you should be at home and vice versa. Fight this," warns Pope. It's not productive.

"Regardless of the scenario you choose, enjoy the journey," she adds. "Be open minded." If something isn't working, be willing to try something else. Remember that nothing is forever—except that you're a parent. At some points in your life, you will be able to spend more time at home; at others, you'll spend more time at work. Learn to be fluid and make sure that over the course of your lifetime there is give-and-take, rather than trying to achieve balance every second of every day.

Maternity Leave: A Primer

Maternity leave is an important time to focus on your new baby. This protected time is essential and, when you're taking the time off, it's important to be present with your little one, and not wondering whether or not your team is floundering without you. As you're preparing to think about starting a family, research your company's policies and determine what setup will make the most sense for you as a new mother. Consider the following:

✓ NEGOTIATE A PLAN THAT MEETS YOUR UNIQUE NEEDS: You may be legally entitled to 12 unpaid weeks off, but only if you work for a company that employs 50-plus people, you've worked for the same employer for the prior 12 months, and you've logged 1,250 hours of service (a little more than 24 hours a week) during that 12-month period. If you work at a small company or part time, this may not be the case. If it doesn't apply, it opens your maternity leave up to negotiation. Regardless of your legal rights, consider negotiating a unique plan. "When I had my third daughter, I came back to work after six days, but worked half days," says Alice + Olivia founder and creative director Stacey Bendet. "I preferred that option over coming back after two months and working late every night trying to catch up."

✓ **NEGOTIATE POSTBABY FLEXTIME:** As flextime becomes more common, especially among moms (see page 157), Elizabeth Cronise McLaughlin says it's not necessary to offer to reduce your pay. Instead, approach flextime negotiations with data on how it will benefit your employer. Offering flexibility helps reduce absenteeism and turnover among employees who can't fit an inflexible job schedule into their other responsibilities, and leads to higher employee engagement and greater loyalty. Assure your boss that working from home (either all the time or occasionally) is as good for her as it is for you—then deliver on that promise.

✓ **CHOOSE A GATEKEEPER:** Find someone trustworthy and capable on your team to act as a gatekeeper once you go on leave. They'll filter through any requests sent your way and determine what's truly important enough to bother you with, as well as take on any nonessential projects in your absence. Leaving things in good hands will give you peace of mind while you're out of the office and, upon your return, make the transition back to work that much easier.

✓ **SCHEDULE CHECK-INS WITH YOUR TEAM:** Some new mothers swear by this; others say it depends on your role within the company, the specifics of your delivery, and your boss's expectations. You can go off the grid completely during maternity leave and be totally within your rights, but staying in the loop and knowing that things are getting done may help you relax and focus on your baby. As with anything, decide what is best for you and your family and know that it will look different for everyone. If you plan to be in touch, choose a day and time that's consistently convenient for you (e.g., when your mother-in-law is on newborn duty) to spend half an hour chatting with your team. If you're planning on taking an extended period of time off, recruiter Jennifer Lenkowsky suggests meeting up with former bosses and colleagues every few months, even just for drinks. "These are the people who will keep you relevant professionally," she says.

Becoming comfortable authentically expressing myself as a female executive with kids was a bit of a journey for me. So many of the women in my life—like my three sisters-in-law, whom I adore (two are stay-at-home moms, the other works outside the home)—had been so unabashed and transparent in embracing their new roles after having children, and yet I was rather guarded. Part of it was a preference for privacy, but another part was grappling with whether being a young female executive with a baby would undermine my authority in the eyes of my colleagues and peers in a very male-dominated industry. I didn't share a single picture of Arabella publicly until after her first birthday, at which point the paparazzi snapped a photo of us at an airport. I didn't want the first photo of my daughter to be sold to the press, so I posted an image myself on one of my social media accounts; after that, I began posting photos of our family more frequently.

I wasn't expecting the overwhelming number of comments I received in response to these candid family snaps. So many people expressed surprise and relief that I was comfortable revealing a more private side of myself. Especially in the first couple of years, I often heard things like, "It's so inspiring that you're such a hands-on mom and not intimidated to show that part of you," and "So amazing! You're not wearing makeup. I'm used to seeing you on *The Apprentice* in a powerful boardroom setting." The contrast was jarring, in a positive way. As professional women, we've traditionally been careful about sharing our personal lives, for very valid reasons. These comments emboldened me to share all aspects of my life—not just my more polished persona—more frequently.

I began to wonder whether I had been doing women who work a disservice by not owning the reality that, because I've got an infant, I'm in my bathrobe at 7 A.M. and there's pureed avocado all over me. I realized that it might be helpful in changing the narrative—even in a small way—to, for example, debunk the superwoman myth by posting a photo that my husband candidly snapped of me digging in the garden with the kids in our backyard, my hair in a messy ponytail, dirt on my cheek. I've been careful not to pretend it's easy because it is not. It took me a while to have the confidence to know that my authenticity as a mother with young children doesn't undermine my professional capabilities or my toughness at the negotiating table; being true to who we are and what our lives look like proves that women who work are real.

Knowing my family is in the spotlight, I decided I was going to embrace it. If I can help celebrate the fact that I'm a superengaged mom and unabashedly ambitious entrepreneur, that yes, I'm on a construction site in the morning and at the dinner table with my kids in the evening, I'm going to do that. Part of what I hope to accomplish with our Women Who Work initiative is for *you* to feel comfortable doing that, too. Together we will debunk the caricature of what it looks like to be a "working woman."

> Don't drive yourself nuts striving for perfection: perfect home, brilliant kids, on and on, just enjoy the everyday and the messiness of it. Laugh a lot, travel a lot, have fun and make memories because childhood is fleeting.
>
> **—Michelle Kohanzo, managing director of The Land of Nod**

ACCEPT THAT BALANCE DOESN'T EXIST

> There is no such thing as work-life balance. Everything worth fighting for unbalances your life.
>
> **—Alain de Botton, author of *On Love***

Hands down, the number one question I'm most frequently asked—by reporters, young women starting out in the workforce, or new mothers—is "How do you balance work and family?"

My answer is: I don't and you can't, so I don't even try.

Work/life balance simply does not exist. The sooner we accept that it's not a feasible goal to pursue, the less stressed we'll be. I really believe that. Balance implies a scale, which by its very nature cannot remain level for more than a brief second, at which point the weights shift and the scale tips. As the actress and author Ali Larter says, "Balance as a modern woman is an impossibility. If you're trying to segment out your time fairly, you will always lose. I believe in taking each moment, investing in it fully, and then forgiving what I cannot get to. You will know intuitively what is most important."

No matter how hard you try, you can't plan for that day, that moment, when the delicate interplay between work and home falters, due to the flu, fever, snowy commute, or downed transportation. As Anne-Marie Slaughter put it, "My schedule was often so finely calibrated that a kid's ear infection could send a week's worth of appointments toppling into one another like dominoes, and I certainly faced days where I felt like I was letting both my family and my work down."

In contrast to striving to achieve balance, I believe the key to living a successful, fulfilled life is twofold: identify your individual goals and priorities, both personal and professional, and structure your time in such a way that you focus the majority of it on meeting those obligations. Christiane Lemieux, founder of DwellStudio and executive creative director of Wayfair, agrees. "Every morning I make a list of both my personal and professional goals and then I rank each task by priority. I work my way down the list. Things fall off, but that's okay because I feel like I am getting the most important things done—even when my life with kids is total blissful chaos."

In navigating my many roles, the demands on my time vary daily. The one constant is that every day I go where I'm most needed. I think about how to best leverage myself for the benefit of both my brand and The Trump Organization. Occasionally that means working late into the night at the office if we are closing a deal; other days it means stepping out midday to take my son to a doctor's appointment. Every Sunday, I reflect back over the week and assess whether I feel more good than bad about how I've allocated my time. University of North Carolina at Chapel Hill professor Barbara Fredrickson says, when we "look under the hood . . . we should be focusing on how we feel from day to day." I like to look at it through the filter of, "Is the life I'm leading consistent with my priorities?" For me, my family is the ultimate litmus test. Have I been present with my children? Was I there for them when they needed me?

Instead of balance, Anne-Marie Slaughter prefers the idea set forth by Cali Williams Yost—speaker, author, and flexible workplace strategist—of "striving toward a good 'work/life fit.' . . . As the term suggests, fitting the demands of work and caregiving together differs day to day, and the only way to do it is to have the flexibility to adapt to continually changing circumstances."

I believe that we each get one life—and it's up to us to live it to the fullest. Jared is a tremendous source of inspiration and support in this arena. He loves to remind me that life is a marathon, not a sprint. Every day won't be perfect, and that's okay; it's the sum of the moments that counts.

Stanford professor Jennifer Aaker's work focuses on the idea that setting obtainable goals (see page 115) is the key to happiness. As Sheryl Sandberg says in *Lean In*, "Instead of perfection, we should aim for sustainable and fulfilling. The right question is not 'Can I do it all?' but 'Can I do what's important for me and my family?'"

Some weeks I do better than others. If I am negotiating a major partnership, I might work three weeks straight. If I'm planning a work trip, I know not to book something the night before I leave or after I return because I want to spend time with my family. Then I have other moments, like if one of the kids is sick, that completely change the dynamic of the day (or the week!). It's about taking a bigger-picture approach and creating a routine that works for you and your family.

When my father was running for president, my schedule was even crazier than usual, but the way I made it work was through meticulous planning. I was incredibly disciplined about looking at my schedule and ensuring that I prioritized plenty of great quality time with my kids. When I agreed to campaign-related travel, the days that I wasn't on the road, I worked from home, which is not customary for me, to make up for the time that I had been away from my family. If I was going to Philadelphia, or on a similarly close jaunt, I'd make sure that I could drop Arabella and Joseph off at school in the morning and that I'd be back by six to do the bedtime routines. In the max peak craziness of October, I was so grateful for the Jewish holidays, which forced me to take a break and allowed me to spend several days focused entirely on my family.

During extremely high-capacity times, like during the campaign, I went into survival mode: I worked and I was with my family; I didn't do much else. Honestly, I wasn't treating myself to a massage or making much time for self-care. I wish I could have awoken early to meditate for twenty minutes and I would have loved to catch up with the friends I hadn't seen in three months, but there just wasn't enough time in the day. And sometimes that happens. Seasons of chaos will undoubtedly come at some point in your life, and throw off even your best-laid plans, but you can go momentarily off track, knowing that you have a solid system in place to return to as soon as possible. The goal is that it's the exception not the norm, and that you're able to get back to healthy habits as quickly as you can.

When you are able, make the pace of your life work for you, rather than base your decisions solely on convention. For me, this applies to vacation. I sprint hard for eight to twelve weeks and then I'll take a long weekend with the aim of resting and recovering. Taking a traditional week or two off happens much less often, but this routine works well for me. As Anne-Marie Slaughter advises, "Working really hard for something and someone you believe in is exhilarating and often necessary. But it can and should be punctuated with periods when you take far better care of yourself." General Colin Powell explains how advocating this approach was part of his management style. "In every senior job I've had, I've tried to create an environment of professionalism and the very highest standards. When it was necessary to get a job done, I expected my subordinates to work around the clock. When that was not necessary, I wanted them to . . . go home at a decent time, play with the kids, enjoy family and friends, read a novel, clear their heads, daydream, and refresh themselves. I wanted them to have a life outside the office. I am paying them for the quality of their work, not for the hours they work. That kind of environment has always produced the best results for me."

Know your priorities and do your best to live your life so that your time is aligned with what's most important to you.

A Balanced Lifetime

> You can't have everything you want, but you can have the things that really matter to you. And thinking that way empowers you to work really hard for a really long period of time.
>
> —Marissa Mayer

While work/life balance on a day-to-day basis may be impossible to achieve, my goal instead is to try to attain balance over my lifetime. Rosie Pope agrees, preferring to look at her life in phases. There was the no-kids, no-husband, workaholic phase of her twenties, which evolved over time to the phase she's in now: the four-kids, great-husband-and-business-partner, successful-entrepreneur phase. No phase is actually balanced at all (or ever), but that's okay—it's about looking at things in terms of your lifetime and adjusting your goals based on where you find yourself at any given moment. Here's her advice on staying sane and seizing each day as it comes:

✓ ENJOY THE MOMENT—IT WON'T LAST: "I wish I had been able to see my life in phases when I was beginning," Pope reflects. "The concept of 'balance' can be misleading. It's okay to be a workaholic when you're young, it's the right time to be. As you become a mom, you can adjust your working schedule and perhaps spend more time at home. Equally, as your kids grow up, it might be the right time to start a new venture."

✓ VISUALIZE YOUR GOALS AND WORK BACKWARD: Building off of the idea of viewing your life as a series of phases, Pope says, "Think about where you want to be at the end of each phase, and then make a game plan by working backward to where you are now. You don't have to have everything mapped out, but think through the first couple of steps. Once you get there, think through the next couple of steps, and so on."

✓ EVALUATE YOURSELF: "When you set goals, say, 'By the end of the year I want to do X,'" Pope advises. "Then commit to checking in in six months. When we don't set a time to self-evaluate, we end up plodding along and doing the same thing for five years without realizing it."

✓ DON'T WALLOW: "Forgive yourself and move on. You will make many mistakes—and some will be massive. Everyone else will get over it when you do, so give yourself the ability to mess up so that you can learn. Knowing when you have erred is part of the skill of succeeding." Stop feeling guilty for whatever you think you aren't doing and embrace what you *are* doing well.

✓ BE CONFIDENT IN YOUR ACHIEVEMENTS: "I know so many amazing women who don't see all the things they've achieved—only the things they haven't. Have confidence in yourself. That doesn't mean you should be arrogant, but it does mean that you should be honest about what it is that you're awesome at and proud of the great work you've done."

From time to time, consciously reframe. Think about your goals and whether you should change them. The formula that worked for you in the past may no longer fit the circumstances.

—Joanna Barsh and Susie Cranston

SET BOUNDARIES AND BE PRESENT

When I became a mother, I realized that in order to juggle the myriad demands of family and career and try to achieve a balanced lifetime, I had no choice but to work smarter, not harder. I also discovered that, in order to be superproductive and efficient, I needed to set healthier boundaries for myself and stick to them.

When we don't set limits, we're communicating that what's important to us—our time with our family, our mental health and wellness—isn't as valuable as the demands of others. This can leave us feeling "less than" and exhausted; it can undermine our confidence and our ability to achieve our dreams.

Because we're all living one life, where work and home blend together, boundaries are less black and white, and more about honoring your priorities. In setting boundaries, I find it's important to know your values, but know your environment, too.

Ideally we're able to openly celebrate the fact that our lives are multidimensional, where work and family coexist in harmony. We've certainly come far as a society, since in generations past, working women didn't talk about their families or interests outside of the office, and men would compete to win the "he who works longest, works best" competition—what Anne-Marie Slaughter dubs "time macho." She calls Dick Darman, Ronald Reagan's budget director, a paragon of it: "Mr. Darman sometimes managed to convey the impression that he was the last one working . . . by leaving his suit coat on his chair and his office light burning after he left for home." I remember at the beginning of my career I would feel self-conscious if I had to leave work early; I'd say I had a meeting when really I had a doctor's appointment. I've stopped doing this, in part because I've achieved a higher level of seniority, but also because that's not sending the right message to the people who look up to me. Plenty of mothers today still feel as if they have to lie and say they're doing something for work in order to attend their child's school play. As women who work, we need to band together to eliminate the old-fashioned "work warrior" mentality and communicate the message to ourselves and to those around us that results are what matter, not face time.

Divorcing ourselves from the reality that we have full lives isn't useful or sincere. The myth of all work, all the time, is a damaging one to perpetuate regardless of gender, but it's especially so for women. Assuming you are the type of person who gets stuff done and isn't using your personal obligations as an excuse to underperform, there's no reason to lie. If you feel you have a boss who doesn't fully support this, have a conversation about the fact that you are completely committed to your work and happy to make up for the lost time, but need to be able to honor your personal obligations, too. Make it clear that you're not asking to work less, just less traditionally (see pages 158–159 on negotiating flextime). I know this isn't always an easy conversation to have, especially in environments where face time still rules. But you owe it to yourself to try. There are always going to be occasions where you need to drill down and grind it out at the expense of your personal life. But it shouldn't be all the time.

If you're in charge, share the fact that you're leaving to pick your daughter up from school in order to create a culture in which others feel comfortable doing the same. I make an effort to swing by both of my offices before holiday weekends when I'm leaving early; every night, I start making the rounds at 5:30 to check in and announce that I'm going home as I leave. My team knows that I trust them to make the right decisions about how they allocate their time, and they would never abuse the privilege. They also know to expect e-mails from me at 11 P.M.—and that I don't expect an answer at that hour, unless they, like me, leave early!

If a leader sends the message that flexibility is tolerated or even embraced, she creates an honest, supportive work environment in which other people feel it's acceptable to acknowledge their lives outside of the office, and are inspired to go beyond what's expected of them to deliver great results.

With these boundaries in place, it's essential that when you're with those you care about, you are present—just as when you're at work, it's important to be focused on work. We've all rushed home from the office to have dinner with our kids, partner, friends, or family and spent half the meal on our phones. If you've made a commitment to be there, *be there.* Try to keep technology off the table, at least during dinner, so you can catch up on the day with your family and enjoy them without distraction.

Sometimes when things get crazy at work it's not always easy to carve out the time you'd like to spend with your children. Certainly there will be times when you need to hunker down and ride out the storm; put on your blinders and close the deal or complete the project. The goal is to enjoy the times that are less harried and strive to make them memorable. Committing to individualized time with each child is a priority for me; as I've mentioned, I make "dates" with each of them separately, just as I do with Jared. They look forward to doing fun things with Mommy by themselves, and I schedule the time in my calendar as I would a meeting—it's just as important to me—so I can be fully focused, present, and not distracted by whatever may or may not be going on at work. For Elizabeth Cronise McLaughlin, "it's bath time and bedtime for each child, separately, every night." She adds, "Unless there's an emergency or an absolutely vital work event . . . I take this precious time with each kid separately every single day. I stick to this ritual even when I'm overwhelmed at work, and have been known to go back to work online as soon as the kids are in bed. As a result, my kids know that they can count on that special time with Mommy every day."

Unlike Elizabeth, I've never really loved bath time, but it falls within our evening routine, so I try to make it special for the kids. I like to give them "spa baths," where I run the shower for steam, play rain forest music on Spotify, lower the lights, and let them add bubble bath to the water. They get a kick out of it and it makes it more fun for us all. And bedtime is one of our favorite times of day. Each of the kids chooses a story, then we say prayers and have cuddle time together. If Jared is working late, we'll FaceTime him so he can share the moment and say good night. If I can't get home one night for bedtime, he does the same for me.

"On occasion, a particularly important work event, speaking engagement or unexpected crisis keeps me away from home at bedtime," shares McLaughlin. "However, in my home we have a ground rule: I never miss bedtime two nights in a row. At times, this has meant that I've turned down an event I might otherwise have attended, or taken a round-trip flight in the same day to get home in time, rather than spending the night in another city after a full day of work. . . . Finishing our day by connecting with our kids before bed sends the message that no matter what is happening for us at work, that connection is priceless."

Communicating to our children that the work we do is valuable—to our families, ourselves, and society—is important as well. McLaughlin says, "When one of my kids says, 'No work, Mommy!' on a given day, I usually respond with something like this: 'I know you don't want me to go to work today . . . I love spending time with you, too! Mommy is going to go to work today, though, to help women who need support in their jobs and with their families. Because of Mommy's job, we get to eat great food, and live in this nice home, and we get to help other people have better lives!' "

In setting boundaries, it's also crucial to prioritize your wellness. Between juggling the demands of work and family, it can be difficult to take time for ourselves. One of the most important components of wellness is sleep. While getting seven to eight hours a night can be challenging, protect your sleep by closing the computer an hour before turning off the lights. When your brain is engaged in an activity, like writing an e-mail, neurons start firing, creating a physiological state that's the opposite of relaxation. Also, the light emitted from your device suppresses the part of your brain that releases melatonin, the hormone that triggers sleep.

Second to sleep, I find exercise another essential aspect of tending to wellness. I love running most. Whether you're into CrossFit or kickboxing, spinning or yoga, invest the time in your own well-being. People who exercise on workdays suffer less stress, and are happier; sometimes even a walk at lunch or an afternoon break can help. A recent study also found that 72 percent of participants cited improvement in time management on exercise days and 74 percent said they managed their workload better when they exercised. When my team and I were training for a half marathon, I convinced Jared to participate and run with me on the weekends (I hadn't told him the race was just for women!). It became a healthy habit. Now we look forward to our weekend run as a time to discuss important things that we may not have had time to get to during our busy weeks. I never listen to music when I run anymore as I so look forward to that time with him.

Just as important is to know what works for you in reducing stress and anxiety, then prioritizing it in your life. We all have those days when we're running in circles, not getting anything done because we're so stressed. There's an irony in that we all stop doing the very things that are good for us when we feel that way, and we all have our different detachments. Sometimes I like turning on *Real Housewives* and sitting in front of the TV eating a giant bowl of pasta with a glass of wine, but if I'm honest with myself, it's kind of counterproductive. It is in these moments especially that we should meditate, soak in the tub, exercise, or take a long walk. I always feel better if, at the end of a harried day, I simply turn off my devices, go into my kids' room, and just watch them sleep. Suddenly, everything's prioritized for me. There is nothing like a peacefully sleeping child to remind you that life is good, and most of what you're worried about is minor and fleeting.

Make sure to make time for whatever it is that helps you find calm and avoid burnout, and if you're having trouble doing so, schedule it on your calendar or to-do list. Prioritize the appointment with yourself as if it were with your boss, client, child, or partner. Remember Dr. Lauren Hazzouri's rule of thumb: treat yourself as you would your number one.

RETURN TO THE WORKFORCE

> We delight in the beauty of the butterfly, but rarely admit the changes it has gone through to achieve that beauty.
>
> —Maya Angelou

Whether you've been out of the workforce for two years or twenty, at no time will you need to be more ready to set boundaries and be present than when you return to work from an extended hiatus. Going back after you've had a baby—or even after you've been home with older children for a significant period of time—is often equal parts emotional and exciting, and requires a certain amount of mental preparation. One of the many skills we must develop as parents is learning how to handle the feeling that you are being split in two. Rosie Pope weighs in with a few tips to smooth the transition:

Accept that it's not easy: "Understand that no matter how much you may think you need to get out of the house, going back to work will be hard," Pope admits. "Acceptance is the first step, so the feeling that you are missing a limb does not come as a shock. It's not easy, but it's normal. A newborn has, after all, been literally attached to you for the better part of a year." With older children, recognize that you've been together for however long they've been alive, so separation anxiety is normal for you both. "Remind yourself why you are working, whether it be for finances, personal ambition and enrichment, or all of those things and more."

Stay connected during the day: Pope suggests "establishing ways that your babysitter or daycare can send you updates and pictures throughout the day." Some of my best photos of the kids were taken by my nanny during the day (I'm sure in ten years I'll convince myself I took them!). "Depending on your work, text or e-mail may be best. Being able to see your baby or children playing, knowing she is napping and staying in tune with all the other milestones of the day will put you at ease and allow you to feel more connected," Pope adds.

Have a breast-feeding strategy: "If you are breast-feeding and would like to continue, make sure you have a plan for pumping," Pope advises. There are regulations that your office must follow for providing you with a private area to do so, but even then, it's never ideal. One of the hardest things about returning to work is trying to continue breast-feeding and watching your milk supply plummet. It creates a terrible cycle, which started to make me feel like an awful parent.

I was really bad at breast-feeding with Arabella because I hadn't done my homework on supply and demand. My milk supply dropped pretty precipitously very early on. Milk reduction also correlates with stress, which is hard to avoid when you're busy and stretching the length of time you go between feeds. The experts talk about playing soft music, dimming the lights, and staring at a picture of your baby's face to increase milk flow, but let's be honest: conditions at work—fluorescent lighting, an ever-growing in-box, and a packed schedule—are hardly conducive to maximizing milk production. By month three, I was never making enough milk to cover the needs of my kids and always had to supplement. I beat myself up over this. With Theodore, I dealt with it best because I cut myself some slack, knew my limitations, and learned from experience that consistency was key.

Just be realistic. Don't be too hard on yourself. We live in a culture in which people think it's okay to judge mothers, based on whether or not you breast-feed and the frequency and ease with which you do so. I have actually had strangers ask me if I nurse. It's really no one's business but yours. Give yourself grace, knowing you're doing the very best you can for your baby.

It's hard to foresee issues like these before they actually happen, but preparing yourself mentally for new challenges is incredibly important in returning to the workforce. Furthermore, consider your current relevance in your industry—and your skill sets. For those who have been out of the workforce for longer than a few months, executive recruiter Jennifer Lenkowsky shares her top tips for planning a (triumphant!) return:

Make yourself relevant and get up to speed: "In the months preceding your job search, consult, temp, start a blog on your area of expertise," offers Lenkowsky. "Get yourself out there and get your name out there. If you're not on social media, start a Facebook profile, Twitter account, and make a LinkedIn profile; if you're already on, make sure your social footprint is professional and ready for potential employers to review."

"You also need to update yourself on your industry; things change all the time. Are you a lawyer? Find out if people are still using Lexis-Nexis. Are you an accountant? Don't talk about the Big Six—we're down to the Big Four. Do your homework so you don't seem out of touch."

You must have a résumé: This should go without saying, but, Lenkowsky says, "I cannot tell you how many people tell me they don't have a résumé. If you are asked to submit a résumé and you do not have one, the answer is never, 'I don't have one.' It's, 'No problem. Can I get it to you by Friday?' Have a résumé that shows the last ten years of your life." If you've been home for that long, have a résumé that captures what you accomplished in the ten years before that, but acknowledge that you've been home. There is no shame in caregiving; own it and use it to your advantage by highlighting skills you developed during that time, such as negotiating, patience, and empathy, that are transferable to the job or industry you're targeting.

Use your resources: "Talk to everyone you know" and let them know that you're looking for work, Lenkowsky advises. "When my best friend went back to work, I called a client and said, 'This is my best friend. I promise you, she'll be amazing.' She got the job and she *was* amazing. Use your contacts. Post to social media. Say, 'I'm going back to work and would love to do XYZ. Anyone looking to hire?'"

Don't put anything beneath you: "We all started somewhere. Unfortunately, when you make a life change that takes you out of the mix for a significant period of time, you may need to start back at the bottom. Be flexible. Do what it takes. Realize that you may be older than your colleagues at the same level but that could be a plus. Be willing to work for free, get an internship or join a temp agency to start gaining experience and building a new network."

Make your skills transferable: "Decide what you want to do," says Lenkowsky, and then comb your life for situations that illustrate those skills. "Perhaps you took a few years off, got married, and moved all over the world to accommodate your spouse's job. You're probably incredibly organized. You can plan an itinerary like a pro. You can set up a house in a day. And you're worldly wise. Need a visa? You know exactly who to talk to and can get one in three days, flat." Present yourself as marketable even if your experience isn't traditional. She adds, "Know what your potential employer is looking for and tailor your experience accordingly."

The secret is there is no secret—just doing the best you can with what you've got.

—Mary Curtis, journalist

ASK FOR FLEXIBILITY

It always seems impossible until it's done.

—Nelson Mandela

In *Lean In*, Sheryl Sandberg tells the story of Cynthia Hogan, who "served as chief counsel for the Senate Judiciary Committee under then-senator Joe Biden before leaving in 1996 after her first child was born. Her plan was to return to the workforce a few years later. But when her second child was born prematurely," Sandberg writes, "those plans changed. A full twelve years later, Vice President-Elect Biden called Cynthia to ask her to join his staff as chief legal counsel in the White House." She wasn't sure "whether she could manage the long hours in the White House and still see her family. . . . 'I knew that whether this would work depended on two men. So first I asked my husband if he could step in and take on more of the responsibility for the kids. . . . And then I told the Vice President-Elect that I really wanted to have dinner with my kids most nights. And his response was, 'Well, you have a phone and I can call you when I need you after dinnertime.' . . . Being forthright led to opportunity."

When you are committed to working smarter—perhaps because you have a family, or a marathon to train for, or a novel you're writing in your free time—you may find you're more motivated to advocate for flexibility at work. Make no mistake: flexibility does not mean working less or working less hard. In fact, in some cases, people who have been granted flexibility find that they end up working harder and longer than they would in an office setting, which unquestionably benefits the company—but can become burdensome for the employee. The convenience of having your work at home means you lose your commute and can easily log in early in the morning or late at night, which adds hours of productivity that a typical office wouldn't afford, but it can make it difficult to set boundaries—for yourself and for others. When structured appropriately, with clear expectations, a flexible setup becomes not just nice to have but also a meaningful business advantage.

While many companies still focus on the hours employees spend in the office—the face time or "butts in seats" mentality—switching to an emphasis on results, where the focus is on achieving goals, not logging hours, heightens employee efficiency, improves quality of life, increases companies' attractiveness to talent, and reduces turnover.

It's not just working mothers who are seeking flexibility; Elizabeth Cronise McLaughlin says, "More and more, I am asked by clients of both sexes how to negotiate for flextime at their jobs. As technology advances and more of us seek a greater work/life balance, flextime can seem like an ideal solution that allows us to still be productive."

Here's the advice McLaughlin gives her clients when negotiating to work more flexibly:

Go into any negotiation for flextime armed with statistics and facts: "As with any negotiation, you always want to go in as prepared as possible to state your case with conviction," counsels McLaughlin. "Flextime is a particularly thorny area, because employers are usually concerned that by allowing you to work a reduced schedule or to work remotely, something is bound to fall through the cracks."

Richard Branson, founder of Virgin Group, is a longtime proponent of flextime, citing increased productivity; a healthier, happier workplace; and more satisfied employees as key benefits. In fact, Branson said that "flexible working is smart working" when he introduced Virgin's unlimited leave policy.

Be very specific in asking for what you want: "Assure your employer that none of your job responsibilities will be neglected should your request be granted, and show your employer the benefits of the arrangement." If they are hesitant, suggest a trial period to reassure them and prove it will work. "Remember," McLaughlin warns, "their interests are what matters. Assure them that you've got your job covered, and you are more likely to get the flextime arrangement you want."

Do not offer to reduce your pay unless you are also asking to reduce your total hours: "Many a working mother in a powerhouse profession like law or finance has bemoaned the flextime arrangement that allows her to work from home one day a week for 80 percent of her pay. These sorts of flextime arrangements often result in working moms working 100 percent of their hours for four fifths of their earlier paycheck.

"In recent months, I've had a number of conversations with female executives"—some mothers, some not—"who have negotiated to work from home one day a week by simply assuming that their employer would allow it without any reduction in pay. The good news is that times are changing, and more and more of them have been able to get an agreement for that arrangement at full pay.

"Do not assume that a flextime arrangement that still has you working full time will require a pay cut. Unless your employer brings up the issue, leave it alone."

If you're in a profession where face time still matters, seek out allies and combat bias: "For many working women in more traditional professions, flextime still carries something of a bias—the assumption being that working remotely means less dedication to the job. If you find yourself in such a workplace," but otherwise love what you do, says McLaughlin, "your only solution may be to work for change." Women executive committees within corporations have made traction recently in addressing these face time concerns by stressing the importance of work/life fit for all employees, regardless of gender and whether or not they've got kids.

Once you've got the flextime arrangement you've asked for, don't drop the ball: "This final point is critical," McLaughlin says. "There's no quicker way to sabotage a good flextime arrangement than by neglecting your job responsibilities or staying out of touch with the office when you know you need to be available. And not only does this harm your career, it also harms the prospects of every other employee who may seek a similar arrangement down the road. Negotiate for what you want, work together, and above all, do your job to the best of your ability, and you'll be a part of the increasing number of women who are making flextime work for all of us."

Working Remotely

> We like to give people the freedom to work where they want, safe in the knowledge that they have the drive and expertise to perform excellently, whether they [are] at their desk or in their kitchen. Yours truly has never worked out of an office, and never will.
>
> **—Richard Branson**

Working remotely is a component of flextime; my editorial director, Sarah Warren, works full time in a nontraditional environment, with monthly visits to our New York office. People feel more engaged with their work if they can live and work where they want. Regardless of the fact that Sarah is almost two thousand miles away instead of down the hall, she is in constant contact with our team; we are a part of each other's lives even if she isn't always physically present in our office.

Whether you're looking to work remotely once in a while or all the time, it's crucial to stay on top of things at the office. Here are five great tips for being effective and impactful when working remotely:

Build a solid team on the ground: "Having a team in the office that's communicative and amenable to a remote setup is essential," says Sarah, who lives and works in New Mexico. "The women I work with do a great job at being inclusive. From calling when something significant and unexpected happens, to FaceTiming me in to a birthday celebration in the conference room, we're very connected." Sarah's team in the office acts as her eyes and ears. "I still get updates—even on trivial things—when I'm not physically present," she says. "I never feel as though I'm out of the loop."

Schedule regular check-ins: Sarah has daily video "touch bases" with her team in the New York office on Google Hangouts. Molly Fienning, who cofounded Babiators, lives in Charleston, and her company's office is in Atlanta. "I have weekly check-ins with the head of each department," she says. "They can use that hour with me to ask specific questions or share updates. Those catch-ups are nonnegotiable."

Set specific hours of availability: "When you're remote, it's essential that you're accessible," says Sarah. "Your presence won't necessarily be seen, so it needs to be felt." During work hours, she's available throughout the day on Google Chat for check-ins—it's the remote equivalent of popping over to someone's desk to ask a question. "Although I come to our New York office once a month, we joke that I'm more accessible when I'm in New Mexico, since I often spend the days in meetings when I'm in the office." Molly Fienning suggests designating a time block for every workday, when your team knows you're sitting at your computer. "Commit to being responsive during that window, so you don't become a bottleneck," she advises.

Sync up: "Technology has enabled us to work better, communicate better, and be engaged remotely," says Anna Auerbach, co-CEO of Werk; she and her partner, Annie Dean, work from New York and Las Vegas, respectively. They swear by Slack, Google Drive, and Google Hangouts for sharing information and staying connected. "Anna and I share a to-do list so we both know what the other is working on," says Dean. "We also share a calendar, which allows us to coordinate across our two time zones."

Be self-motivated: "The gig economy and subsequent remote workforce is the way of the future," says Sarah, "but for companies to take the leap, it's essential that remote employees don't abuse the freedom." She warns that you may need to work twice as hard to build your reputation and prove your trustworthiness, because you don't have the advantage of people seeing you put in the effort. "If you say you're going to do something, make sure you do it," she advises, and adds that working remotely has actually made her incredibly effective and efficient. "I haven't had to sacrifice personal relationships with my team, but I'm not bombarded by unnecessary distractions, either," she says. "I'm able to work faster and focus better as a result." That said, be sure to arrange for occasional in-person visits, which are necessary for building and cementing relationships.

> All companies can benefit from fostering a more flexible environment (creating a place where the most talented, industrious, and entrepreneurial people want to work) and relinquishing hierarchical control to favor a results-oriented meritocracy.
>
> **—Maynard Webb, author of *Rebooting Work***

REMEMBER WHAT MATTERS MOST—TO YOU

> What you do makes a difference, and you have to decide what kind of difference you want to make.
>
> **—Jane Goodall**

Much like success, what matters most varies for each and every one of us. Who or what matters most to you? How are you honoring them daily? Prioritizing our families and our personal passions is a key way senior executive women are changing the conversation around women and work.

For instance, Elizabeth Cronise McLaughlin recounts how Sallie Krawcheck, the former chief financial officer of Citibank, once famously put six hundred managers on hold to take a call from her daughter concerning the location of her pink nail polish, fulfilling a promise to her kids that they could always reach her, no matter what. This may seem like an extreme example—and it isn't something I would recommend unless you're the boss—but as a leader, Krawcheck demonstrated to her team that it was okay to have priorities other than work. She led by example. Be true to what's important to you, as long as you kick ass at work, too!

BE IRREPLACEABLE—THEN ASK FOR WHAT YOU WANT

The best way to influence a traditionally corporate environment is to become indispensable and deliver results. Prove that you're an A++ player, make yourself irreplaceable, then ask for what you want. You can't change the culture if you don't ask—and you're not going to get what you want if you aren't creating high value for your company.

A few years ago, Jared interviewed someone for a senior position on his development team who said at their first meeting, "I have four kids. I have to be home every day by five." To which he replied, "It doesn't bother me when you leave so long as you get the work done well. If you don't get the work done, you won't last—just like anyone else." He told me about the conversation that evening and praised the woman for being forthright and clear about her priorities. Flash forward several years and it turns out she is a machine—one of the most loyal and hardworking employees he has, and she has never once short-circuited the system despite her considerable obligations at work and at home.

If you're already at the company, you may have to prove your worth by pointing out to your boss how much you're doing and how well you're doing it if you think she's unaware. In some companies, achievements that are out of sight are out of mind. Countless studies show that women don't often tout our accomplishments, but we can't just assume that our employers really know how much we're taking on and how well we are performing. Make sure your boss knows your value and your contributions, then tell her what you need. She'll be far more likely to accommodate your request if she doesn't want you to leave.

CREATE MEMORABLE RITUALS

One of the ways I'm setting an example for a different kind of corporate culture in my company is by involving my kids—and spending quality time with them *at the office.* I had a standing lunch date with Arabella every Wednesday before she started kindergarten. We called it our "working lunch." She came into the office—she prefers my "pink" Ivanka Trump office to my real estate one, in part because it has a kids' desk that folds out of the wall, complete with treats, toys, colored pencils, and markers. We'd play for a bit—she has a doll called "Office Baby," and sometimes I think she's more excited to visit Office Baby than me! Then we'd go downstairs to the Trump Grill for lunch; I'd bring paper, crayons, and little games, but her favorite thing to do was draw on project floor plans—so I'd also bring layouts down for her to color. She'd use a crayon to draw where the bed or shower is, then she'd color it in and add special details, like flowers on a bedside table.

I love finding ways to incorporate my children into my work routine, and living so close to the office makes it easy to do. In a traditional setting, I might feel uncomfortable if my boss heard me FaceTiming with my son or saw him in my office, eating ice cream, midday, but as Shawn Achor says, "All these practices provide exactly the kinds of quick bursts of positive emotions that can improve our performance on the job." By occasionally bringing my kids to the office, I'm sharing what I love to do with them but also sending the message to my team that I prioritize my family and they can, too. It doesn't just set the tone that kids are welcome; it acknowledges that having a family is a part of the fuller lives that we're all living, in the same way that we sometimes need to take a conference call on a Sunday or reply to e-mails late at night. So I say, take that call, have that treat. Make memories and make the time you have together count. It's good for you, it's good for your kids, and it's good for your company.

> While we try to teach our children all about life, our children teach us what life is all about.
>
> **—Angela Schwindt, mother and entrepreneur**

ESTABLISH A CODE OF VALUES
AND LEAD BY EXAMPLE

> As human beings, our greatness lies not so much in being able
> to remake the world . . . as being able to remake ourselves.
>
> —Mahatma Gandhi

In his book *The Secrets of Happy Families*, Bruce Feiler shares how Stephen Covey adapted the organizational and personal mission statements for which he was well known to apply to the family. Covey's concept was to articulate what matters most to you and your partner—and to codify those values you ideally want your children to uphold.

The Feiler family's mission statement, which Bruce drafted with his wife and twin daughters, is: "May our first word be adventure and our last word love. We live lives of passion. We dream undreamable dreams. We are travelers not tourists. We help others to fly. We love to learn. We don't like dilemmas; we like solutions. We push through. We believe! We know it's okay to make mistakes. We bring people together. We are joy, rapture, yay!"

I loved this idea so much that I shared it with many of the mothers who work with me, as well as Jared and the kids. We enjoyed riffing on our core values, like never giving up, embracing challenges, being grateful, and giving back. Arabella was three at the time, and she has always felt very passionately about wanting to help the homeless and children in need, so adding those sentiments was important to her. "At the end of the day, you want your children to be truly happy. And that's what this is trying to do," says David Kidder, a father Feiler interviewed for his book. "I believe words matter, even a few words. Maybe they'll matter when the kids are young; maybe they'll matter when they're eighty. Who knows? But this puts onto one piece of paper all the words that matter to their parents."

Establishing a code of values as a family serves as a guiding light for your children; it inspires you to stay on course when the going gets tough, and clarifies your purpose should it ever get murky.

Create Your Family Mission Statement

You can create your own family mission statement in a few simple steps. Feiler recommends starting by asking each member of the family: "What do you stand for?" Let the phrase "This is what our family is about" be a part of the conversation that leads you to your core values. Use these four questions to help you define your family's compass:

1. What words best describe our family?

2. What is most important to our family?

3. What are our strengths as a family?

4. What sayings best capture our family?

In brainstorming the statement, Feiler says, "Make it authentic. Keep it concise. Keep it positive. Emphasize what the family should do. Make the drafting of it a special occasion. Display it in a prominent place," such as the kitchen or above the mantel so you can see it and reference it often.

The family mission statement serves another function, too. It reminds us to embody these values and model them daily as an example to our children. If a solid work ethic is among your core values, don't just tell your children about your passion for your work, show them how that passion gets you out of bed every morning. Demonstrate grit in the face of challenge, flawless integrity, and a desire to succeed. It's noble to say, for example, that your family values experiences over material objects, but that doesn't just apply to the kids' toys—that goes for you, too. Kids are quick to pick up on the old contradiction, "Do as I say, not as I do." If kindness matters to your family, don't just talk about it, live it in your interactions with others, and not just when it's easy, but when it's hard. When your spouse or your kids seem at their least lovable—when they are hungry, crabby, tired, bickering—that's when they need your compassion and caring most.

These positive messages create a chain reaction that multiplies beyond your immediate family to impact the world around you. As Elizabeth Cronise McLaughlin says, "When we practice compassion, we change corporate practices that make it harder for women to succeed when they have children. When we practice compassion, we explore alternative models of success that include things like flextime and balance instead of eighty-hour work weeks that break individuals and families. When we practice compassion, we invest in education and communities and the health of the planet. The future depends on raising children who *care*. Being the best example we can be for our daughters—and our sons—requires us to live into a model of success that includes respect for ourselves, for others, and for the world. Leading by example, and showing our daughters what's possible, means that we will raise proud, compassionate, confident women, who will make the world a better place."

YOU ARE A WOMAN WHO WORKS AT— TIPPING THE SCALE

You are a woman who works at prioritizing your family and your passions alongside your professional aspirations. And though you may not even realize it, doing so is helping to change the conversation around women and work. By setting a positive precedent for generations to come, you are helping to create a work environment that is aligned with our values as people and more supportive of our choices, whatever they are and however they vary for each of us. Corporate environments have typically been too rigid to support women who prioritize passions and relationships outside of work, which is why, for generations, many working mothers felt they had no choice but to leave a traditional work setting. As Stanford professor Deborah Gruenfeld says in *Lean In*, "We need to look out for one another, work together, and act more like a coalition. . . . Working together, we are fifty percent of the population and therefore have real power."

The workplace revolution we are launching is quiet, deliberate, and essential. It's a call to action not just for mothers currently working but also mothers who are at home (either by choice or because they had no other viable, realistic options) and for women who are not mothers but are passionate about their equally multidimensional lives.

One by one, we must fight for ourselves, for our rights not just as workers but also as women. We must prioritize our families and passions. We must serve as role models for the peers and colleagues for whom this issue may not yet feel relevant, who may not be ready or able to take a stand themselves. And we must lead change to benefit our daughters *and* our sons. Work is changing for men as much as it is for women; men want and expect to be a bigger part of their children's lives, and there's no reason in the world why they shouldn't be.

As an executive—and the founder of a company dedicated to celebrating women who work at all aspects of their lives—I've found that to attract and, more important, retain this next generation of talent, it's no longer enough to build a good business. To achieve meaningful, lasting success, we must build a great company for which great people want to work. As leaders we need to create and cultivate a culture that truly embraces women and the roles we play both in our family lives and our business lives, a culture that allows multidimensional women to thrive.

> The message of this [female] model of leadership is that if we
> know what we want, and ask for it with careful negotiation, we can
> indeed have lives that are in alignment with what we value most.

> —Elizabeth Cronise McLaughlin

NEVER DOUBT THAT
A SMALL GROUP OF
THOUGHTFUL
COMMITTED CITIZENS
CAN CHANGE THE
WORLD.
INDEED, IT IS
THE ONLY THING
THAT EVER HAS.

MARGARET MEAD

CHAPTER SIX

Lead with Purpose

Changing the Conversation
Around Women and Work

B y the time you arrive at this point in your career, you will likely
have made choices—some difficult, some less so—about working
smarter versus harder. Perhaps you're employed in a corporate
work environment, or working flexibly or remotely some of the time;
maybe you've left the workforce to raise your family or work indepen-
dently from home. No matter what your day to day looks like, creating
a more positive and inclusive workforce benefits us all: professionals and
parents, women and men.

Innovative companies—those creating policies that support people
who prioritize their lives outside of the office—are fostering environments where employees flourish. They are engendering loyalty by allowing parents to feel less conflicted about meeting their responsibilities to
their families while wanting and needing to devote themselves to fulfilling work. They are also encouraging those without families to pursue
their passions outside of their careers, resulting in happier employees.
Contrary to the concerns of some traditional organizations, these companies know that working in a new way doesn't mean fewer hours or
less commitment from their workforce; rather, they realize that trust
and empowerment lead to lower turnover, diminished absenteeism, reduced health-care costs, and bigger profits.

How do we create a culture—both in our organizations and also in our country—that truly embraces our diverse priorities and passions, at work and at home? How do we cultivate a support system that allows multidimensional women (and men) to thrive? By celebrating the enormously positive contributions that women make every day to the world of work—no matter their level or title—and building on those accomplishments. By deliberately creating a climate of trust and flexibility that replaces the archaic concept of face time in favor of benchmarking performance based on excellent results. By working to address barriers that disproportionately affect women—a lack of access to safe, quality childcare, among them—to allow more women to remain in the workforce, grow in their careers, and contribute to the economy. By telling meaningful narratives about *why* our companies exist, not just "what" we make, do, or sell. And by starting and funding female-run businesses where these cultural ideals are bred in the seedlings of ideation and steeped in the companies' DNA.

All that you've learned and accomplished thus far has led you to this point: identifying your passions; parlaying them into a job you love; establishing yourself as a leader by communicating clearly and connecting sincerely with your colleagues and bosses; breaking through the glass ceiling by networking, hiring, managing, and negotiating thoughtfully and effectively; working smarter to prioritize your time and interests and aligning your personal and professional goals in support of your relationships and family.

You are living one life to the fullest. Now it's time to create an environment that is conducive to others doing the same.

Whether within a company for which you work, or at the helm of a venture you create, you are a woman who leads with purpose. "Leading, however, means that others willingly follow you—not because they have to, not because they are paid to, but because they want to," Simon Sinek says. In this chapter, the tremendous contributions women are making at every level within their organizations are explored, from instituting family-supportive policies and procedures to reframing their company's mission in a more inspiring, meaningful way. You'll meet successful female entrepreneurs who are figuring out innovative new ways to blend their passions, families, and businesses, and hear their timely advice, which may help with your own entrepreneurial journey. Even if you don't want to venture off on your own, these groundbreaking entrepreneurial experiences offer important insight into leading with purpose within an organization.

CREATE A ONE-LIFE CORPORATE CULTURE

> It's not the size and might that make a company strong; it's the culture—the strong sense of beliefs and values that everyone, from the CEO to the receptionist, share.
>
> **—Simon Sinek**

In my experience creating a company and building businesses, and in studying the cultures of other organizations I respect and admire, I believe the answer to fostering a positive corporate culture is found less in rules and routines and more in the actions of leaders and the people they employ.

With high-performance self-starters in place, you *can* foster a mostly informal culture that emphasizes self-discipline over rigid, top-down rules; you *can* clearly communicate the expectation of mutual trust and measurable deliverables alongside the perks of flexibility and autonomy. Rather than police your team, populate it with like-minded A+ talent at every level, and trust them to act responsibly and in the company's best interests. I believe that the best leaders get great results not through control, but by setting an appropriate context via their culture.

In 2009, Netflix CEO Reed Hastings and then chief talent officer Patty McCord created a 127-slide PowerPoint deck in which they outlined a revolutionary perspective on shaping culture and motivating performance. The slide show went viral—it's since been viewed more than five million times online, and Sheryl Sandberg referred to it as one of the most important documents ever to have come out of Silicon Valley.

The deck changed my whole perspective on corporate culture; I reread it every year, and, while I don't agree with everything outlined, I took several of its ideas to heart when I began to build my business. At its foundation, the deck was doggedly insistent on the concept of running a business based on common sense: hiring exceptional players, "fully formed adults" who would act in the company's best interests, operate with integrity, and create great teams. Rather than institute cumbersome policies to police the 5 percent of employees who might abuse vacation days and office hours, I focus on hiring the best and most passionate people, who I then empower and trust to orchestrate their time off responsibly.

I have extremely high expectations for myself and for my team. I want my employees to think of the greater organization; to support the smartest, most innovative ideas, no matter whose they are; and to help their colleagues, even when it isn't convenient to do so. I expect my team to be known for its honesty and directness, even—or especially—if that means admitting a mistake. I have seen us all grow, in our jobs and as people, by inspiring one another and celebrating team and individual accomplishments, big and small. I trust that everyone will face hard problems and big challenges with equal parts optimism and practicality; that they'll challenge the "it's what's always been done" attitude when they see a better way; that they'll continue to deliver world-class results even as the bar is set higher and higher.

Our mission is clear, our goals are defined, our results are measurable, and my team gives me—and one another—their absolute best, facilitating a supportive one-life environment without the need for strident rules and regulations.

That hardly sounds like the diminished commitment that traditional companies fear in moving toward a more flexible culture.

In return, I provide my team with purpose and the autonomy to be brilliant at what they do. As President Theodore Roosevelt said, "The best leader is the one who has sense enough to pick good men [or women!] to do what he wants done, and the self-restraint to keep from meddling with them while they do it." I try to give my employees the support, the latitude, and the training to succeed. It's not always easy—I joke that I'm a frustrated art director or copywriter, sometimes micro-managing Instagram crops and wordsmithing pieces of content we create—but I try never to forget that delegating is essential to scaling my business and to imparting a sense of ownership and pride to my team.

Beyond a competitive salary and full benefits, my team gets stipends to offset their cell phone costs (because they can work from anywhere, anytime, and often do) and gym membership (the benefits of exercise on health and stress are well documented). I stock the fridge with healthy snacks (thanks to my awesome mother-in-law, who does grocery runs for us!). I don't have a formal vacation or sick-day policy; I believe people should take a break when they need it and rest when they're ill. People outside the company always seem surprised when I tell them this, but we don't track how many hours we're working per day or per week (including late nights and weekends), so why would we track the days we don't work per year? I focus on hiring people who have no interest in abusing this policy and use their time off wisely so they can perform at their best.

We have many parents on staff. To accommodate them—whether they're married or single—and their growing families, my company offers eight weeks of paid time off for maternity, paternity, or adoption leave; we also allow them to ease back into work in the months that follow. There's a children's area in the office—stocked with art supplies and (somewhat healthy) sweets, in case someone needs to bring her child to work, because babysitters get sick, too.

As a goal-oriented company, our deliverables and deadlines determine our hours. Sometimes we work more, sometimes less. I apply my own sprint/rest theory to my business; when we're working on a big project, I expect my team to give 100 percent. When we aren't in crunch mode, I don't mind if they leave early for a date night or a midday jog in Central Park, and they know that.

Because of technology, face time is not as essential as it used to be in our highly connected world; it's a nonissue for me if someone isn't at her desk at the stroke of nine or leaves at six. I encourage my employees to set their own schedules, so they can walk their kids to school or pick them up at the end of the day, for example. We're a performance-based environment and results aren't subjective. I believe that as long as you are passionate, working hard, and committed to excellence, you will succeed.

So how do we build cohesion among our team members if people are coming and going at different times, or, like my editorial director, Sarah, working full time from New Mexico when the rest of us are in New York? We are constantly connected, by e-mail, Google Chat, or Google Hangouts, during the workday, but as needed after hours, too. In the office, we believe in collaboration, and that all ideas are worth sharing, so we work in open-space zones; there is not a single office with a door, although we do have dedicated quiet zones for making calls and doing uninterrupted work. Every other Tuesday, we eat lunch together in the conference room so we can touch base and review all current company projects. I host a monthly series called #LunchBreaks, where I bring in leaders of industry to speak to my team on myriad topics instrumental to their personal and professional growth: we studied Transcendental Meditation with one of the most experienced teachers in the world, Bob Roth; trained for a half marathon with Olympian and running coach John Henwood; and learned about how to organize our personal finances with Alexa von Tobel, the founder and CEO of LearnVest. I host an annual retreat at a Trump hotel or golf property where we review our business, reflect on the prior year's achievements (and what we could have done better), and set goals for the year ahead. We may all be working on a flexible schedule, but our connections are meaningful, and we share a clear, common purpose. We all want the team—and one another—to excel!

As a leader and a mother, I feel it's as much my responsibility to cultivate an environment that supports people—and the roles we hold, both in our family and business lives—as it is to post profits. One cannot suffer at the expense of the other—they go hand in hand. I also believe that the culture of my company is as important to our success as the products we offer. An inspiring, mission-driven organization is essential to attracting—and retaining—top talent; and I'm pretty obsessed with building an organization for which multifaceted go-getters love to work. In recruiting, we use our uniqueness as a competitive advantage; our company is a place that encourages you to prioritize whatever it is that's meaningful to you outside of work, in tandem with your professional responsibilities. We also deliberately tap a dramatically underutilized recruitment pool—well-qualified parents who have stepped out of rigid roles because they find the strain on their families to be a deal breaker. By making my company extremely family friendly, we have been able to assemble a world-class team that delivers high-quality work on time without compromising their commitments to their spouses and children.

The companies that learn to focus on what their employees accomplish, not on how many days or hours they've spent in the office, are those that will attract and retain the greatest talent. To build a healthy, productive corporate culture, hire the right people and treat them well. To achieve meaningful, lasting success, build a company that great people want to work for—especially women.

> Some leaders are born women.
>
> **—Geraldine Ferraro, first female vice-presidential candidate**

Women Who Work Improve Organizations

It seems inconceivable that as women we still have to prove our worth in the workplace, but the advent of work/life initiatives has prompted new questions from traditional employers; there are still many heads of companies, and even heads of HR, who feel that supporting women is too much trouble, too expensive, and not a professional concern. The evidence stands on its own, proving the overwhelmingly positive impact women have in corporations:

✓ WOMEN ENHANCE PERFORMANCE: "European telecommunications giant Deutsche Telekom mandates that at least one-third of its top jobs be filled by women," notes Mika Brzezinski in *Knowing Your Value*. The company has said, "Taking on more women in management positions is not about the enforcement of misconstrued egalitarianism; having more women at the top will simply help us operate better." Similarly, as Sheryl Sandberg and Adam Grant wrote in the *New York Times*, "an analysis of the 1,500 Standard & Poor's companies over 15 years demonstrated that, when firms pursued innovation, the more women they had in top management, the more market value they generated."

✓ **WOMEN ARE MORE COST CONSCIOUS:** Research shows that when more women are on the board of directors, companies are less likely to pay outrageous compensations. A study by the University of British Columbia's Sauder School of Business revealed that female CEOs and female company directors tend to pay less in corporate takeovers, reducing debt, and saving their shareholders money. This very reason is why Norway passed a law requiring that at least 40 percent of their public boards of directors be female.

✓ **WOMEN FACILITATE BETTER DECISION MAKING:** Bruce Feiler refers to a group of researchers at Carnegie Mellon, MIT, and Union College who in 2010 published a study in *Science* that found that groups make better decisions than individuals; specifically, groups that had a higher proportion of females were more effective. These groups were more sensitive to input from everyone, more capable of reaching compromise, and more efficient at making decisions.

✓ **WOMEN TAKE FEWER UNNECESSARY RISKS:** Part of what drives better decision making may be women's tendency not to take risks where they aren't needed. A 2001 study in the *Quarterly Journal of Economics* found that women investors traded stocks 45 percent less frequently, giving them a net outcome of 50 percent higher returns a year compared with men.

✓ **WOMEN ENCOURAGE TEAMWORK:** Feiler also notes that a growing body of evidence has shown the more women on a team, the better the team works. "In 2006, researchers at Wellesley conducted extensive research on women who served on the boards of Fortune 1000 companies." The study found that "a lone woman on a board can make a substantial contribution, but two are better than one. . . . Lead researcher Sumru Erkut summed up the findings, 'Women bring a collaborative leadership style that benefits boardroom dynamics by increasing listening, social support and win-win problem-solving.'"

✓ WOMEN CREATE OPPORTUNITIES FOR WOMEN: "On corporate boards, despite having stronger qualifications than men, women are less likely to be mentored—unless there's already a woman on the board," observe Sandberg and Grant. "And when women join the board, there's a better chance that other women will rise to top executive positions."

LEAD WITH PURPOSE FROM ANY LEVEL

If your actions inspire others to dream more, learn more, do more, and become more, you are a leader.

—John Quincy Adams

What if you aren't senior enough within your company to change policy? You might be wondering if you can still positively influence the culture. Leadership skills can and should be learned and cultivated at every level, regardless of rank or stature. "Leadership has little to do with titles and everything to do with influence," says Chris Guillebeau.

Becoming a leader doesn't start the day you're promoted to a senior position within your organization; it starts the minute you decide you want to make a difference. There are plenty of leaders who have little official influence and are incredibly effective because, as Simon Sinek puts it, "leaders are the ones willing to look out for those to the left of them and those to the right of them." I encourage my employees to have one another's backs by always doing what's best for the team: supporting one another's ideas and aspirations, being forthright with constructive feedback, and celebrating team wins while learning from failures. My hope is to create a culture of leaders at every level, who are accountable not just to me but also to one another. As noted by Bruce Feiler, in 2012, scholars from MIT published groundbreaking research in the *Harvard Business Review* revealing that "the most effective teams are not dominated by a charismatic leader. Instead, members spend as much time talking to one another as to the leader, they meet face-to-face regularly, and everyone speaks in equal measure." In my company's culture, leadership flows laterally as much as top down. My goal as a leader is, as Sinek says, "to create an environment in which great ideas can happen."

In contrast, there are plenty of examples, past and present, of people in senior positions who may have been running the company, but certainly were not *leading* their people in the pure sense of the word. "Leadership requires people to stick with you through thick and thin. Leadership is the ability to rally people not for a single event, but for years," says Sinek. Companies whose leaders don't spark enthusiasm in their employees, engender loyalty, or summon respect pay the price in lost talent and productivity. Shawn Achor writes, "Studies have found that the strength of the bond between manager and employee is the prime predictor of both daily productivity and the length of time people stay at their jobs; when this relationship is strong, companies reap the rewards." Chris Guillebeau states: "If you're a leader, never forget that your followers are real people who have a lot to contribute. Wherever your leadership journey takes you, always remember that your followers are not just a number."

> Wherever you are in the pecking order, you can make a profound impact. It takes a bit of extra effort but it's worth it. Never underestimate your own agency.
>
> **—Rachel Haot, former chief digital officer for New York State**

Share the Why Behind Your Business to Create Leaders at All Levels

> If you hire people just because they can do a job, they'll work for your money. But if you hire people who believe what you believe, they'll work for you with blood and sweat and tears.
>
> **—Simon Sinek**

It's not just women in senior positions who are changing the conversation around women and work; in order to inspire leaders at every level, it's critical to share your company's purpose to build a one-life corporate culture. The best way to do that is to clearly articulate not just what it is that your company does, but *why* you do it. Think about that for a moment. "When a WHY is clear," explains Sinek, "those who share that belief will be drawn to it and maybe want to take part in bringing it to life."

In his book *Start with Why* and associated TED Talk, "How Great Leaders Inspire Action," Sinek introduces and explains the Golden Circle, his seemingly simple diagram of three concentric circles that reveals why we are loyal to certain brands beyond what we might think about what they make and sell.

Within the three rings, "what" a company does is represented by the outside circle, "how" the company does it rests inside the what, and "why" the company exists is at the very center. Most organizations think from the outside in, starting with the what; advertising and marketing campaigns focus primarily on what the organization makes or sells, and the narrative within the company begins and ends there, too. Although it may seem that what your company does is important in carving out a niche in a crowded market, whether you make handbags or hotels, that's not memorable enough on its own to generate significant recall from your target customer—and it certainly isn't enough to inspire action from your employees. A great leader communicates the why behind her company's existence—to her people and through her marketing—in order to create a culture that inspires her customers and employees to join the mission.

Take Apple, an example Sinek uses in his talk. Apple doesn't start by saying, "We make phones, computers, and other electronics." That's their what—but it's no different from Samsung's or Lenovo's what. Apple instead talks about what they really believe in—creating products that disrupt the status quo. They could talk about the specs and features (the what of their products), but instead they talk about their belief system (the why). "When a company clearly communicates their why—what they believe—and we believe what they believe . . . we feel a kinship with others," and their brand mentality becomes a natural outgrowth of the company's culture.

The cult of Apple doesn't exist because their technology is so far superior to, say, Samsung's. It exists because, as Sinek says, "people don't buy *what* you do, they buy *why* you do it." Culturally, for decades, Apple has fostered a like-mindedness among its employees, creating a ripple effect among its customers that converted them to disciples. Its renegade spirit is part of the company's ethos. The culture feeds the brand and vice versa, resulting in a major competitive advantage. Apple could sell almost anything and we would buy it—which is not the case with its competition.

Under Armour is another great example of a company whose "why" has inspired leaders at all levels, saturating its culture from the inside out with its brand mission, and motivating its employees through its clear reason for being. Having long been the scrappy underdog, UA became known for perseverance, for working hard to overcome challenges, for emerging victorious—and never giving up. The tagline "I will" sums up its tenacity and determination; in emphasizing its "why," the company is selling an attitude more than performance footwear and apparel. What's more, Under Armour's rule-breaking spirit isn't a slogan or a brand strategy but an honest, sincere extension of its dogged and resourceful company culture. As Kevin Plank, the founder, chairman, and CEO says, "Culture's an incredibly important thing in every organization. . . . Too often, we start with what's not possible, or what can't happen or here's the limitations or here's the glass ceilings. . . . That idea of progress over perfection, of having the courage and the guts to frankly progress versus having something be perfect—that is important and entrepreneurial." That cultural philosophy—Under Armour's "why"—is what's translated into their advertising, like the "I Will What I Want" commercial, in which American Ballet Theatre ballerina Misty Copeland is shown dancing, accompanied by the voice-over of a young girl reading the actual rejections Copeland herself received. The message isn't "Buy our athletic wear," but rather, stories of strength that portray that women can do anything if they work hard, believe in themselves, and never give up, a logical extension of the "why" that has informed the company's culture and inspired its people from its inception.

"When you have a higher purpose in mind and it's shared by the team, leading is easier," say Joanna Barsh and Susie Cranston. "You are not tripped up by the little stuff—who is ahead of you, or what department is outperforming yours, or a million other distractions. . . . 'When you have your purpose in life,' adds Geraldine Laybourne, serial entrepreneur and cofounder of Katapult, 'you're making a difference for the people around you.'"

Culture Confab: Alice + Olivia

Alice + Olivia CEO and creative director Stacey Bendet has successfully established an apparel brand that women want to work for. Here are her four key takeaways for creating a culture that truly supports her fellow females:

✓ BE NICE, NO MATTER WHAT: "I require niceness at my office," says Bendet. "People need to feel comfortable to do their best work. I want women who work here to feel good about themselves."

✓ SUPPORT PROFESSIONAL GROWTH: "I want my employees, especially women, to feel like they can have it all, and I want them to grow," she adds. "The only limits are the ones you place on yourself." Create opportunities for talented women to evolve within the company. Bendet has former interns who are now executives; she's had assistants go on to work in Alice + Olivia's photography department.

✓ SET AN EXAMPLE: "My business partner had kids before I did, and she showed me that you can be a powerhouse executive and a nurturing mother at the same time," shares Bendet. "We try to set an example for our employees without judgment or expectation. Not everyone is going to come back six days after giving birth like I did," even to a modified schedule. And that's okay. For Bendet, easing in slowly made more sense than working late nights playing catch-up after two months away.

Umber Ahmad, the banker-turned-baker/entrepreneur from Chapter One, echoes this sentiment. Mah-Ze-Dahr is not just a bakery—it's a brand. "I think of this business as an enterprise, not a one-door shop," says Ahmad. "Growing up, food was a way to communicate and explore. I'd travel and learn about people and cultures through the food. . . . This is a food business that's accessible to everyone (rather than tethered to one neighborhood location). It's about creating a language for people who normally wouldn't have an opportunity to connect. In all of the decisions I make for this business, I ask myself, 'How do I create that language for people? How do I introduce them to things that matter in other parts of the world through food?' That's the foundation of the Mah-Ze-Dahr brand."

Similarly, I am enormously proud of the success of my brand, but apparel, accessories, and footwear are more the "what" to the "why" of my mission—to inspire and empower women to create the lives they want to live. I designed a company around a larger mission, so whether you're trying on a pair of my heels or perusing my Web site for interviewing tips, my "why" is to provide you—a woman who works—with solutions and inspiration. Even the reason for writing this book goes beyond the how and what of building a life you'll love to the greater cause of changing the dialogue around women and work and helping erase the caricature of what a "working woman" looks like. It's the "why" behind the Women Who Work initiative and my brand that gets me out of bed at the crack of dawn every morning, and is what most deeply motivates my team.

Do you know your company's "why"? Do all of your employees and coworkers? If so, how is it communicated, internally as well as to the outside world? Is the how and what of your organization in alignment with the why? If not, in what ways can you influence this positively? While you certainly want to think about how your company's purpose is being communicated to your target audience, you first want to consider how it's being shared with your employees and whether and how it aligns with their passions—and yours. Your company's story, and how everyone who works there feels about it, is the key to developing leaders who lead with purpose at every level.

If you're in a senior role, looking to inspire leaders at every level of your organization, find those self-appointed champions who live and love your company's purpose and are motivated to enthusiastically share your story—with peers, customers, vendors, even shareholders. Consider creating a brand book that captures the essential elements of your vision and goals so that every member of your team is on the same page and can internalize your company's mission. In tandem with my team, I created a brand book that we carefully cultivated to align the different functions of our businesses (design, marketing, content, creative, et cetera) with our brand attributes: "We are smart, polished, purposeful, invested, alluring, strong." We spent time writing a brand manifesto—a statement of intentions and beliefs we hold to be true and strive to fulfill: "The greater the challenge, the bigger the opportunity. Be bold. Act purposefully. Embrace the future, respect the past. Lead with purpose. Prove smart is sexy. Invest in each other. Be inspired and inspiring. Own your femininity. Stake your claim. Dream and do. Go all in. You get one life. Live it to the fullest." Finally, we distilled our core values and created an acronym to make them easy to recall. (See box on page 186.)

Purposefully creating an authentic, meaningful narrative enhances employee engagement and customer commitment; those who are clear about their company's mission feel they are a part of something important, something larger than themselves, and something they deeply believe in. This is what provides the foundational passion—the quintessential building blocks—for inspiring leaders at every level of your organization, who will together help to disrupt the dialogue around women and work.

We DREAM and DO.

We are . . .

DETERMINED—we embody the mission of the brand and we lead by example.

RESPECTFUL—we are well mannered and strive to act graciously, always.

ENGAGED—we're in this together and we trust each other.

AMBITIOUS—we're intellectually curious and always learning. We swing for the fences.

MOTIVATED—we believe that success is up to us.

DEDICATED—we're accountable to each other in achieving our shared goals.

OPTIMISTIC—we see challenges as opportunities.

LEAD YOUR OWN ORGANIZATION WITH PURPOSE

Entrepreneurs have a great ability to create change, be flexible, build companies and cultivate the kind of environment in which they want to work.

—Tory Burch, fashion designer and businesswoman

As much as you may care about the company you're working for, there may come a time when the desire to start your own company, consultancy, or freelance business grows too strong to ignore. Maybe you're seeking more creative freedom or greater autonomy. Perhaps, in the face of traditional schedules and corporate mandates, you feel that going out on your own is the only way to truly make work and life fit. Or there's the pull toward entrepreneurship because you see a market opportunity, as I did, ready to be seized. Sometimes it's as simple as wanting to be the boss and spend all of your time doing something you love. As Rachel Blumenthal says, "For me, being an entrepreneur means that there is really no line between work and play, and I love everything that I do . . . who doesn't want to enjoy what they're doing every day and have fun doing it?"

Whatever the reason, founding a business can be a whirlwind: liberating, exhilarating, overwhelming, gratifying, and terrifying—sometimes all at once. But take heart; all the skills you've mastered thus far are excellent preparation for making the big leap. Entrepreneurship is one of those areas in business where one's experience can differ enormously from someone else's, depending on your industry, financial backing, whether you have a partner or are going solo, whether you have a family, and more. To best capture the many facets of the entrepreneurial experience, I've called upon inspiring executives, as well as women who have founded innovative start-ups, to reflect upon the various components of building a successful business.

One by one, female-owned businesses are changing the world of work for the better. We are creating enterprises that, from inception, embody the new rules of success, rules that support women in all that we aspire to and all that we do. Together, we are raising the bar for other companies to follow suit.

> It's important to be willing to make mistakes. The worst thing that can happen is you become memorable.
>
> —Sara Blakely, founder of Spanx

THE NEW RULES OF ENTREPRENEURSHIP

> The glass ceiling that once limited a woman's career path has paved a new road toward business ownership, where women can utilize their sharp business acumen while building strong family ties.
>
> —Erica Nicole, founder and CEO of *YFS Magazine*

Think you don't have the constitution to start your own business? In his book *Originals*, Adam Grant turns the common belief that to be an entrepreneur "you need to take radical risks" on its head. Despite the fact that the term "entrepreneur" means "bearer of risk," as defined by economist Richard Cantillon, Grant says that the idea that people who start businesses are "all-in" from the beginning is false; many aspiring entrepreneurs hedge their bets—certainly financially—and refine their ideas over time before fully committing. They often get started on their concept while working at a full-time job (and saving money), sometimes for *years*. In fact, entrepreneurs who kept their day jobs had 33 percent lower odds of failure than those who quit. "Having a sense of security in one realm gives us the freedom to be original in another," he says, which despite the additional workload can be a very freeing perspective for a would-be entrepreneur.

> The only skills you need to be an entrepreneur are: an ability to fail, an ability to have ideas, to sell those ideas, to execute on them, and to be persistent so even as you fail you learn and move onto the next adventure.
>
> —James Altucher, entrepreneur and author of *Choose Yourself*

Set your goals.

"You may be working fourteen hours a day, but at least you get to pick when you work those fourteen hours," says Angela Benton. Launched in 2011, Benton's start-ups have raised more than $20 million. "I had my oldest daughter when I was sixteen so I worked literally my whole life. But when I finally decided to become an entrepreneur, all of a sudden I had freedom and choice and my kids weren't the first kids to be dropped off at before care and the last kids to be picked up at after care. I could pick them up from school if I wanted to. That might mean working at 9 P.M. because I'm doing those things during the day, but the point is, I have a choice."

I'm a workhorse by nature and I was raised to work hard at everything

I do. That said, it wasn't until I built my own business from the ground up that I understood the vastness of launching your own enterprise. Amanda Steinberg, who's started multiple businesses, including the popular career and finance site DailyWorth, counsels, "Know what you're signing up for. I think back to the first year of DailyWorth. I had a newborn and five full-time employees at my engineering company, Soapbxx, and I was publishing content on DailyWorth every day. I lost my mind. There were so many nights of tears. It feels crazy-impossible sometimes. If you really want to be an entrepreneur and run your own show, you can, but it's really painful for a long time. There's beauty in getting a paycheck . . . but becoming successful as an entrepreneur can be done. It's just harder, and that's okay."

Even during the painful periods of growing your business, it's so important to prioritize personal time. I'm not great at this, frankly—for me, the hardest thing to do is to work less. I have to make a concerted effort to create healthy boundaries, to make time for date nights with Jared when I'm exhausted from parenting and there are hundreds of unopened e-mails in my in-box. Particularly when the business is yours, when you feel that its ultimate success or failure depends largely on you—your vision, your effort, your leadership—it's hard to take breaks and easy to burn out.

Annabella Daily, founder of Map My Beauty and mother of two, adds: "In the start-up world, every single call and every single meeting is extremely important. It's all too easy to get into a pattern of working without any flexibility for yourself, but it's important to live in a way that aligns with your values. Don't sacrifice beautiful moments with your children and miss all the firsts, because that's time you'll never get back. Create rules for yourself to protect the time that's important to you, whether that's time when you need to be 100 percent focused on your business or 100 percent focused on your family." Daily is originally from Finland and says, "I moved to the U.S. when I was nineteen with nothing but a suitcase." After consulting for YouTube and creating the playbook for their fashion and beauty vertical, she launched Hearst's YouTube channel and spearheaded Condé Nast's digital transformation.

As the mother of a then toddler, with a second child on the way, Daily craved a personalized beauty experience but realized that a trip to the beauty counter was no longer resonating—or realistic with two kids in tow. It occurred to her that she could re-create that which she was seeking virtually, so she set out to design Map My Beauty, an app that provides virtual instructions for various beauty looks and the ability to shop recommended products on your phone.

Find an idea that will solve a common problem.

We all have lots of ideas for products and businesses, some of which are better than others. How do you know which to pursue?

Marcela Sapone and Jessica Beck cofounded Hello Alfred—a service that, according to their Web site, "pairs busy individuals with organized, knowledgeable, intuitive people who handle all of life's necessities: from groceries and dry cleaning to tailoring and sending packages." Says Sapone, "When I started my career, I worked at McKinsey and later at a private equity firm; I worked long hours and had little time for anything else. Coming home after a long day to a messy apartment, wrinkled work clothes on the floor, and an empty fridge wears on you. Jessica and I asked other busy professionals how they made it all work, and the near-unanimous answer was hired help. When we hired someone on Craigslist to take care of each of our basic home-keeping chores, everyone in our building wanted to get in on it. It was the first iteration of Alfred. We started small and realized that there was actually a huge demand for accessible, affordable, automatic hired help."

Sapone and Beck's team of Alfreds are vetted pros who take care of household chores and errands, freeing up your time, energy, and mental space. Not only is Hello Alfred's product revolutionary, its business model is radical, too. Sapone and Beck hire only W-2 employees—people who earn salaries and are eligible for benefits, as opposed to 1099 contract workers, who aren't afforded the same rights. It's a first in the on-demand space, and a rarity in the hired help industry as a whole. "We've essentially created a new class of jobs," Sapone says.

In 2014, the year Hello Alfred officially launched, the team won the prestigious TechCrunch Disrupt San Francisco start-up competition and, by 2016, had raised $12.5 million in venture capital funding.

Create the product you wish existed—just as Sapone and Beck did, just as Spanx founder Sara Blakely did. Blakely was getting ready for a party when she realized she didn't have the right undergarment to provide a smooth look under her white pants. With the snip of a scissor, she cut the feet off a pair of control top pantyhose and launched a multimillion-dollar business.

Seek knowledge and support from other people.

Much as I have always done, and will always do—first in real estate and then in building my own brand—you need to talk to lots of different people, both in your industry and outside of it, in order to gain perspective and figure out what it is that you don't know. Angela Benton says, "Find subject matter experts. Learn how things have been done in the past so that you can be innovative moving forward. Don't limit yourself to your industry. If you're building a textile company and need help with financial projections, look for an expert in finance. Put together a list of potential advisors that can help you along the way—LinkedIn is a great resource. You don't have to take their advice, but you need to be open to receiving it. . . . Critical feedback might be hard to hear, but it could change your business for the better."

You can reject the advice you receive from others and draw your own conclusions, but be sure to solicit the opinions of a wide variety of smart people first. My dad is a great example of this. One of the reasons he has thrived as a builder is that he listens to everyone. He's certainly known for having very strong opinions; what's less known is how he forms them—by asking the people doing the work for their feedback. When he walks a construction site, he'll ask the super, the painter, the engineers, and the electricians for their candid impressions of the project, whether they think something should be done differently or done better. Sometimes he'll learn, for example, that the mechanical plans are overdesigned or that the architect drew something on the plans that the builders in the field think is a mistake. The key is to ask for advice and when you get it, listen. Ask thoughtful questions. Say thank you. You don't have to follow the advice, but you should internalize it and make your own determination of whether you're going to accept or reject the recommendations. Also, avoid talking solely to people who will only reinforce your own viewpoint or bias.

Don't just talk to others about the specifics of launching your business; also talk about the challenges you face personally as a new entrepreneur. Annabella Daily recommends seeking a supportive network and looking for advice in unexpected places. "I had big career goals and I didn't know anyone, so I had to build my network from scratch and work my way up," she says. "Launching a start-up can be a lonely existence, and when you're a founder and a new mother, you're juggling two completely new things. A supportive network of other working or entrepreneurial moms is priceless. Meet up regularly to share stories and swap advice. The support of other working parents was, unexpectedly, one of my most helpful assets when I was starting Map My Beauty. I'm always blown away by how much expertise people have in their unique fields. I've met people in the elevator in my building and in baby music class (those music classes are better than any networking happy hour!) who have helped me with everything from making financial projections to creating content."

Lauren Bush Lauren, CEO and cofounder of FEED Projects, is quick to acknowledge that to feed a village it takes a village. "Although you should set the mission and overarching vision for what you are trying to manifest and bring into the world, it is so important to surround yourself with really smart, dedicated people who probably know a lot more than you do in certain realms," Lauren says. "I have been fortunate to have met amazing people in starting and growing FEED over the last eight years—people who have been extremely gracious to make connections, help me work through problems, and strategize the best way forward. To have that support system, whether it's friends, mentors, or capable and dedicated teammates—and hopefully it's all of the above—is valuable for any entrepreneur. Starting any venture takes a village, so make sure that your village is made up of people you respect and can learn from and grow with along the way."

Lauren, as a sophomore at Princeton, traveled to Guatemala with the UN World Food Programme as part of an effort to raise awareness of world hunger. "It was so eye-opening," she says. "We went to really rural, impoverished parts of the country and visited children who were very hungry and malnourished. That's when I really got hooked. I knew this would become a part of my life in one way or another—trying to help."

Lauren began spending vacations, long weekends, then a month between her junior and senior year doing research and visiting countries where hunger was impacting entire communities. "It was such a gift to be able to go to these places and visit with these families and children firsthand."

"I graduated without a job, but with the idea for a FEED bag and the initial development done," she says. When her plan of passing the idea to the World Food Programme fell through—after she'd made her first sale to Amazon.com—Lauren decided to start the company herself. "I had put in the work to make a product and a brand that I thought was quality, and we had an order to fill. That was the moment that I started FEED Projects."

To date, FEED has provided tens of millions of meals to children around the world through the World Food Programme and Feeding America. FEED supports global nutrition programs and launched the nonprofit FEED Foundation, which is working alongside other organizations to fight hunger and eliminate malnutrition worldwide.

Invest in your team.

I have learned as much about leadership from junior members of my team as I have from my father himself—leaders come at every level of the organization, which is why it pays dividends to invest in your team.

In my experience, the best way to support your team is to put people in environments where they're growing, empower them to excel, and show them respect. Whether that means offering education and inspiration like we do with our monthly #LunchBreaks series or being cognizant of their workload, I'm trying to provide meaning and purpose along with a paycheck.

Another crucial part of leadership and maintaining a great team is caring about your employees' lives and understanding what motivates them to do what they do. Do they feel like they're on a growth path? What are their goals, dreams, and aspirations? Help your best people turn a job into a career by knowing what lights them up and forging a path for them to become their best selves.

"It's key to have a really capable team that can fully support you and drive the business," shares Annabella Daily. "A great team is very cohesive; they're on the same page and have the same clear goal of making the business a success."

To grow organically, without lowering the quality of your services, you need to train people, suggests Marcela Sapone. With contract workers, you can't do that. This is why, at Hello Alfred, Sapone and her partner opted to hire salaried W-2 employees. "Doing this communicates that our Alfreds are the core of our business. They take pleasure in their job, they're compensated well, and they're proud to do high-quality work."

Be resilient.

"As an entrepreneur, you're going to be told 'no' in a lot of different ways," warns Angela Benton. "It's not going to be easy. Resiliency will be a skill you'll need throughout your entire entrepreneurial career."

Ali Maffucci, founder of *Inspiralized*—a popular healthy food blog dedicated to turning veggies and fruit into spiralized noodles—says it's "how you interpret rejection that's important. When I first started, spiralizing wasn't very popular. People didn't get it yet, and they rejected me, but that was okay. I made a mental note to check back in six months, and my resilience and persistence have paid off."

Maffucci was in her midtwenties, working in business development for the airline industry, when she discovered that her mom, a Type 1 diabetic, was experimenting with raw veganism. She made Ali, an Italian American pasta purist, an Asian-inspired "noodle" dish with spiralized zucchini noodles—and Ali couldn't believe how similar they tasted to the real thing. Maffucci took her mom's spiralizer home that night to test it out; after a few months of sharing recipes with her friends and posting about her newfound passion on Instagram, she quit her day job and, the next day, bought the domain for inspiralized.com.

"When I started thinking about developing my own spiralizer, I cold-called the company that made the spiralizer I was using. I thought, maybe I can talk to the company about improving the product and making an Inspiralized brand version. It didn't work out, but it was a first step in the process of creating my own product." Maffucci has since also published a cookbook.

Marcela Sapone concurs that being told no can be a gift. "Let doubt make you more resilient," she says. "When you face doubt, that's all the more reason to reinforce your convictions. Write down your overarching goal and come back to it every day; keep your company's mission in mind with every decision you make. Ask yourself and people you trust why you're getting pushback. Is there really something you could be doing differently? It forces you to make your case to others—and yourself—which will only strengthen your resolve."

For Annabella Daily, the challenge of raising money for her business was complicated by the fact that she was already a mother—and pregnant. "Potential investors often doubt your ability to commit to growing a business while you're starting a family," she says. "When I closed my early seed funding rounds for Map My Beauty, I was seven and a half months pregnant with my second child. The key was to clearly communicate my goals and intentions for growing my business—and then deliver on those goals. I had to show people that it is possible to mix business and babies. If you don't take no for an answer and you're focused on your goals, you can always make them happen."

Being resilient applies to your personal life as an entrepreneur, too. "Schedule time for the unschedulable, like impromptu meetings that can't be delayed or picking up a sick kid at school," says Angela Benton. "The good news about running your own ship is that you *can* be flexible, you'll just pick up the slack later."

Get scrappy.

Amanda Steinberg of DailyWorth says, "If you really want to start something, learn to do things for yourself. This is especially helpful if it's digital—it's not that hard to learn HTML if you're willing to commit the time. It's best to become as independent as possible, because if you have to pay someone every time you need something done, you're never going to get there."

Ali Maffucci's husband calls her the most resourceful person he's ever met. "I taught myself how to use the Adobe Creative Suite just using Google and YouTube. With the help of the Internet, you can figure almost anything out as long as you do the research, spend the time, and stick to it. If you're willing to work, you can do anything." And save yourself money in the process.

Find a partner.

Your spouse isn't the only significant "other" in your life; when you're launching a business, sometimes a business partner can be critical to your new venture's success. As Ashley Wayman, formerly of Petit Peony puts it, she went back to school after a stint in finance to open her mind to other industries. "I found myself falling in love with small businesses and start-ups," she recalls. She went on to head up operations at Rent the Runway just as the now megabusiness was getting off the ground, before moving to Boston to run Rue La La's mobile marketing team during the flash-sale-site boom. Then, after leading the promotions team for two years at home goods e-commerce site Wayfair, Wayman got pregnant.

"I realized that I wasn't going to be able to balance corporate life with being a mom and see both of those endeavors through the way I wanted to," she says. She looked through her contacts to find something more entrepreneurial, where she could still work hard and make an impact while keeping flexible hours. Wayman's brother introduced her to his next-door neighbor in Vermont, Kate Bowen, who had started a girls' dress business. Using local seamstresses to produce her designs, Bowen took her samples on a boutique road show in New England and attended the ENK Children's Club trade show at the Javits Center in New York. Boutiques went wild for the youthful prints and wholesome designs.

"It's pretty unheard of for a new brand to be successful at a first trade show like that, but people loved Petit Peony," says Wayman. She was intrigued. "Then I found out I was pregnant with a girl, and it all clicked."

After Wayman left her full-time job, she and Bowen had five months before her due date to get the ball rolling on growth plans for Petit Peony; they changed production facilities (the whole line is manufactured in Massachusetts) and rebranded the business before Wayman's daughter was born.

The secret to running a successful business while starting a family, according to Wayman, is a great business partner. "When I met Kate and talked to her, I instantly realized how perfect our partnership would be because our skillsets were so complementary," she says. "She inspired me with her creativity and fearlessness, and, most important, when my daughter was born, she understood the demands of early motherhood." Since they met, the business has been enormously successful.

"Building a business, especially with a new baby, is a leap of faith," Wayman says. "Every day it's a roller coaster of emotions. Choosing the right person to ride it out with makes all the difference." Here are five top qualities to look for in a business partner:

✓ A SKILL SET THAT'S THE YIN TO YOUR YANG: "Your partner should bring something different to the table and have a skill you don't have yourself, but that's important to the business," says Wayman. "While it's nice to have some things in common, finding a balance and being able to divide and conquer based on expertise has proven to be a recipe for success."

✓ STRONG COMMUNICATION AND CONFLICT-RESOLUTION SKILLS: "Honest and real-time communication is so important to a healthy partnership," shares Wayman. "Look to see how your partner resolves conflict. Find someone who reaches agreements with others using logical, data-driven approaches. The more Kate and I understood each other, the better—it allows us to inspire and support each other."

✓ A SHARED VISION AND GOALS: "While you and your partner might be motivated by different things, it's vital to align on common goals and a vision for the business. Be comfortable with these things changing over time, but, again, communicate and align on your priorities weekly, if not daily. Building a business comes with many challenges and requires an around-the-clock effort, so it can be easy to lose track of your big-picture goals. A partner who is both aligned on and passionate about your company's purpose is your best ally," Wayman advises.

✓ TRUSTWORTHINESS AND A KIND HEART: "In any good partnership, whether it's a business relationship or a life partnership, there must be trust," shares Wayman. "I have always looked to work with and for kindhearted people who value honesty. Honesty leads to more informed decision making, healthy partnerships, and, above all, a moral and transparent work culture. These are simple but essential qualities to look for. When I was looking for this opportunity, I felt really strongly about working with someone who had a great moral compass. I was drawn to Kate because I knew she'd make decisions from a position of kindness and fairness—it showed in the way we ran our business and treated our customers."

✓ A SIMILAR LIFE STAGE TO YOUR OWN: "Kids or no kids? Married or single? Being in a similar life stage as your partner's can help you avoid tension," adds Wayman. "For example, a single guy who works hard and plays hard likely won't pair well with a father of twins. At the time, Kate had three children under five, and I had a seven-month-old daughter. If one of her kids was sick and she needed to take a step back for the day, I completely understood and was happy to pick up the slack. A situation like that may build resentment if the partners are at conflicting stages in their lives. We related to each other and supported each other's lives outside of the business."

Raise and manage your money.

Entrepreneurs face a unique amount of uncertainty and risk when it comes to their finances, particularly in the throes of early-stage entrepreneurship. Typically, the number one reason that people don't start their own company is they fear they can't afford to raise enough money to do so. The second reason? Not knowing how to manage their money once they do.

After her success as a consultant, serial chief technology officer, and founder of a handful of companies (including the Web consultancy Soapbxx and DailyWorth, a financial media company for women), Amanda Steinberg was earning more money than her peers, but wasn't able to create any kind of stability—because she was living well beyond her means. "I was raised by a single mom who always stressed the importance of being able to take care of myself," says Steinberg. "But, in spite of my relative success, I couldn't."

Fed up, she attended a workshop her friends were offering on financial management for women. When she walked out, she knew she had to share what she'd learned—and DailyWorth was born. On the site, Steinberg provides her million-plus subscribers with access to the financial and career expertise she wished she'd had when she was first starting out. In launching a financially smart business while protecting your personal funds, Steinberg recommends that you save before you self-fund your business. "Not many entrepreneurs are able to save before they launch a business unless they live at home with their parents," she says. "I've been able to do it twice, both times due to the fact that I had another job. I worked a full-time job in order to fund Soapbxx. You can even have a part-time job that doesn't require a lot of energy, so you can focus your efforts on your business. Having that consistent income when you're getting started is critical, because start-ups often don't make money in the first couple of years. It really might take that long to plant all the seeds and see them pop."

Once you've raised the money you need, it's crucial to manage it well. "Separate your personal and business accounts," advises Steinberg. "People don't do that! Money comes into their business and they drop it right into their personal checking account, and then when it comes time for taxes and deductions and understanding what your income is, it's really hard to discern. It's important for clarity between personal and business. Businesses get really expensive and you have to spend money on a business, but if you get confused about the distinction, you'll never be able to manage the money effectively."

She also recommends giving yourself a simulated "salary." "When you do get paid into your business, you have to put yourself on some sort of consistent monthly draw. You're the head of the company, so it's not a salary technically, but you need to get into a rhythm of knowing how much you have. The economic patterns of any business look like an EKG chart—constantly up and down. If you spend everything on the up, you won't have anything on the down. Giving yourself a 'salary' helps you avoid treating your business income like personal income."

Separating your flexible and fixed expenses into different accounts is important, too. "In addition to my general checking account, I have one for flexible spending (nonessential things like shopping and entertainment). I pay bills and other fixed monthly expenses from my general account. I take a set amount of money—let's just say a thousand dollars—out of my paycheck and move that into my flexible spending account, which has its own debit card. That way, I can look up on my phone the balance of that account, so I'm never in a position where I'm spending money that should be allocated to something essential, like paying bills, on something nonessential, like new clothes."

Finally, be sure to set up accounts for unexpected costs. "I have four accounts in total. In addition to the two spending accounts, I have one that I call my 'curveball' account and one for my emergency fund. It's kind of like hiding cash from yourself so that it's there when you need it. I put two hundred dollars a month into my curveball account, until it gets to at least five hundred. That's for the little stuff that happens, like my kids needing their school lunch plan renewed, for example. It's the things you don't think about and that don't fit into the monthly expenses you've planned for. I spend it when I need it, and then build it back up. The other account holds my emergency fund, which is for bigger unexpected things like medical emergencies. I've had to wipe it out before, which can feel really demoralizing, but thank goodness it was there."

A Venture Capitalist's Perspective

My brother-in-law, Joshua Kushner, founder of the successful venture capital firm Thrive Capital (whose investments include Instagram, Warby Parker, Spotify, and Oscar), shares what he looks for when investing in start-ups:

How does an entrepreneur catch your eye?
I am most drawn to entrepreneurs who are solving big problems. Often, these problems are not immediately apparent, or could involve more traditional industries that many may initially find mundane, like insurance or infrastructure. Disrupting these industries requires time, patience, and a great deal of hard work in order to compete with incumbents who typically enjoy a head start that's decades long. I find myself most drawn to the founders who are focused on the most challenging issues, who are transforming and working to better our world.

Beyond the idea, what do you look for in an entrepreneur that makes you want to invest your money?
I look for a genuine personal connection to the idea. I like to understand the stories and circumstances that inspired an entrepreneur to pursue a particular opportunity in the first place. I have found that this ultimately becomes the driving force behind the entrepreneur in both good times and bad. For instance, Mario Schlosser, CEO of Oscar Health, became passionate about changing health care when he had his first baby and realized how convoluted the health insurance industry was.

What's the best way for an entrepreneur to prove her value?
Head down, ignore the noise, and continue to execute on your vision above all else.

Take time to recharge and celebrate small wins.

"Women never feel we have the luxury of taking time to ourselves, and being an entrepreneur brings that time squeeze into great relief," says Angela Benton. "However, it pays to think of it practically: having a hobby can make you more creative in your business, giving your brain the chance to disconnect and recharge. Make friends who have nothing to do with your profession, which will give you a break from talking about work and perhaps bring a new and different perspective to what you do."

Annabella Daily agrees. "As women, we tend to be quite tough on ourselves. When you're ambitious and want everything to happen quickly, it's important to celebrate the little moments, both in your business and personal life, and to appreciate the progress you're making. The small wins really make all your hard work worth it."

Photographer Abbey Drucker adds, "As a freelancer, you need to take care of yourself. You'll be on the go, dedicating many hours to your work. It's time away from family and loved ones. You have to make time to recharge.

"Whatever your passion, whatever you're devoting yourself to, as much as you love it, when you do it professionally it becomes a job. Half the time you'll be creating, but the other half—more than half, really—you'll be running a business. Tracking invoices, generating estimates, budgeting, accounting, taking meetings and appointments, and managing a team. Scheduling is so important: set aside blocks of time and say, these three hours are for accounting, these two hours are going for photo editing.

"You are the one person who will be most passionate about your work. If you get run down, you won't be performing at your fullest potential. Rest, meditation, and healthy eating can be some of the most refreshing and rewarding things you can do for yourself and your career."

Stay optimistic.

Learning to become more resilient by knowing what we *can* change, versus what we can't, is a lesson all leaders need to learn. If you focus on a growth mind-set—which is when you believe that your abilities, talents, even your IQ! can be positively influenced through learning, dedication, and hard work—and encourage your team to do the same, you will create a far stronger reserve against setbacks and stress. The more typical fixed mind-set dictates that you're born good or bad at something and that can't be changed, no matter what.

"When the going gets tough, some people respond in healthy ways while others experience defeat and a dead end," says Dr. Samantha Boardman. Inoculating yourself against stress—or, what researcher Suzanne Kobasa calls becoming "stress hardy"—will make you a more effective leader and a happier person.

"The good news is that you don't have to be born stress hardy to become stress hardy," says Boardman, who recommends Kobasa's three C's—commitment, control, and challenge—in cultivating greater resiliency. "People are less stressed when they feel a genuine purpose and passion for what they do," she says. (That's commitment.) "Stress hardy people are committing to living the life they lead and the work they do . . . a life in concert with their values."

With respect to control, Boardman says that the people who manage stress best focus on what they have control over, rather than what they don't. "They recognize that they choose their attitude in any situation." Especially stressful ones, which is where the third C, challenge, comes in. "When difficulty arises, stress hardy people ask, can I learn something from this?" focusing on the positive, not the negative.

Shawn Achor adds that optimists "also cope better in high-stress situations and are better able to maintain high levels of well-being during times of hardship—all skills that are crucial to high performance in a demanding work environment." Stress begets stress; the worse you handle it, the more stressed you become, the more likely you are to engage in unsupportive and unhealthy behaviors, like social isolation and overconsumption of food and drink.

Whether you face obstacles with positivity and resilience, or negativity and overwhelm, your attitude trickles down to your team and over to your family in ways you may not even notice. It literally pays to focus on the positive. "Happiness can improve our physical health, which in turn keeps us working faster and longer and therefore makes us more likely to succeed," says Achor. "Companies and leaders who take measures to cultivate a happy workplace will not only have more productive and efficient workers—they'll have less absenteeism and lower healthcare expenditures."

When I reflect upon what being an entrepreneur means to me, I think about how far I've come as a professional and how much I've changed since college. Until I was twenty-five, my full professional focus was on real estate. It was all I knew. As I got older, the aperture opened on my life and my experience, and I started noticing entrepreneurial opportunities all around me. When I first recognized the chance to disrupt traditional industries like fine jewelry and apparel, I got excited about the viability of the business idea. But once I began to execute and grow my business, I realized I was building a larger mission. The values I wanted to communicate to my customers and women at large far transcended what my company was selling.

As I dug deeper, and reflected more on what was really motivating me in the retail space, I realized that clothing and accessories were my "what"—but my "why" was really about inspiring and empowering women, for all that we are and all that we can be, beyond the stereotypes of what we look like, how we dress, what we do at work, and for whom we care. I cultivated my passions by being curious, experimenting, working hard, finding success, thinking bigger picture, grinding it out, and arriving at my life's mission: to change the conversation around women and work for us and for those who follow.

> I think we, as women who work, have a tremendous opportunity in terms of creating workspaces that are sane. We're leading teams that are comprised of women and men; we have to both get the work done and do it in a way that sets an incredibly positive example in terms of family and life and self-care.
>
> **—Dr. Nadine Burke Harris**

CHANGE THE CONVERSATION

> The equality we fought for isn't livable, isn't workable, isn't comfortable. . . . We have . . . to get on to the second stage: the restructuring of our institutions on a basis of real equality for women and men, so we can live a new "yes" to life and love, and can choose to have children.

> —Betty Friedan

In the history of long-distance running, 1954 was a truly remarkable year. It was the year a British runner named Roger Bannister ran a four-minute mile—which was deemed impossible, from the first Olympic Games in 776 B.C. until that fateful day, May 6, 1954. Yet once Bannister broke the record, he held it for only forty-six days. Suddenly, every top runner was able to run a four-minute mile; once it had been achieved by Bannister, it was perceived as attainable by others—and, therefore, they, too, accomplished this once seemingly impossible goal.

That same year, a Czechoslovakian named Emil Zátopek became the first runner to break the twenty-nine-minute barrier for 10,000 meters— "an arguably tougher accomplishment," said the *Wall Street Journal*, "given how much longer the agony must be endured." Over his lifetime, Zátopek would win an astonishing five Olympic medals and set eighteen known world records. "In 2013, *Runner's World* magazine named him 'the greatest runner of all time,'" as noted by the *Journal*.

I love both these stories, and not just because I've become a runner in the last few years and can only imagine the strength and endurance such feats require; or even because Zátopek was from Zlin, the town in which my mother was born and my grandmother still lives. I love these stories because Bannister's and Zátopek's accomplishments manifest the ultimate in passion and determination, dedication, hard work, stamina, and grit. I love them because they remind me of that French proverb: "To believe a thing impossible is to make it so," and the opposite—from Churchill—that is also true: "The positive thinker sees the invisible, feels the intangible and achieves the impossible."

These men, against all odds, broke through psychological barriers by sheer force of will to accomplish the impossible, raising the bar for runners worldwide. Similarly, we must summon the fortitude to persevere—and overcome—the seemingly insurmountable challenges we face in the world of work, and serve as an example for women everywhere.

As female leaders, many of us are already demanding change on some of the issues explored in this book—flexible schedules, equal pay, and family-friendly cultures with far more supportive leave policies, to name a few. Know that real change can start small and build incrementally. Influencing the policies at your company contributes to the big picture. Every win matters.

So how do we make real strides toward change?

Engage women at higher levels in business: Women make up more than half the world's population, yet, in 2015, there were only twenty-one female CEOs in the Fortune 500. Research has shown that the increasing number of women on corporate boards is leading to more ethical workplaces and fewer corporate scandals. Even with the pros clearly identified, many traditional workplaces still make it difficult for women to stay and succeed in the long run. It's one of the reasons we continue to see women leaving corporations after having children. Those who persist still often experience tension trying to fit two separate lives together. We must demand equal representation in leadership in order to effect change.

Embrace, support, and fund female entrepreneurship: Women are critical job creators in our country. In the last fifteen years, we've seen a substantial increase in female entrepreneurs who are achieving impressive levels of success, yet women still face many unique barriers, including a lack of access to capital, education, networks, affordable childcare, and paid maternity leave. While the amount of early-stage investment in companies with a woman on the executive team has tripled (to 15 percent from 5 percent), only 2.7 percent of venture capital–funded companies have a female CEO. Strangely enough, women entrepreneurs outperform men at raising money through crowdfunding campaigns. The reason female founders receive much less venture capital than men may have a lot to do with the fact that venture capital networks are dominated by male investors.

Female entrepreneurs need to feel supported and part of a community that understands, firsthand, the challenges and opportunities that come with being a woman who works. We must continue to foster engaging, dynamic discussions with and about these entrepreneurs, to create awareness and learning. Our site shines a spotlight on many of these women, introducing new role models to our audience, while empowering and inspiring other women who work.

Invest in female-run business initiatives and education: Female-owned enterprises consistently produce positive results and inspire innovation across industries; time and again it is proven that investing in the education and business initiatives of women and girls is one of the highest-return opportunities, especially in emerging markets, where their success has a direct impact on economic growth. Some institutions are taking notice and taking action. In an interview with CNN, Dina Habib Powell of Goldman Sachs's 10,000 Women Initiative said, "Over the last several years, what was once rightly a justice issue, or a human rights issue, has become smart economics. The investment in female entrepreneurs around the world is the single best way to drive job creation and growth."

Investing in the future of adolescent girls is a significant and exciting way to change the conversation around women and work—and change the world. When I think about the opportunities Arabella will have available to her in the United States, compared with some of the six hundred million girls growing up in developing countries, I'm even more inspired to make a difference. Empowering adolescent girls is the key to eliminating poverty, achieving social justice, stabilizing the population, and preventing humanitarian crises.

We must realize the enormous untapped potential of female entrepreneurship and the power of capitalizing on it in the early stages of growth. So many investors—and female entrepreneurs—are missing out.

Protect and promote women in corporations: In addition to appreciating the value of female entrepreneurs, we must also consider the cost of not retaining women in corporations. Not every woman has a passion for starting her own business. So where does that leave her, and where does that leave corporate America?

Women and men in leadership positions within traditional corporate environments must create and cultivate work environments that encourage a new generation to thrive. The tide is turning; businesses need to get on board or they will lose some of their best talent. At The Trump Organization, there are more female than male executives, and women are paid equally for the work we do; but as an executive and as a mother, I realize that isn't the norm. So I sought to create a company to attract and retain this next generation of incredible talent. Our corporate culture positively influences our success as women, as much as it informs the products and services we build.

As leaders, we set culture cues, so we need to create and cultivate environments that recognize the blending of work and life, and that endorse women's professional goals, passions, personalities, and pursuits beyond the office. Only this will allow multidimensional women (and men) to thrive.

Work toward making stereotypes and assumptions irrelevant: The "overwhelm was never just a 'mommy issue,'" wrote Brigid Schulte, "it's a father's issue. A children's issue. A workplace issue. A household issue. A family issue. A human rights issue. It's an issue for society, especially one that purports to value families so highly. The overwhelm is an issue for everyone, really, living in a country whose very mission is to guarantee the right of its citizens to pursue happiness." Debora Spar, president of Barnard College and author of *Wonder Women*, writes, "'Fixing the women's problem' is not about fixing the women. . . . It's about fixing the organization—recognizing a diversity of skills and attributes, measuring them in a concrete way, and rewarding people accordingly." Part of "fixing the organization" involves cultivating a culture where the burden of menial, administrative, and support tasks isn't thrust disproportionately upon women. As Adam Grant and Sheryl Sandberg note, teams place greater demands on their female coworkers, who can make the mistake of addressing others' needs before caring for themselves, leading to a high rate of burnout. The way to fix this, they say, involves women "putting self-concern on par with concern for others," and men using "their voices to draw attention to women's contributions" and "doing their share of support work."

Shedding light on what it really means to be a woman who works is one step toward eradicating stereotypes. We must start early by educating girls *and* boys, young women *and* men, that there is another, better way that benefits us all. Kunal Modi, former copresident of the Harvard Business School Student Association, "urged his fellow male students to 'man up' for economic and egalitarian reasons," according to Anne-Marie Slaughter. "Raising children and running a household are not 'women's roles,'" he says, and "treating them as such is counterproductive to your family's economic well-being." Millennial men are seeking more well-rounded lives, too. Even the most traditional firms are changing their policies to help in recruitment and retention.

CREATE A MORE ENLIGHTENED WORLD OF WORK

My parents raised my siblings and me to be passionate, committed, and to work hard at whatever we set our minds to. They taught us the importance of leading by example, dealing with challenges, and striving for excellence in all that we do. I really don't know another way, and I'm grateful for that. Neither of my parents wanted to raise entitled children who didn't know the satisfaction of a job well done—and they didn't.

Now that I am a parent, it's important to me and to Jared to impart those same values to our children. I was inspired to create the Women Who Work initiative to change the conversation around work and family so that we might model a healthier, more balanced, more fulfilling work/life fit for all of our children—girls and boys alike. And I am hopeful that by doing so collectively, we might leave an even more enlightened world of work as our legacy—where the overstressed, one-dimensional "ideal" worker of the twentieth century is replaced by an inspired, multidimensional human being who is engaged by work and passionate about life. It may sound idealistic, but it's possible—and it is happening! I witness it daily as I watch my own team work and thrive, professionally and personally.

The ultimate goal is to create a society where gender-based stereotypes are a thing of the past. As Elizabeth Cronise McLaughlin says, "The shift in gender roles we're seeing today truly benefits us all, because as we are opened up to becoming more prominent leaders and earners, men are opened up to becoming more than just a salary to their families and in the world. . . . When we work together toward equality, we all benefit."

When children see mothers who are working and fulfilled in their lives because they are supported by their culture, companies, and partners; when children see men living one life because they have prioritized their relationships and their passions alongside their professional goals, then—and only then—will the boys and girls of tomorrow be able to create a world of work in which gender won't matter.

When I think about how much my work means to me, and how important my family is to me, I'm so grateful that I don't have to choose between doing work I love and being a hands-on mother and devoted wife. But I know that I am far more fortunate than most. As much as motherhood is a joy to so many of us, it is also the *greatest* predictor of wage inequality between men and women in our country. Forty-seven percent of the U.S. labor force is female; 40 percent of women are their family's primary breadwinner. Yet research shows that in 2014, single women without children earned 94 cents for each dollar earned by a man, whereas married mothers made only 81 cents. Seventy percent of mothers with children at home also work in a professional capacity, and 64 percent of these mothers have kids age six and under. The number of households led by single mothers has doubled in the last thirty years, and about two thirds of these women work in low-wage jobs that offer neither flexibility nor benefits. As a society, we need to recognize these important realities and create policies that champion parents, enabling the American family to thrive.

I AM A WOMAN WHO IS PRIVILEGED TO ADVOCATE FOR WOMEN AND FAMILIES

My father's presidential campaign afforded me an unprecedented opportunity to advocate for change relating to issues that are of critical importance to me and to all women, particularly those with children. I was raised to hold strong convictions and to pursue solutions to problems. As someone who has made it her life's mission to empower women in all aspects of their lives, I felt it was my duty and obligation to take a stand on issues that contribute to wage inequality such as our country's failure to mandate paid leave for American workers and the lack of safe, affordable, high-quality childcare. It is one of the biggest challenges facing American families, a failure of public policy that's left an increasing number of parents unsupported and unable to take the steps necessary to better their lives and those of their families. While I never expected to have this heightened platform—and stepping into the political fray was daunting—I recognized both the privilege and the opportunity to use my voice to dramatically advance an important conversation that benefits parents and families nationwide.

The current federal policies that are in place to benefit families have not undergone fundamental change for sixty-five years and don't address modern realities such as dual-income households, which today account for about two thirds of married couples. The cost of childcare is the single greatest expense for many American parents—even exceeding the cost of housing in much of the country. Whether you have a family, are planning for one, or run a company that employs parents, it's a crucial issue to consider, as the status quo is unsustainable. This is not a women's issue, although mothers in particular are disproportionately affected and suffer the most financially; it is a family issue: an issue that affects men, women, children, and businesses nationwide.

Current U.S. law also does not require companies to offer paid maternity, paternity, or adoption leave and, as a result, only 10 percent do. My company is one of them. I also provide the employees of my brand with flexible work schedules to accommodate various caregiving and personal responsibilities and priorities, as well as the ability to work from home when necessary. I recognize that not everyone has a job that affords these flexibilities, which is why it's imperative to advocate for new and better solutions for working men and women.

We need to fight for change, whether through the legislature or in the workplace. Over the course of my father's campaign, I was proud to have helped encourage bipartisan discussions on these critical issues, improving the likelihood that antiquated laws and policies will change. Whether you're working in the home or out of it, we're all women who work—and we *all* deserve the opportunity to make the best decisions we can for ourselves, our families, and our lives, inevitably helping our country, companies, and culture to thrive.

Acknowledgments

As a mother, I've always recognized that you can't do it alone; when it comes to raising a family, the right support system is essential. It turns out that's the case for writing a book, too. This book is at once deeply personal and incredibly public. It's the continuation of a conversation that started, and continues, on IvankaTrump.com, fueled by the voices of incredible women and men, many of whom I'm fortunate to consider mentors, colleagues, and friends. They've shared their stories and given strategic advice in order to further our mission of inspiring and empowering modern women who work—at all aspects of their lives.

This book would not have been possible without Sarah Warren, who brought tremendous energy, creativity, passion, dedication, and intelligence to this project—from our very first pitch meeting to the final word. Thank you to my agent, Mel Berger, who introduced me to the fantastic team I was fortunate to work with at Portfolio, including Adrian Zackheim, who has been a great champion and partner. Thank you to my editor, Stephanie Frerich, who pushed us in a direction we didn't know we needed to go until we'd arrived there.

The content within these pages was informed by the contributions of the Entrepreneurs in Residence we've had on IvankaTrump.com. Adam Grant, Elizabeth Cronise McLaughlin, Rosie Pope, Samantha Boardman, and Alexa von Tobel have all given their time, wisdom, and expertise, making this book materially better, and for that I'm forever appreciative. Stephen Covey, Simon Sinek, and Angela Duckworth are other thought leaders who have guided my thinking, both personally and professionally.

If I'm a "highly effective person," know my "why," and am embracing and cultivating my inner *grit*, it's because of them.

Abigail Klem and Amanda Miller have been with me from the beginning of my brand. They continue to help me realize its potential and I'm grateful for their commitment and vision. Over the course of the unprecedentedly chaotic last year, they've often helped focus me on my mission and they've kept me on track; along with Suzie Acosta, who skillfully has kept all of the balls I'm juggling in the air.

It is said that behind every successful woman are more successful women, and I'm eternally grateful to my girlfriends—Maggie, Bara, Tamara, and Wendi—and sisters—Dara, Nikki, Vanessa, Lara, and Tiffany. You inspire me always. Babi and Seryl, thank you for being available for hugs (and good food!) at all times. You keep me well fed and remind me how thankful I am for family.

It was my mother who first personified for me what it meant to be a modern woman who works. Mom, you've led by example your entire life and you remain a role model to me today. My mother also recognized the importance of bringing up a family in community and I have been grateful to know and love Dorothy and Bridget, who helped raise my siblings and me. To Liza and Xixi, who are helping me raise my own children, thank you for being a part of our extended family and enabling me to do what I do.

Dad, you never cease to amaze me! You have taught me to dream big and then surpass those goals—and to never, *ever* give up.

To Don Jr. and Eric, thank you for pushing me hard—as only brothers can—to be my best. Josh, David, and Joseph, I'm fortunate to have married into your families; I won the lottery with you three. Love and hugs to my sweet brother Barron, who's maturing into a wonderful young man. Melania, you are an unbelievable mother with a heart of gold. You give generously of your time and attention and I appreciate your support and friendship.

Charlie, you have been a gift in my life. You always focus your attention on the right priorities—and you keep me focused on mine as well.

Thank you, Jared, for being my fiercest advocate and greatest source of strength. I love you more than I can possibly express. Thank you,

Arabella, for reminding me daily of why it's so important to have this conversation and push this dialogue further. Joseph, thank you for brightening each day with your sweet smiles; and Theodore, you won't remember this, but thank you for your snuggles and for keeping me company as a newborn while I worked on this book late into many, many nights. Nothing compares with the fortune I've found in my family—and the privilege of being a wife and mother.

However you define success and whatever it looks like to you, I hope this book has helped you clarify your priorities, elucidate your goals, and determine the next steps on your own individual path. Thank *you*, for being with me on this journey. Here's to a future of bright tomorrows!

The Reading List

To dig deeper into the topics covered in this book, visit WomenWhoWork.com for links to the books, articles, TED Talks, and resources that have helped to shape my thinking. It is a single-stop destination for furthering the dialogue that's started here and I encourage you to check it out and join in on the conversation.

CHAPTER ONE: DREAM BIG

BOOKS

The Happiness Advantage: The Seven Principles of Positive Psychology That Fuel Success and Performance at Work, Shawn Achor

How Remarkable Women Lead: The Breakthrough Model for Work and Life, Joanna Barsh and Susie Cranston

The Road to Character, David Brooks

The 7 Habits of Highly Effective People: Powerful Lessons in Personal Change, Stephen R. Covey

Grit: The Power of Passion and Perseverance, Angela Duckworth

The Element: How Finding Your Passion Changes Everything, Ken Robinson with Lou Aronica

Start with Why: How Great Leaders Inspire Everyone to Take Action, Simon Sinek

ARTICLE

James C. Collins and Jerry I. Porras, "Building Your Company's Vision," *Harvard Business Review,* September–October 1996.

TED TALKS

"Should You Live for Your Résumé . . . or Your Eulogy?," David Brooks

"Your Elusive Creative Genius," Elizabeth Gilbert

CHAPTER TWO: MAKE YOUR MARK

BOOKS

TED Talks: The Official TED Guide to Public Speaking, Chris Anderson

Confessions of a Public Speaker, Scott Berkun

Give and Take: Why Helping Others Drives Our Success, Adam Grant

Difficult Conversations: How to Discuss What Matters Most, Doug Stone, Bruce Patton, and Sheila Heen

TED TALKS

"Your Body Language Shapes Who You Are," Amy Cuddy

"Why We Do What We Do," Tony Robbins

"How to Speak So That People Want to Listen," Julian Treasure

WEB SITES

levo.com

themuse.com

nonviolentcommunication.com

positiveprescription.com

CHAPTER THREE: STAKE YOUR CLAIM

BOOKS

The Emotionally Intelligent Manager: How to Develop and Use the Four Key Emotional Skills of Leadership, David R. Caruso and Peter Salovey

Getting to Yes: Negotiating Agreement without Giving In, Roger Fisher and William Ury

Leading Teams: Setting the Stage for Great Performances, J. Richard Hackman

Thinking, Fast and Slow, Daniel Kahneman

The Paradox of Choice: Why More Is Less, Barry Schwartz

Bargaining for Advantage: Negotiation Strategies for Reasonable People, G. Richard Shell

Topgrading: The Proven Hiring and Promoting Method That Turbocharges Company Performance, Bradford D. Smart, PhD

Multipliers: How the Best Leaders Make Everyone Smarter, Liz Wiseman with Greg McKeown

TED TALKS

"How to Make Hard Choices," Ruth Chang

"The Career Advice You Probably Didn't Get," Susan Colantuono

"As Work Gets More Complex, Six Rules to Simplify," Yves Morieux

WEB SITES

levo.com, "A Step-by-Step Guide to Negotiating Your Salary," Career Contessa, www.levo.com/articles/career-advice/a-step-by-step-guide-to-negotiating-your -salary

womenintheworkplace.com

CHAPTER FOUR: WORK SMARTER, NOT HARDER

BOOKS

Getting Things Done: The Art of Stress-Free Productivity, David Allen

The Power of Habit: Why We Do What We Do in Life and Business, Charles Duhigg

Essentialism: The Disciplined Pursuit of Less, Greg McKeown

Deep Work: Rules for Focused Success in a Distracted World, Cal Newport

The Happiness Project: Or, Why I Spent a Year Trying to Sing in the Morn[...] Clean My Closets, Fight Right, Read Aristotle, and Generally Have N[...] Fun, Gretchen Rubin

I Know How She Does It: How Successful Women Make the Most of Their [...] Laura Vanderkam

TED TALKS

"What Makes a Life Worth Living?," Mihaly Csikszentmihalyi

"All It Takes Is 10 Mindful Minutes," Andy Puddicombe

"Inside the Mind of a Master Procrastinator," Tim Urban

WEB SITES

bulletjournal.com

tm.org

wholehealthyglow.com

CHAPTER FIVE: TIP THE SCALE

BOOKS

The Secrets of Happy Families: Improve Your Mornings, Tell Your Family History, Fight Smarter, Go Out and Play, and Much More, by Bruce Feiler

Sleeping with Your Smartphone: How to Break the 24/7 Habit and Change the Way You Work, by Leslie A. Perlow

How to Have a Good Day: Think Bigger, Work Smarter and Transform Your Working Life, by Caroline Webb

TED TALKS

"Why Work Doesn't Happen at Work," Jason Fried

"How to Make Work-Life Balance Work," Nigel Marsh

"Work-Life Balance: Balancing Time or Balancing Identity?," Michelle Ryan

"The Power of Time Off," Stefan Sagmeister

"Off-Balance on Purpose: The Future of Engagement and Work-Life Balance," Dan Thurmon

CHAPTER SIX: LEAD WITH PURPOSE

BOOKS

How Will You Measure Your Life?, Clayton M. Christensen

Originals: How Non-Conformists Move the World, Adam Grant

Leading Change, John P. Kotter

Overwhelmed: How to Work, Love and Play When No One Has the Time, Brigid Schulte

Leaders Eat Last: Why Some Teams Pull Together and Others Don't, Simon Sinek

Unfinished Business: Women Men Work Family, Anne-Marie Slaughter
Zero to One: Notes on Startups, or How to Build the Future, Peter Thiel with Blake
Masters

TED TALKS
"The Happy Secret to Better Work," Shawn Achor
"Listen, Learn . . . Then Lead," Stanley McChrystal
"Why We Have Too Few Women Leaders," Sheryl Sandberg
"How Great Leaders Inspire Action," Simon Sinek

WEB SITES
hbr.org, "How Netflix Reinvented HR," Patty McCord, www.hbr.org/2014/01/
how-netflix-reinvented-hr
levo.com, "Four Steps to Assessing Cultural Fit Before Getting Hired," Paula T. Edgar,
www.levo.com/posts/4-steps-to-assessing-cultural-fit-before-getting-hired
makers.com
women2.com
yfsmagazine.com

Notes

INTRODUCTION: WOMEN WHO WORK—REWRITING THE RULES FOR SUCCESS

xii **"Define success on your own terms":** Anne Sweeney, "A Lesson in Leadership," *Stanford Review*, stanfordreview.org/article/anne-sweeney-a-lesson-in-leadership/.

2 **A meager 12 percent:** Pietro Mazzola, Gaia Marchisio, and Joe Astrachan, "Strategic Planning in Family Business: A Powerful Developmental Tool for the Next Generation," *Family Business Review*, Volume 21, Issue 3 (September 2008): 239–58.

3 **Forty-seven percent:** U.S. Department of Labor, Women's Bureau, Data & Statistics, Latest Annual Data, Women of Working Age, 2015 Annual Averages, www.dol.gov/wb/stats/latest_annual_data.htm.

3 **70 percent of all mothers:** U.S. Department of Labor, Women's Bureau, Data & Statistics, Mothers and Families, Labor Force Participation, 2015, www.dol.gov/wb/stats/mother_families.htm.

4 **40 percent of American households:** Wendy Wang, Kim Parker, and Paul Taylor, "Breadwinner Moms," Pew Research Center, May 29, 2013, www.pewsocialtrends.org/2013/05/29/breadwinnermoms/.

5 **"The size of your dreams":** Ellen Johnson Sirleaf, Harvard commencement address, *Harvard Gazette*, May 26, 2011, news.harvard.edu/gazette/story/2011/05/text-of-ellen-johnson-sirleafs-speech.

7 **"Women leaders are moving":** Elizabeth Cronise McLaughlin, "The New Paradigm of Feminine Leadership—and What It Means for You," ivankatrump.com, December 7, 2015, www.ivankatrump.com/elizabeth-cronise-mclaughlin-new-paradigm-feminine-leadership/.

8 **"If family comes first":** Anne-Marie Slaughter, *Unfinished Business: Women, Men, Work, Family* (New York: Random House, 2015), 224.

9 **"As female leaders":** McLaughlin, "The New Paradigm of Feminine Leadership."

10 **"If you do work you love":** Oprah Winfrey, www.oprah.com.

11 **"Authenticity is not something":** Brené Brown, "Authenticity," November 26, 2014, tribalsimplicity.com/2014/11/26/brene-brown-authenticity/.

12 **Facebook COO and author of *Lean In*:** Sheryl Sandberg, *Lean In: Women, Work, and the Will to Lead* (New York: Knopf, 2013), 132.

12 **"What is success?":** Alexa von Tobel, original interview, September 23, 2014.

13 **"If you don't see a clear path":** Mindy Kaling, quoted in David Beattie, *Just Saying: Laylah Talks: Season 1* (n.p.: David Beattie, 2016), "My Dream Apartment."

CHAPTER ONE: DREAM BIG—IDENTIFY YOUR PASSIONS TO CREATE A LIFE YOU'LL LOVE

16 "Passion comes from": Simon Sinek, *Start with Why: How Great Leaders Inspire Everyone to Take Action* (New York: Portfolio, 2009), 111.

18 As Grammy Award–winning musician: Angela Duckworth, *Grit: The Power of Passion and Perseverance* (New York: Scribner, 2016), 46.

19 "The biggest mistake": Malcolm Forbes, quoted in Dr. Purushothaman, *Words of Wisdom* (Volume 41): *1001 Quotes to Quotations* (Kollam, Kerala, India: Centre for Human Perfection, 2014), 17.

19 "What we spend our time and mental energy": Shawn Achor, *The Happiness Advantage: The Seven Principles of Positive Psychology That Fuel Success and Performance at Work* (New York: Crown, 2010), 12.

19 "New research in psychology": Ibid., 15.

19 doctors in a positive mood: Ibid.; Barbara L. Frederickson provides more background in her broaden-and-build theory of positive emotions, www.ncbi.nlm.nih.gov/pmc/articles/PMC3122271/.

19 "It's really about following your gut": Rachel Blumenthal, original interview, September 23, 2014.

20 "One of the biggest drivers of success": Achor, *The Happiness Advantage*, 129–30.

20 "pleasure combined with": Ibid., 39.

20 The Greek philosopher Aristotle: Ibid., 40.

20 "Recognize the way": Nadine Burke Harris, original interview, September 23, 2014.

21 "Many think that happiness": The Dalai Lama, official Twitter account, twitter.com/dalailama/status/648429542202191872.

21 "Your life doesn't just 'happen'": Stephen R. Covey, www.stephencovey.com/7habits/7habits-habit1.php.

22 Optimistic, proactive people . . . *I can, I plan to, I trust*: Adapted from Covey, www.stephencovey.com/7habits/7habits-habit1.php, and Stephen R. Covey, *The 7 Habits of Highly Effective People: Powerful Lessons in Personal Change* (New York: Free Press, 2004), 85–93.

22 Proactive people are: Ibid.

22 *Bridge of Spies*: *Bridge of Spies*, directed by Steven Spielberg (Glendale, CA: DreamWorks Pictures 2015), film; www.youtube.com/watch?v=Yylz3pHE5Vc.

22 Reactive people tend to dwell: Adapted from Covey, www.stephencovey.com/7habits/7habits-habit1.php and Covey, *The 7 Habits*, 85–93.

23 here's an exercise: Adapted from Achor, *The Happiness Advantage*, 100–102.

23 Make a daily list: Ibid., 100.

23 "over a decade": Ibid.

23 "three good things": Ibid.

23 "scan the last 24 hours": Ibid.

23 five minutes a day: Ibid., 101.

23 One study found that: Ibid.; original source of study per Achor: M. E. P. Seligman, T. A. Park, and C. Peterson, "Positive Psychology Progress: Empirical Validation of Interventions," *American Psychologist,* Issue 60 (2005), 410–21.

23 Best of all, Achor notes . . . boss at work": Achor, *The Happiness Advantage*, 101.

23 "One glanced up": Ibid., 91.

24 "If you carefully consider": Covey, *The 7 Habits*, 105.

24 What do you hope to have accomplished?: Inspired by Covey's thinking on visualizing your retirement, in *The 7 Habits*, 139.

25 "[People] may forget": Carl W. Buehner, quoted in Richard L. Evans, *Richard Evans' Quote Book* (Salt Lake City, Utah: Publisher's Press, 1971), 244. (Verified

with scans per quoteinvestigator.com/2014/04/06/they-feel/; with thanks to the librarians of Harold B. Lee Library, Brigham Young University, Provo, Utah.)

25 Or, as David Brooks: David Brooks, "The Humanist Vocation," *New York Times*, June 20, 2013, www.nytimes.com/2013/06/21/opinion/brooks-the-humanist -vocation.html?_r=0.

25 Should you live for your eulogy or your résumé: David Brooks, "Should You Live for Your Résumé . . . or Your Eulogy?", March 2014, www.ted.com/talks /david_brooks_should_you_live_for_your_resume_or_your_eulogy.

25 We all know someone: Inspired by Covey, *The 7 Habits*, 105.

25 "To begin with an end in mind": Ibid.

26 "Have you ever wondered": Joanna Barsh and Susie Cranston, *How Remarkable Women Lead: The Breakthrough Model for Work and Life* (New York: Crown Business, 2009), 206–7.

26 In his book: Bruce Feiler, *The Secrets of Happy Families: Improve Your Mornings, Tell Your Family History, Fight Smarter, Go Out and Play, and Much More* (New York: William Morrow, 2013), 56.

26 "A clear sense of WHY": Sinek, *Start with Why*, 147.

26 As Feiler notes: Feiler, *Secrets of Happy Families*, 71.

26 "If you don't have your own frame": Ibid.

26 it must contain ruminations: Adapted from Covey, *The 7 Habits*, 113.

27 they should reflect timeless and enduring principles: Ibid., 115.

27 the basis for making: Ibid.

27 "We are more in need of a vision or destination": Ibid., 108.

27 happiness "cannot be pursued": Viktor E. Frankl, *Man's Search for Meaning* (Boston: Beacon Press, 2006), 138.

28 "The quieter you become": Ram Dass, "Ram Dass Quotes," Ram Dass Web site, www.ramdass.org/ram-dass-quotes/; Ram Dass, *Be Here Now* (Questa, NM: Lama Foundation, 1971).

28 "Writing or reviewing": Covey, *The 7 Habits*, 137.

29 "I really became interested": Tina Wells, "Three Steps to Building Your Personal Brand," ivankatrump.com, January 11, 2016, www.ivankatrump.com /tina-wells-buzz-marketing-personal-brand/.

29 "After the financial crisis": Ibid.

29 "The happiest people I know": Ibid.

29 "They've built careers": Ibid.

29 "Your personal brand statement": Ibid.

29 "I'm passionate about pop culture": Ibid.

29 "Whatever your dreams are": Barbara Sher, *Wishcraft: How to Get What You Really Want* (New York: Ballantine Books, 1979); as recollected by Chris Guillebeau, *The Art of Non-Conformity: Set Your Own Rules, Live the Life You Want and Change the World* (New York: Perigee, 2010), 30.

30 "what we eventually accomplish": Duckworth, *Grit*, xiv.

30 Most people don't serendipitously: Ibid., 100.

30 they don't usually become passionate about something: Ibid., 105.

30 "Our vanity, our self-love": Friedrich Nietzsche, *Human, All Too Human: A Book for Free Spirits,* trans. R. J. Hollingdale (Cambridge, UK: Cambridge University Press, 1986), 80; Duckworth, *Grit*, 39.

30 "exploring several different interests": Duckworth, *Grit*, 100.

31 "One of the huge mistakes": Rob Walker, *Inc.*, April 1, 2004, www.inc.com /magazine/20040401/25bezos.html; Duckworth, *Grit*, 104.

31 In fostering a passion: Duckworth, *Grit*, 99.

31 Duckworth recommends the following: Bullets summarized from ibid., 104–5.

31 "Enthusiasm is common": Ibid., 58.

31 "There are no shortcuts": Ibid., 54.

31 "It all takes time": Ibid.

31 "Before you can leverage": Adam Grant, "How to Discover Your Strengths," ivankatrump.com, November 19, 2015, www.ivankatrump.com/discover-your -strengths-adam-grant/.

32 heavily researched Reflected Best Self Exercise: Laura Morgan Roberts, Gretchen Spreitzer, Jane E. Dutton, Robert E. Quinn, Emily Heaphy, and Brianna Barker, "How to Play to Your Strengths," *Harvard Business Review*, January 2005, hbr.org/2005/01/how-to-play-to-your-strengths.

33 "I can close my eyes": Abbey Drucker, "Abbey Drucker on the Business of Art," ivankatrump.com, October 21, 2014, www.ivankatrump.com/abbey-drucker -photographer/.

33 "Fast forward to sixth grade": Ibid.

33 "I wake up every day": Ibid.

35 historic Old Post Office: Find a Building: Search, www.gsa.gov/portal/ext/html/ site/hb/category/25431/actionParameter/exploreByBuilding/buildingId/803.

35 walk-through of the building: Jonathan O'Connell, *Washington Post*, August 17, 2012, www.washingtonpost.com/business/how-the-trumps-landed-the-old-post -officepavilion/2012/08/17/54cbf1da-bbdd-11e1-9134-f33232e6dafa_story.html.

38 "Do work you love": Angela Benton, "The Essentials of Entrepreneurship," ivankatrump.com, November 18, 2014, www.ivankatrump.com/essentials-of -entrepreneurship/; original interview, September 23, 2014.

38 "Life is a verb": Charlotte Perkins Gilman, *Human Work* (Oxford: AltaMira Press, 2005), 208.

40 Honor yourself: Inspired by Barsh and Cranston, *How Remarkable Women Lead*, 29.

40 "Purpose is what drives you": Ibid., 46.

40 "When you have purpose in life": Ibid., 51.

40 "If you're being given": Cynthia Nixon, quoted in *Fast Company*, Special Edition, The Fast Company Innovation Festival, August 30, 2016, www.fastcompany-digital .com/fastcompany/fast_company_innovation_festival_highlights?pg=10#pg10.

41 Lynda Gratton and Andrew Scott: Anne-Marie Slaughter, *Unfinished Business: Women Men Work Family* (New York: Random House, 2015), 189–90.

41 "people in their twenties": Ibid., 190.

41 These so-called explorers: Ibid.

42 Reshma Saujani's story: girlswhocode.com/our-team/.

42 Debbie Sterling founded GoldieBlox: Jena McGregor, "The Brains Behind the Viral GoldieBlox Video," *Washington Post*, November 21, 2013, www.washing tonpost.com/news/on-leadership/wp/2013/11/21/the-brains-behind-the-viral -goldieblox-video/.

43 "Dream bigger. Think about": Alexa von Tobel, original interview, September 23, 2014.

44 "You need passion": Guillebeau, *The Art of Non-Conformity*, 83.

44 Umber Ahmad, master baker and creator: All quotes from "Take the Leap," ivankatrump.com, February 23, 2015, www.ivankatrump.com/umber-ahmad -mah-ze-dahr/.

46 "My daughter was eight months old": Jenna Fain, "Michelle Kohanzo of the Land of Nod," The Everygirl, theeverygirl.com/feature/michelle-kohanzo.

46 "I loved the idea": Ibid.

46 "My mentor gave me": Ibid.

47 "Don't ask yourself": Dr. Howard Thurman, quoted in Gil Bailie, *Violence Unveiled: Humanity at the Crossroads* (New York: Crossroad Publishing Company, 1996), xv.

48 "The most courageous act": Coco Chanel, Mariel Reed, *Marie Claire*, October 4, 2016, www.marieclaire.co.uk/fashion/coco-chanel-s-25-snappiest-quotes-54026.

49 "You can have brilliant ideas": Lee Iacocca with William Novak, *Iacocca: An Autobiography* (New York: Bantam Books, 2011), 16.

50 whether you participate: Matthew Hutson, "Why New Yorkers—and Everyone Else—Should Pursue Small Talk More," *New York*, July 23, 2014, nymag .com/scienceofus/2014/07/why-new-yorkers-should-small-talk-more.html.

50 "it weaves and reweaves": David Roberts, "Why Small Talk Is So Excruciating," Vox, November 26, 2016, www.vox.com/2015/7/7/8903123/small-talk.

50 "to *do* something": Ibid.

51 "As for me, all I know": Socrates, as quoted in Plato, *Republic*, 345b–c (conclusion of Book I).

51 stimulates the same pleasure centers: Robert Lee Hotz, "Science Reveals Why We Brag So Much," *Wall Street Journal*, May 7, 2012, www.wsj.com/news/articles /SB10001424052702304451104577390392329291890?mg=reno64-wsj&url= http%3A%2F%2Ftopics.wsj.com%2Farticle%2FSB10001424052702304451 10457739039232929291890.html.

51 "When you ask a 'what' question": Samantha Boardman, MD, "8 Ways to Make Meaningful Small Talk," goop.com/8-ways-to-make-meaningful-small -talk/.

52 "When you talk": The Dalai Lama, quoted in Robin Koval, "Want to Ace a Job Interview? Be Nice to the Receptionist," *Fortune*, August 24, 2015, fortune.com /2015/08/24/robin-koval-building-a-strong-team/.

52 effective listening involves: Quotes from Boardman, "8 Ways to Make Meaningful Small Talk."

52 "Consider reframing the situation": Ibid.

52 Heed the 20-second rule: Ibid.

53 "When we are feeling powerless": Amy Cuddy, *Presence: Bringing Your Boldest Self to Your Biggest Challenges* (New York: Little, Brown, 2015), 158.

53 "Carrying yourself in a powerful way": Ibid., 207.

53 When you can admit that you don't know something: Paragraph inspired by Mircea Samoila, "Curiosity," Active Listening, Episode #3, gohighbrow.com /portfolio/active-listening/.

53 "If you had to identify": Dave Barry, *Dave Barry Turns Fifty* (New York: Crown, 1998), 183.

54 Jim Kochalka . . . before it breaks up: All quotes from "Make Your Next Meeting a Better Meeting," ivankatrump.com, January 27, 2016, www.ivankatrump .com/jim-kochalka-efficient-meetings-tips/ and original transcript, May 26, 2016.

56 "Be sincere; be brief": Franklin D. Roosevelt, quoted in Paul L. Soper, *Basic Public Speaking* (Oxford: Oxford University Press, 1963), 12.

56 "There are only two types": Mark Twain as quoted by Richard Branson, "Richard Branson on How to Calm Public Speaking Jitters," *Fortune*, January 12, 2015, fortune.com/2015/01/12/richard-branson-on-how-to-calm-public-speaking-jitters/.

56 "There are always three speeches": Dale Carnegie/Dale Carnegie Training, *Stand and Deliver: How to Become a Masterful Communicator and Public Speaker* (New York: Simon & Schuster, 2011).

56 Researchers trace the sweaty-palmed: E. Dunnigan, "The Very Real Science Behind Your Fear of Public Speaking," accentonbusiness.net/the-very-real-science -behind-your-fear-of-public-speaking/.

58 Classic studies by: Adam Grant, "Five Ways to Squash Your Public Speaking Nerves," ivankatrump.com, February 7, 2016, www.ivankatrump.com/skill-set-public-speaking/.

58 Consultant John Paul Engel: Gwen Moran, "Seven Habits of the Best Public Speakers," *Fast Company*, February 26, 2016, www.fastcompany.com/3057007/how-to-be-a-success-at-everything/7-habits-of-the-best-public-speakers.

58 "The single most important thing": Ibid.

58 "Don't try to calm down . . . about tackling the challenge at hand": Grant, "Five Ways to Squash Your Public Speaking Nerves," original source: Alison Woods Brooks, "Get Excited: Pre-Performance Anxiety as Excitement," *Journal of Experimental Psychology: General*, Volume 143, Number 3 (2014): 1144–58, www.apa.org/pubs/journals/releases/xge-a0035325.pdf.

59 "The goal is to provide": Guy Kawasaki, *Enchantment: The Art of Changing Hearts, Minds, and Actions* (New York: Portfolio, 2012), 162.

59 "I define connection": Brené Brown, *The Gifts of Imperfection: Let Go of Who You're Supposed to Be and Embrace Who You Are* (Center City, MN: Hazelden 2010), 19.

60 "Meaning-making . . . [provides]": Adam Grant, "Three Lies About Meaningful Work," ivankatrump.com, March 6, 2016, www.ivankatrump.com/3-lies-about-meaningful-work/.

60 "people with strong networks": Joanna Barsh, Susie Cranston, and Rebecca A. Craske, "Centered Leadership: How Talented Women Thrive," *McKinsey Quarterly*, September 2008. www.mckinsey.com/global-themes/leadership/centered-leadership-how-talented-women-thrive.

60 a 2013 Gallup report: Steve Crabtree, "Worldwide, 13% of Employees Are Engaged at Work," www.gallup.com, October 8, 2013.

60 "The people we surround ourselves": Matthew Kelly, *The Rhythm of Life: Living Everyday with Passion and Purpose* (Boston: Beacon Press, 2015), 56.

60 "There are two ways": Edith Wharton, "Vesalius in Zante (1564)," *North American Review* (November 1902), 631, archive.org/details/jstor-25119328.

61 "Authenticity [is] the new currency": Elizabeth Cronise McLaughlin, "How to Be More Authentic at Work and Why It's So Important," ivankatrump.com, April 10, 2016, www.ivankatrump.com/be-more-authentic-at-work-elizabeth-cronise-mclaughlin/.

61 Authenticity means being yourself: Ibid.

61 If you're struggling: Ibid.

61 Authenticity is fundamentally: Ibid.

61 "When we're focused": Adam Grant, in an e-mail to Ivanka Trump; also "The Dangers of Being Authentic," LinkedIn/Pulse, June 6, 2016, www.linkedin.com/pulse/dangers-being-authentic-adam-grant.

62 "Building relationships is part": Joanna Barsh and Susie Cranston, *How Remarkable Women Lead: The Breakthrough Model for Work and Life* (New York: Crown Business, 2009), 125–26.

62 "more women than ever before are refusing": Elizabeth Cronise McLaughlin, "Five Ways to Work Well on a Team," ivankatrump.com, February 14, 2016, www.ivankatrump.com/workingwith-a-team-tips/.

62 "Look around your workplace": Ibid.

63 "Gossip inevitably blows back": Ibid.

63 "Place your attention": Ibid.

63 "We don't accomplish anything": Sandra Day O'Connor, quoted in Dennis Abrams, *Sandra Day O'Connor: U.S. Supreme Court Justice* (New York: Infobase Publishing, 2009), 41.

65 "Never argue with a fool!": Mark Twain, quoted in Daniel Coenn, *Mark Twain: His Words* (n.p.: Daniel Coenn, 2014).

65 evaluate your own role: All text and quotes on pages 69–70 are from Elizabeth Cronise McLaughlin, "Four Steps for Working Through Office Conflict," ivanka trump.com, February 7, 2016, www.ivankatrump.com/work-through-office -conflict-elizabeth-cronise-mclaughlin/.

66 "It's not what you know": Anonymous, quoted in James Edwards and Richard Bramante, *Networking Self-Teaching Guide* (New York: John Wiley & Sons, 2009), 403.

67 "People influence people": Mark Zuckerberg, quoted in the American Society of Association Executives (ASAE), *Membership Essentials: Recruitment, Roles, Responsibilities, and Resources* (New York: John Wiley & Sons, 2016), 175.

67 "Focus on just building": Tony Hsieh, *Delivering Happiness: A Path to Profits, Passion, and Purpose* (New York: Grand Central Publishing, 2010), 81.

68 as Adam Grant recommends: Adam Grant, "Finding the Hidden Value in Your Network," ivankatrump.com, October 7, 2015, www.ivankatrump.com/net working-tips-wharton-adam-grant/.

68 "weak ties" . . . sociologist Mark Granovetter: Mark S. Granovetter, "The Strength of Weak Ties," *American Journal of Sociology*, Volume 78, Issue 6 (May 1973): 1360–80, sociology.stanford.edu/sites/default/files/publications /the_strength_of_weak_ties_and_exch_w-gans.pdf.

68 58 percent more likely: Ibid.

68 "Strong ties tend": Grant, "Finding the Hidden Value in Your Network."

68 what Grant calls "dormant ties": Ibid.

68 when hundreds of executives: D. Z. Levin, J. Walter, and J. K. Murnighan, *Organization Science*, Volume 22, Number 4 (July–August 2011): 923–39, www.levin.rutgers.edu/research/dormant-ties-paper.pdf.

69 "Colleagues are a wonderful thing": Junot Díaz, quoted in Keith Walker and Bob Bayles, *Reflections on Facilitating Learning in Prairie Spirit* (Wellington, NZ: Turning Point, 2016), 81.

70 You're full of ambition: Section based on ivankatrump.com post by Alice Shroeder; tips from Angie Chang, "Mentorship: A How-to with Angie Chang," ivankatrump .com, November 19, 2014, www.ivankatrump.com/mentorship-tips-angie-chang/.

72 "A sponsor is often a senior-level person": "5 Ways to Find Your Career Sponsor," ivankatrump.com, July 3, 2016; www.ivankatrump.com/career-sponsor/.

72 "They may put your name": Ibid.

72 Weinberg suggests building relationships: Ibid.

72 McLaughlin suggests simply: Ibid.

73 Adam Grant notes: Ibid.

73 If you show senior members: Ibid.

CHAPTER THREE: STAKE YOUR CLAIM— MAXIMIZE YOUR INFLUENCE AT WORK

76 "The magic works": Mike Dooley, official Twitter account, twitter.com/mike dooley/status/337237942747660288.

78 "Opportunities multiply as": Sun Tzu, *The Art of War*, trans. Philip Martin McCaulay (Raleigh, NC: LuLu, 2010), 25.

78 "We are what we": Will Durant, *The Story of Philosophy: The Lives and Opinions of the World's Greatest Philosophers* (New York: Pocket Books, 1991), 76.

79 "When we have a community": Shawn Achor, *The Happiness Advantage: The Seven Principles of Positive Psychology That Fuel Success and Performance at Work* (New York: Crown, 2010), 176.

79 In his TED Talk: Simon Sinek, "Why Good Leaders Make You Feel Safe," May 2014, www.ted.com/talks/simon_sinek_why_good_leaders_make_you_feel_safe? language=en.

80 "We cannot lead numbers": Simon Sinek, www.facebook.com/simonsinek /posts/10154214426641499.

82 "If you can hire people": Stephen R. Covey, *The 8th Habit: From Effectiveness to Greatness* (New York: Free Press, 2004), 76–77.

83 "The best leaders are able": Elizabeth Cronise McLaughlin, "How to Be More Authentic at Work and Why It's So Important," www.ivankatrump.com/be-more -authentic-at-work-elizabeth-cronise-mclaughlin/.

85 As Bradford D. Smart: Bradford D. Smart, PhD, *Topgrading: The Proven Hiring and Promoting Method That Turbocharges Company Performance* (New York: Portfolio, 1999, 2005), 75.

86 "forced choice question": Adam Grant, e-mail to Ivanka Trump, August 15, 2016.

86 Top Hiring Dos and Don'ts: Deirdre Rosen, senior vice president of Human Resources, Trump Organization, e-mail to Sarah Warren, ivankatrump.com.

89 If someone starts: Ivanka Trump, *The Trump Card: Playing to Win in Work and Life* (New York: Simon & Schuster, 2009), 139.

90 In corporations everywhere: Ibid.

90 "external hires" get significantly lower performance evaluations: "Why External Hires Get Paid More and Perform Worse Than Internal Staff," Knowledge@ Wharton, March 28, 2012.

91 "Hard work is nice": Lee E. Miller and Jessica Miller, *A Woman's Guide to Successful Negotiating*, second edition (New York: McGraw-Hill Education, 2010), 32.

92 determined that women who: Linda Babcock and Sara Laschever, *Women Don't Ask: Negotiation and the Gender Divide* (Princeton, NJ: Princeton University Press, 2003), 6, www.womendontask.com/stats.html.

92 Moreover, she cites another study: Ibid., 7; study from Robin L. Pinkley and Gregory B. Northcraft, *Get Paid What You're Worth: The Expert Negotiator's Guide to Salary and Compensation* (New York: St. Martin's, 2003).

92 Adam Grant frequently gets requests for advice: Section from Adam Grant, "Negotiate Your Salary Without Playing Hardball," ivankatrump.com, September 16, 2015, www.ivankatrump.com/negotiate-your-salary-adam-grant/.

93 "studies conducted by researcher Katie Liljenquist": Katie A. Liljenquist, PhD, "Resolving the Impression Management Dilemma," Northwestern University, 2010, gradworks.umi.com/34/02/3402210.html.

94 "Every time I sat": Mika Brzezinski, *Knowing Your Value: Women, Money, and Getting What You're Worth* (New York: Weinstein Books, 2012), 4.

94 "Ask for what you want": Maya Angelou, *The Heart of a Woman* (New York: Random House, 2009), 29.

94 Linda Babcock says that women ask for raises: Linda Babcock, "Salary Stats: Women vs. Men," *Washington Post*, November 7, 2008, www.washingtonpost .com/wp-dyn/content/article/2008/11/06/AR2008110602982.html.

94 "Their perception [is] that": Babcock and Laschever, *Women Don't Ask*, 20.

94 Women in the Workplace 2016: Sheryl Sandberg, "Women Are Leaning In—But They Face Pushback," *Wall Street Journal*, September 27, 2016, www.wsj.com/ articles/sheryl-sandberg-women-are-leaning-inbut-they-face-pushback-147496 3980; the source for the original study: womenintheworkplace.com/.

95 A 2011 McKinsey report also noted: Joanna Barsh and Lareina Yee, "Special Report: Unlocking the Full Potential of Women in the U.S. Economy," McKinsey & Company, April 2011, 6, www.mckinsey.com/Client_Service/Organization /Latest_thinking/Unlocking_the_full_potential.aspx.

96 "It is only by being bold": Richard Branson, *Losing My Virginity: How I've Survived, Had Fun, and Made a Fortune Doing Business My Way* (New York: Crown Business, 2011).

97 "If you don't ask": Nora Roberts, *Tears of the Moon: Book Two of the Gallaghers of Ardmore Trilogy* (New York: Berkley Books, 2000), 64.

97 Pamela Weinberg says: "Five Tips for Negotiating Your Severance Package," ivanka trump.com, May 22, 2016, www.ivankatrump.com/severance-negotiation-tips/.

97 "You'll likely be caught off guard": Ibid.

97 formula to calculate severance: Ibid.

98 "Remember: relationships matter": Ibid.

98 Be prepared to be asked: "Five Tips for Getting Laid Off Gracefully," ivanka trump.com, April 10, 2016, www.ivankatrump.com/layoffs-career-advice/.

98 "Thank her for all you've learned": Ibid.

98 "If your company was simply downsized": Ibid.

99 "Do some soul-searching": Ibid.

99 "Reach out to headhunters": Ibid.

100 "Negotiating is something": Bruce Feiler, *The Secrets of Happy Families: Improve Your Mornings, Tell Your Family History, Fight Smarter, Go Out and Play, and Much More* (New York: William Morrow, 2013), 80.

100 "Before any challenging": Elizabeth Cronise McLaughlin, "How to Negotiate Anything and Win," ivankatrump.com, September 28, 2015, www.ivankatrump .com/negotiate-anything-and-win-elizabeth-cronise-mclaughlin/.

101 "Anticipate the challenges": Ibid.

101 Know that your personality . . . counterproductive: Ivanka Trump, *The Trump Card*, 165.

101 My brothers and I . . . negotiation: Ibid.

102 A 2015 study: Max Nisen, "You Are Almost Certainly Starting Salary Negotiations Wrong," *Quartz*, March 16, 2015, qz.com/356612/you-are-almost-certainly -starting-salary-negotiations-wrong/; Daniel R. Ames and Malia F. Mason, "Tandem Anchoring: Informational and Politeness Effects of Range Offers in Social Exchange," *Journal of Personality and Social Psychology*, Volume 108, Number 2 (February 2015): 254–74, psycnet.apa.org/journals/psp/108/2/254/.

102 "means setting a fairly ambitious number": Ibid.

102 research shows, when given a range: Ibid.

104 "Negotiation is the stuff of life": Feiler, *The Secrets of Happy Families*, 88.

104 "We keep moving forward": Walt Disney, quoted in Jane Sutcliffe, *Walt Disney* (Minneapolis: History Maker Bios/Lerner, 2009), 45.

104 men apply for jobs: Tara Sophia Mohr, "Why Women Don't Apply for Jobs Unless They're 100 Percent Qualified," *Harvard Business Review*, August 25, 2014, hbr.org/2014/08/why-women-dont-apply-for-jobs-unless-theyre-100-qualified.

104 "Growth and comfort": Andrew Nusca, "IBM's Rometty: Growth and Comfort Don't Coexist," *Fortune*, October 7, 2014, fortune.com/2014/10/07/ibms -rometty-growth-and-comfort-dont-coexist/.

105 "A recruiter is like any great ally": "How to Recruit a Recruiter," ivankatrump .com, February 10, 2015, www.ivankatrump.com/recruit-a-recruiter/.

105 "You want someone who's": "Five Tips for Getting the Most Out of Your Recruiter," ivankatrump.com, March 25, 2016, www.ivankatrump.com/recruiter -relationship-tips/.

105 "no more than three": "How to Recruit a Recruiter."

106 Employers value your ability to speak articulately: From a Bloomberg business study and "The Skills Recruiters Really Look For," ivankatrump.com, March 31, 2015, www.ivankatrump.com/the-skills-recruiters-really-look-for/, and www .bloomberg.com/graphics/2015-job-skills-report/; Akane Otani, "These Are

the Skills You Need if You Want to Be Headhunted," www.bloomberg.com, January 5, 2015; and www.bloomberg.com/news/articles/2015-01-05/the-job -skills-that-recruiters-wish-you-had.

106 Results from the study: Ibid.

106 "Some unemployed candidates choose": "Five Tips for Getting the Most Out of Your Recruiter."

106 "Recruiters will be drawn": Ibid.

106 "I can't tell you": Ibid.

106 "If you're not actively looking": Ibid.

106 "I have candidates": Ibid.

106 Start by checking: "Five Tips for Making Big Career Decisions," ivankatrump .com, April 17, 2016, www.ivankatrump.com/career-decisions-tips/.

107 "Select and prioritize": Ibid.

108 Reacquaint yourself with who you are: Ibid.

108 "No one can pigeonhole you": Ibid.

108 Ahmad says her tenure: "Take the Leap," ivankatrump.com, February 23, 2015, www.ivankatrump.com/umber-ahmad-mah-ze-dahr/.

108 "Make a list of things": Ibid.

108 "Wake up every day excited": "Lauren Bush Lauren Is FEED-ing the World," ivankatrump.com, January 28, 2015, www.ivankatrump.com/lauren-bush -lauren-feed/.

109 "If you want to achieve": Eddie Colla, "Ambition," www.eddiecolla.com/col lections/editions/products/ambition-24x36-poster.

110 "A leader is best": Michael Shinagel, "The Paradox of Leadership," Harvard Division of Continuing Education, www.dce.harvard.edu/professional/blog /paradox-leadership.

110 "It takes 20 years": Brad Tuttle, "Warren Buffett's Boring, Brilliant Wisdom," *Time*, March 2010, business.time.com/2010/03/01/warren-buffetts-boring -brilliant-wisdom/.

111 "I didn't get there": Estée Lauder, quoted in Robert Grayson, *Estée Lauder: Businesswoman and Cosmetics Pioneer* (Edina, MN.: Essential Library, 2013), 101.

CHAPTER FOUR: WORK SMARTER, NOT HARDER—BOOST YOUR PRODUCTIVITY TO MAKE TIME FOR WHAT MATTERS MOST

112 "Bit by bit": Toni Morrison, *Beloved* (New York: Random House, 2004), 111.

114 "The key is not": Stephen R. Covey, *The 7 Habits of Highly Effective People: Powerful Lessons in Personal Change* (New York: Free Press, 2004), 170.

114 Laura Vanderkam suggests: "Five Better Ways to Manage Your Time," ivanka trump.com, February 28, 2016, www.ivankatrump.com/time-management/.

114 "Keeping track of our time": Ibid.

114 "A lot of people think": Ibid.

115 "People think a lot about": Ibid.

115 "people set a goal": "Five Ways to Set Achievable Goals," ivankatrump.com, May 8, 2016, www.ivankatrump.com/goal-setting-tips/.

115 "Make sure that the payoff": Ibid.

115 "Breaking down your goals": Ibid.

115 "Successful goals are SMART": Ibid.

115 "Surround yourself with people": Ibid.

115 "As women, we often try": Ibid.

115 "It's easier to stay accountable": Ibid.

116 "We have the same mission and goals today": Ibid.

116 "Obstacles are those frightful things": Henry Ford, quoted in Stephen Kraus, *Psychological Foundations of Success: A Harvard-Trained Scientist Separates the Science of Success from Self-Help Snake Oil* (Baltimore: Next Level Science, 2003), 74.

116 "The high-minded Greeks called leisure *skole*,": Brigid Schulte, *Overwhelmed: Work, Love, and Play When No One Has the Time* (New York: Farrar, Straus & Giroux, 2014), 51.

117 Bill Gates reportedly did this: Robert A. Guth, "In Secret Hideaway, Bill Gates Ponders Microsoft's Future," *Wall Street Journal*, March 28, 2005, www.wsj .com/articles/SB111196625830690477.

118 Covey's four-quadrant time management grid: Summary based on Covey, *The 7 Habits*, 159–63.

118 "Importance . . . has to do with results": Ibid., 160.

118 In contrast to Quadrant 1: Ibid., summary.

119 "to-stop-doing list": Chris Guillebeau, *The Art of Non-Conformity: Set Your Own Rules, Live the Life You Want, and Change the World* (New York: Perigee, 2010), 177.

120 "Your time is limited": Steve Jobs, quoted in Anthony Imbimbo, *Steve Jobs: The Brilliant Mind Behind Apple* (Destin, FL: Life Portraits, 2009), 96.

120 "How we schedule": Gretchen Rubin, *Better Than Before: What I Learned About Making and Breaking Habits—to Sleep More, Quit Sugar, Procrastinate Less, and Generally Build a Happier Life* (New York: Crown, 2015), 90.

121 "On a macro level": "Hot Mama: Eva Chen," ivankatrump.com, April 10, 2015, www.ivankatrump.com/eva-chen/.

122 "Others inspire us": Ester Buchholz, *The Call of Solitude: Alonetime in a World of Attachment* (New York: Simon & Schuster, 1999), 239.

122 "Even the most left-brain": "Ten Ways to Boost Your Creativity at Work," ivanka trump.com, September 2, 2015, www.ivankatrump.com/brit-and-co-brit-morin -boost-your-creativity/.

122 "77 percent of adults": Ibid.

122 "Creativity has verifiable": Ibid.

123 "Steve Jobs was well known": Ibid.

123 Research shows that "walking outdoors": May Wong, "Stanford Study Shows Walking Improves Creativity," *Stanford News*, April 24, 2014; news.stanford .edu/2014/04/24/walking-vs-sitting-042414/; original study, Marilyn Opezzo and Daniel Schwartz, "The Positive Effect of Walking on Creative Thinking," *Journal of Experimental Psychology*, Volume 40, Number 4 (2014): 1142–52, www.apa.org/pubs/journals/releases/xlm-a0036577.pdf.

123 "Studies show that our brains": Kate Thorn, "This New Study Says Music Makes You Smarter," Brit + Co, August 3, 2015, www.brit.co/music-makes-you-smarter/.

124 Highlight on Your Hobbies: Summaries on calligraphy, chess, dancing, and learning a language informed by Barrie Davenport, "Forty Hobbies for Women to Strengthen Your Brain and Body," www.liveboldandbloom.com, liveboldandbloom.com/09/self-improvement/ hobbies-for-women.

125 "Learning to take care of yourself": Dr. Lauren Hazzouri, "Self Care Is Not Selfish," ivankatrump.com, June 29, 2015, www.ivankatrump.com/self-care-lauren -hazzouri/.

125 Treat yourself in the same way: Ibid.

125 "Start by accepting": Ibid.

126 Tempted to clean your house: Ibid.

126 ask, "Would this be okay for X?": Ibid.

126 "In the midst of movement": Deepak Chopra, "Deepak Quotes," deepakchopra .com, March 14, 2014.

126 "Tranquility comes from": "Five Tips for Staying Calm and Collected at Work," ivankatrump.com, March 25, 2016, www.ivankatrump.com/stress-management -dorit-jaffe/.

126 "Stressing over a situation": Ibid.

126 "You have clearer thoughts": Ibid.

127 Jaffe recommends the following: Ibid.

127 "We know exercise is good": Jessica Hullinger, "Why Do We Pace When We're Thinking?," mentalfloss.com, May 28, 2015, mentalfloss.com/article/64404 /why-do-we-pace-when-were-thinking.

127 "Think of this daily ritual": "Five Tips for Staying Calm and Collected at Work."

127 "gives you the clarity": Ibid.

127 "Take twenty minutes": Ibid.

127 "When you become overwhelmed": Ibid.

128 "Get a massage": Ibid.

CHAPTER FIVE: TIP THE SCALE—LET GO OF BALANCE BY SEIZING MEANINGFUL MOMENTS

130 "A true balance": Michael Thomas Sunnarborg, *21 Keys to Work/Life Balance: Unlock Your Full Potential* (distributed by Creative Consulting, 2013), 10.

131 "When we learn": Dr. Lauren Hazzouri, "It's Time to Learn How to Live," ivankatrump.com, May 13, 2015, www.ivankatrump.com/learn-how-to-live/.

133 "It's important to have": Angela Benton, original interview, September 23, 2014.

133 "When you define yourself": Rosie Pope, "Five Ways to Be Pro Mom," ivankatrump .com, October 14, 2015, www.ivankatrump.com/five-ways-to-be-pro-mom-rosie -pope-2/.

133 in 2015 nearly two thirds: "Employment Characteristics of Families 2015," U.S. Department of Labor, Bureau of Labor Statistics, May 22, 2016, www.bls.gov /news.release/famee.htm.

134 "[Women] somehow wear": Rachel Blumenthal, original interview, September 23, 2014.

134 "The most important career decision": Anne-Marie Slaughter, *Unfinished Business: Women Men Work Family* (New York: Random House, 2015), 24.

134 Consider this scenario: Summarized and adapted, ibid., 202.

134 What are your deepest personal aspirations . . . Who do you hope to be: Summarized, ibid., 203.

134 Similarly . . . Do you want children: Summarized, ibid.

135 Once you find the courage . . . even if you aren't sure about having children: Summarized, ibid., 205.

135 "You must be sure": Slaughter, *Unfinished Business*, 24.

135 6,500 Harvard Business School grads: Ibid., 56; original study, Robyn Ely, Pamela Stone, and Colleen Ammerman, "Rethinking What You 'Know' About High-Achieving Women," *Harvard Business Review*, December 2014, hbr.org /2014/12/rethink-what-you-know-about-high-achieving-women.

135 "You need someone who adores you": Elizabeth Cronise McLaughlin, "We Become the Company We Keep," ivankatrump.com, September 2, 2015, www .ivankatrump.com/elizabeth-cronise-mclaughlin-company-we-keep/.

136 "Always strive to give": Dave Willis, DaveWillis.org.

136 Hanna Rosin calls "seesaw marriages": Hanna Rosin, *The End of Men: And the Rise of Women* (New York: Riverhead Books, 2012).

136 this shift in gender roles: Section adapted from Elizabeth Cronise McLaughlin, "The Rise of Primary Breadwinner Women," ivankatrump.com, January 11,

2016, www.ivankatrump.com/elizabeth-cronise-mclaughlin-rise-of-primary-bread
winner-women/.

137 "The best way to make room": Sheryl Sandberg, *Lean In: Women, Work, and the Will to Lead* (New York: Knopf, 2013), 126.

137 "The richest and fullest": Erik Erikson, quoted by Doris Kearns Goodwin, "Learning from Past Presidents," February 2008 www. tech.com/talks/doris -kearns-goodwin-on-learning-from-past-presidents.

138 "I don't remember making": Rosie Pope, "Career, Baby or Both?" ivankatrump .com, March 20, 2016, www.ivankatrump.com/career-baby-rosie-pope/.

138 Now, as a busy mother . . . come together: Ibid.

138 "This is what I know now, that I wish I had known then": Quotes in section from Pope, "Career, Baby or Both?"

140 Maternity Leave: A Primer: Adapted from "Five Ways to Prepare for Maternity Leave," ivankatrump.com, March 20, 2016, www.ivankatrump.com/maternity -leave-preparation-tips/.

141 Elizabeth Cronise McLaughlin says it's not necessary: Ibid.

141 recruiter Jennifer Lenkowsky suggests: Ibid.

142 "If you've been at home": Ibid.

143 "Don't drive yourself nuts": "Hot Mama: Michelle Kohanzo," ivankatrump.com, April 17, 2015, www.ivankatrump.com/michelle-kohanzo/.

143 "There is no such thing": Alain de Botton, quoted in Jenn Aubert, *Women Entrepreneur Revolution* (Indianapolis: Balboa Press, 2014), 162.

144 "Balance as a modern woman": "Hot Mama: Ali Larter," ivankatrump.com, April 21, 2015, www.ivankatrump.com/ali-larter/.

144 "My schedule was often": Slaughter, *Unfinished Business*, 20.

144 "Every morning I make a list": "Hot Mama: Christiane Lemieux," ivankatrump .com, April 22, 2015, www.ivankatrump.com/christiane-lemieux/.

145 when we "look under the hood": Shawn Achor, *The Happiness Advantage: The Seven Principles of Positive Psychology That Fuel Success and Performance at Work* (New York: Crown, 2010), 51.

145 "striving toward a good": Slaughter, *Unfinished Business*, 186.

145 Stanford professor Jennifer Aaker's work: Sandberg, *Lean In*, 138; Melanie Rudd, Jennifer Aaker, and Michael I. Norton, "Leave Them Smiling: How Small Acts Create More Happiness Than Large Acts," facultysb.stanford.edu /aaker/pages/documents/LeaveThemSmiling_RuddAakerNorton12-16-11.pdf.

145 "Instead of perfection": Sandberg, *Lean In*, 138–9.

146 "Working really hard for something": Slaughter, *Unfinished Business*, 69.

146 "In every senior job I've had": General Colin Powell with Tony Koltz, *It Worked for Me: In Life and Leadership* (New York: HarperCollins, 2012), 40.

147 "You can't have everything": Marissa Mayer, "How to Avoid Burnout: Marissa Mayer," Bloomberg, April 12, 2012, www.bloomberg.com/news/articles /2012-04-12/how-to-avoid-burnout-marissa-mayer.

147 Here's her advice on staying sane: All quotes from "Finding Balance, One Phase at a Time," ivankatrump.com, April 1, 2015, www.ivankatrump.com/rosie-pope -balance-life-phases/.

148 "From time to time": Joanna Barsh and Susie Cranston, *How Remarkable Women Lead: The Breakthrough Model for Work and Life* (New York: Crown Business, 2009), 112.

149 dubs "time macho": Slaughter, *Unfinished Business*, 66–7.

149 "Mr. Darman sometimes managed": Ibid, 67.

151 "it's bath time and bedtime": Elizabeth Cronise McLaughlin, "Five Ways to Be a Great Mom Even When You're Overworked," 40percentandrising.com,

January 6, 2015. 40percentandrising.com/2015/01/06/five-ways-to-be-a-great-mom-even-when-youre-overworked/.

151 "Unless there's an emergency": Ibid.

152 "we have a ground rule": Ibid.

152 "'No work, Mommy!'": Ibid.

152 When your brain is engaged: Heather Hatfield, "Power Down for Better Sleep," webmd.com, www.webmd.com/sleep-disorders/features/power-down-better-sleep#1.

152 People who exercise on workdays: "People Who Exercise on Workdays Suffer Less Stress, Are Happier and Are More Productive," www.dailymail.co.uk/news/article-1095783/People-exercise-work-days-happier-sufferstress-productive.html#ixzz3OtzT6Cyp; study originally published by University of Bristol, Department of Exercise, Nutrition & Health Sciences, in the *International Journal of Workplace Health Management*, Volume 1, Issue 3 (2008).

152 72 percent of participants: Ibid.

153 74 percent said: Ibid.

153 "We delight in the beauty": Maya Angelou, *Rainbow in the Cloud: The Wisdom and Spirit of Maya Angelou* (New York: Random House, 2014).

154 learning how to handle the feeling: Rosie Pope, "Six Tips for Going Back to Work Post-Baby," ivankatrump.com, May 22, 2016, www.ivankatrump.com/going-back-to-work-post-baby-rosie-pope/.

154 Rosie Pope weighs in: Ibid., all quotes in section.

155 Lenkowsky shares her top tips: All quotes from "The Return to the Workforce," ivankatrump.com, January 27, 2015, www.ivankatrump.com/return-to-the-workforce/.

157 "The secret is": As noted in Sandberg, *Lean In*, 139; original source, Mary C. Curtis, "There's More to Sheryl Sandberg's Secret," *Washington Post*, April 4, 2012, www.washingtonpost.com/blogs/she-the-people/post/theres-more-to-sheryl-sandbergs-secret/2012/04/04/gIQAGhZsvS_blog.html.

157 "It always seems impossible": Nelson Mandela, quoted in Kathryn and Ross Petras, *It Always Seems Impossible Until It's Done: Motivation for Dreamers and Doers* (New York: Workman Publishing Company, 2014), 166.

157 Cynthia Hogan, who "served": Sandberg, *Lean In*, 154.

157 A full twelve years later: Ibid., 154–55.

157 "Being forthright led": Ibid., 155.

158 "More and more, I am asked": Elizabeth Cronise McLaughlin, "Flextime: What You Need to Know," ivankatrump.com, October 23, 2015, www.ivankatrump.com/flextime-elizabeth-cronise-mclaughlin/.

158 Here's the advice McLaughlin gives: All quotes from ibid.

158 "flexible working is smart working": Richard Branson, "Flexible Working Is Smart Working," *Virgin*, February 3, 2015, www.virgin.com/richard-branson/flexible-working-is-smart-working.

160 "We like to give people": Richard Branson, "Give People the Freedom of Where to Work," *Virgin*, February 25, 2013, www.virgin.com/richard-branson/give-people-the-freedom-of-where-to-work.

161 "I have weekly check-ins": "Five Tips for Working Remotely," ivankatrump.com, June 5, 2016, www.ivankatrump.com/working-remotely-tips/.

161 "Commit to being responsive": Ibid.

161 "Technology has enabled us": Ibid.

161 "Anna and I share a to-do list": Ibid.

161 "We also share a calendar": Ibid.

162 "All companies can benefit": Maynard Webb, Business Performance Improvement Resource (Centre for Organisational Excellence Research [COER]);

Massey University, www.bpir.com/flexible-work-arrangements/menu-id-71/words
-of-wisdom.html.

162 "What you do makes a difference": Jane Goodall, official Twitter account,
twitter.com/janegoodallinst/status/790946408941559810.

162 For instance, Elizabeth Cronise McLaughlin recounts how Sallie Krawcheck:
McLaughlin, "Be a Great Mom Even When You're Overworked" original
source, Abigail Jones, "Sallie Krawcheck Wants to Take Women to the Top of
Business," *Newsweek*, December 23, 2014, www.newsweek.com/2015/01/02
/sallie-krawcheck-wants-take-women-top-business-294332.html.

164 "All these practices": Achor, *The Happiness Advantage*, 57.

164 "While we try to teach": Angela Schwindt, quoted in Allie Ochs, *Are You Fit to
Love?: A Radically Different Approach to Successful Relationships* (Beverly
Hills: Little Moose Press, 2003), 23.

165 "As human beings, our greatness lies": Mahatma Gandhi, quoted in Yogesh
Chadha, *Gandhi: A Life* (New York: John Wiley & Sons, 1997), vii.

165 Feiler shares how Stephen Covey adapted: Bruce Feiler, *The Secrets of Happy
Families: Improve Your Mornings, Tell Your Family History, Fight Smarter,
Go Out and Play, and Much More* (New York: William Morrow, 2013), 56.

165 The Feiler family's mission statement: Ibid., 69.

165 "you want your children to be truly happy": Ibid., 61.

166 Use these four questions: Ibid., 271.

166 "Make it authentic": Ibid.

167 "When we practice compassion": Elizabeth Cronise McLaughlin, "Five Ways to
Be a Great Role Model for Your Daughter—And Your Son," ivankatrump.com,
July 6, 2015, www.ivankatrump.com/be-a-great-role-model/.

167 "We need to look out": Sandberg, *Lean In*, 160.

168 "The message of this [female] model of leadership": Elizabeth Cronise McLaughlin, "The New Paradigm of Feminine Leadership—and What It Means for You,"
ivankatrump.com, December 7, 2015, www.ivankatrump.com/elizabeth-cronise
-mclaughlin-new-paradigm-feminine-leadership/.

CHAPTER SIX: LEAD WITH PURPOSE—CHANGING THE CONVERSATION AROUND WOMEN AND WORK

170 "Never doubt that a small group": Margaret Mead, quoted in Nancy Lutkehaus,
Margaret Mead: The Making of an American Icon (Princeton, NJ: Princeton
University Press, 2008), 4.

172 "Leading, however, means that others": Simon Sinek, *Start with Why: How Great
Leaders Inspire Everyone to Take Action* (New York: Portfolio, 2009), 85.

173 "It's not the size": Ibid., 90.

173 127-slide PowerPoint deck: Patty McCord, "How Netflix Reinvented HR," *Harvard Business Review*, January–February 2014, hbr.org/2014/01/how-netflix
-reinvented-hr.

174 "The best leader": Kevin Kruse, "100 Best Quotes on Leadership," *Forbes*,
October 16, 2012; www.forbes.com/sites/kevinkruse/2012/10/16/quotes-on
-leadership/#584418dd7106.

177 "Some leaders are born women": Geraldine Ferraro, "The Future of Women in
Politics," speech at the 92nd Street Y, New York, NY, February 20, 1991.

177 "European telecommunications giant Deutsche Telekom": Mika Brzezinski,
Knowing Your Value: Women, Money, and Getting What You Are Worth (New
York: Weinstein Books, 2012), 58.

177 "Taking on more women in management positions": Nicola Clark, "Goal at
Deutsche Telekom: More Women Managers," *New York Times*, March 15, 2010,

www.nytimes.com/2010/03/16/business/global/16quota.html?_r=0; Brzezinski, *Knowing Your Value*, 58.

178 Similarly, as Sheryl Sandberg and Adam Grant wrote: Sheryl Sandberg and Adam Grant, "How Men Can Succeed in the Boardroom and the Bedroom," *New York Times*, March 5, 2015, www.nytimes.com/2015/03/08/opinion/sunday /sheryl-sandberg-adam-grant-how-men-can-succeed-in-the-boardroom-and-the-bedroom.html?_r=0.

178 when firms pursued innovation: Cristian L. Dezso and David Gaddis Ross, "Does Female Representation in Top Management Improve Firm Performance? A Panel Data Investigation," *Strategic Management Journal*, Volume 33, Issue 9 (September 2012): 1072–89.

178 A study by the University of British Columbia's: Sarah Green Carmichael, "Boards with More Women Pay Less for Acquisitions," *Harvard Business Review*, December 20, 2013, hbr.org/2013/12/boards-with-more-women-pay-less-for -acquisitions; Brzezinski, *Knowing Your Value*, 58.

178 This very reason is why: Ibid.

178 a group of researchers at Carnegie Mellon: Bruce Feiler, *The Secrets of Happy Families: Improve Your Mornings, Tell Your Family History, Fight Smarter, Go Out and Play, and Much More* (New York: William Morrow, 2013), 122–23; original source, A. W. Woolley, C. F. Chabris, A. Pentland, N. Hashmi, and T. W. Malone, "Evidence for a Collective Intelligence Factor in the Performance of Human Groups," *Science*, October 29, 2010, www.chabris.com /Woolley2010a.pdf.

178 45 percent less frequently: Brad M. Barber and Terrance Odean, "Boys Will Be Boys: Gender, Overconfidence, and Common Stock Investment," *The Quarterly Journal of Economics*, Volume 116, Number 1 (February 2001): 261–92.

178 "researchers at Wellesley": Feiler, *The Secrets of Happy Families*, 123.

179 "On corporate boards": Sheryl Sandberg and Adam Grant, "Sheryl Sandberg on the Myth of the Catty Woman," *New York Times*, June 23, 2016, www .nytimes.com/2016/06/23/opinion/sunday/sheryl-sandberg-on-the-myth-of-the -catty-woman.html.

179 "If your actions inspire": John Quincy Adams, quoted in Pat Williams, *The Paradox of Power: A Transforming View of Leadership* (New York: Warner Books, 2002), 49.

179 "Leadership has little to do": Chris Guillebeau, *The Art of Non-Conformity: Set Your Own Rules, Live the Life You Want, and Change the World* (New York: Perigee, 2010), 128.

179 "leaders are the ones willing": Simon Sinek, *Leaders Eat Last* (New York: Portfolio, 2014), 66.

179 in 2012, scholars from MIT: Feiler, *The Secrets of Happy Families*, 30; original source, Alex "Sandy" Pentland, "The New Science of Building Great Teams," *Harvard Business Review*, April 2012, hbr.org/2012/04/the-new-science-of -building-great-teams.

180 "to create an environment in which great ideas can happen": Sinek, *Start with Why*, 99.

180 "Leadership requires people": Ibid., 28.

180 "Studies have found that the strength . . . reap the rewards": Shawn Achor, *The Happiness Advantage: The Seven Principles of Positive Psychology That Fuel Success and Performance at Work* (New York: Crown, 2010), 189.

180 "If you're a leader": Guillebeau, *The Art of Non-Conformity*, 128.

180 "Wherever you are in the pecking order": "Rachel Haot on Government + Tech," ivankatrump.com, November 6, 2014, www.ivankatrump.com/rachel-haot.

180 "If you hire people": Simon Sinek, "How Great Leaders Inspire Action," September 2009, 7:29, www.ted.com/talks/simon_sinek_how_great_leaders _inspire_action?language=en.

181 "When a WHY is clear": Sinek, *Start with Why*, 136.

181 "How Great Leaders Inspire Action": Summary of Simon Sinek's the Golden Circle informed by both *Start with Why*, 39–49, and www.ted.com/talks/simon_ sinek_how_great_leaders_inspire_action?language=en.

181 "When a company clearly communicates": Sinek, *Start with Why*, 54.

182 "people don't buy *what* you do": Ibid., 64.

182 Under Armour is another great example: David Aaker, "I Will vs. Just Do It: The Under Armour Success Story," www.prophet.com/thinking/2014/08 /i-will-vs-just-do-it-the-under-armour-success-story/.

182 As Kevin Plank, the founder: "The Sit-Down: Under Armour," *SportsBusiness Daily*, June 8, 2015, www.sportsbusinessdaily.com/Journal/Issues/2015/06 /08/People-and-Pop-Culture/Sit-Down.aspx.

183 "When you have a higher purpose": Joanna Barsh and Susie Cranston, *How Remarkable Women Lead: The Breakthrough Model for Work and Life* (New York: Crown Business, 2009), 50–51.

183 Culture Confab: Alice + Olivia: All quotes in this section from "Companies We Love: Alice and Olivia," ivankatrump.com, March 6, 2016, www.ivankatrump .com/women-friendly-office/.

184 Mah-Ze-Dahr is not just a bakery: "Take the Leap," ivankatrump.com, www .ivankatrump.com/umber-ahmad-mah-ze-dahr/.

186 "Entrepreneurs have a great ability": Tory Burch, "Tory Burch to Entrepreneurs: Embrace Change," interview with Kristine Hansen on *CNN Money*, June 24, 2011, money.cnn.com/2011/06/23/smallbusiness/Tory_Burch_small_business/.

187 "For me, being an entrepreneur means": Rachel Blumenthal, original interview, September 23, 2014.

187 "It's important to be willing": Sara Blakely, quoted in Kara Cutruzzula, "My Favorite Mistake: Spanx Founder Sara Blakely," *Newsweek*, May 7, 2012, 52.

187 "The glass ceiling": Erica Nicole, quoted in Natalie MacNeil, "Entrepreneur ship Is the New Women's Movement," *Forbes*, June 8, 2012.

188 In his book *Originals*, Adam Grant: Adam Grant, *Originals: How Non-Conformists Move the World* (New York: Viking, 2016).

188 the term "entrepreneur": Ibid., 14.

188 entrepreneurs who kept their day jobs: Ibid., 17; original study, Joseph Raffiee and Jie Feng, "Should I Quit My Day Job? A Hybrid Path to Entrepreneurship," *Academy of Management Journal*, 2014, 936–63.

188 "Having a sense of security": Ibid., 19.

188 "The only skills": James Altucher, *Choose Yourself: Be Happy, Make Millions, Live the Dream* (n.p.: James Altucher, 2013), 102.

188 "You may be working fourteen hours": Angela Benton, "Angela Benton on the Essentials of Entrepreneurship," www.ivankatrump.com/essentials-of-entre preneurship/.

188 "I had my oldest daughter": Angela Benton, original interview, September 23, 2014.

189 "Know what you're signing up for": "How to Manage Your Money While Starting a Business," ivankatrump.com, February 1, 2016, www.ivankatrump.com /finance-tips-entrepreneurs/.

189 "In the start-up": "Seven Tips for Entrepreneurial Moms," ivankatrump.com, May 22, 2016, www.ivankatrump.com/tips-new-moms-entrepreneurs/.

189 "I moved to the U.S.": Ibid.

190 "pairs busy individuals": Nicole Boyer, "10 Impressive Startups Founded by Women Entrepreneurs," *YFS Magazine*, May 5, 2016, yfsmagazine.com/2016

/05/05//10-impressive-startups-founded-by-female-entrepreneurs/. www.helloal
fred.com/.

190 "When I started my career": "How to Launch a Truly Disruptive Start-Up,"
ivankatrump.com, April 17, 2016, www.ivankatrump.com/marcela-sapone
-hello-alfred/.

190 "We've essentially created": Ibid.

191 "Find subject matter experts": Benton, "Angela Benton on the Essentials of Entrepreneurship."

192 "I had big career goals": "Seven Tips for Entrepreneurial Moms."

192 "Although you should set the mission": "Lauren Bush Lauren Is FEED-ing the
World," ivankatrump.com, January 28, 2015, www.ivankatrump.com/lauren
-bush-lauren-feed/.

193 "It was so eye-opening": Ibid.

193 "It was such a gift": Ibid.

193 "I graduated without a job": Ibid.

194 "It's key to have": "Seven Tips for Entrepreneurial Moms."

194 "Doing this communicates": "How to Launch a Truly Disruptive Start-Up."

194 "As an entrepreneur": Benton, "Angela Benton on the Essentials of Entrepreneurship."

194 "how you interpret rejection": "New Rules for Young Entrepreneurs," ivanka
trump.com, April 5, 2015, www.ivankatrump.com/ali-inspiralized-entrepreneur
-advice/.

195 "developing my own spiralizer": Ibid.

195 "Let doubt make you more resilient": "How to Launch a Truly Disruptive Start-Up."

195 "Potential investors often doubt": "Seven Tips for Entrepreneurial Moms."

195 "Schedule time for the unschedulable": Benton, original interview, September
23, 2014.

196 "If you really want to start something": "How to Manage Your Money While
Starting a Business."

196 "I taught myself": "New Rules for Young Entrepreneurs."

196 As Ashley Wayman . . . puts it: All quotes and information in this section from
"Five Qualities to Look for in a Business Partner," May 15, 2016, www.ivanka
trump.com/petit-peony-business-partner/.

199 "I was raised by a single mom": "How to Manage Your Money While Starting
a Business."

199 "Not many entrepreneurs": Ibid.

199 "Separate your personal and business": Ibid.

200 "When you do get paid": Ibid.

200 "In addition to my general checking account": Ibid.

200 "I have four accounts": Ibid.

201 A Venture Capitalist's Perspective: All content and quotes in this section are
from an e-mail to Sarah Warren.

201 "Women never feel we have the luxury": Benton, "Angela Benton on the Essentials of Entrepreneurship."

202 "As women, we tend to be": "Seven Tips for Entrepreneurial Moms."

202 "As a freelancer, you need to take care": Abbey Drucker, "Abbey Drucker on the
Business of Art," www.ivankatrump.com/abbey-drucker-photographer/.

203 "When the going gets tough": Dr. Samantha Boardman, from a brochure distributed to the Ivanka Trump team.

203 Suzanne Kobasa calls becoming "stress hardy": S. Kobasa, S. Maddi, and S.
Kahn, "Hardiness and Health: A Prospective Study," *Journal of Personality
and Social Psychology*, Volume 42 (January 1982): 168–77, dx.doi.org/10.1037
/0022-3514.42.1.168.

203 "The good news": Boardman, brochure.

203 Kobasa's three C's: S. Kobasa et al., "Hardiness and Health."

203 "They recognize that they choose": Boardman, brochure.

203 optimists "also cope better": Achor, *Happiness Advantage*, 98.

203 "Happiness can improve our physical health": Ibid., 42–3.

203 "Companies and leaders": Ibid., 43.

204 "I think we, as women who work": Nadine Burke Harris, original interview September 23, 2014.

205 "The equality we fought for": Betty Friedan, *The Second Stage: With a New Introduction* (Cambridge, MA: Harvard University Press, 1998), 29.

205 "'greatest runner of all time'": Michael Shermer, "The Greatest Runner of All Time, *Wall Street Journal*, June 3, 2016, www.wsj.com/articles/the-greatest-runner -of-all-time-1464981368.

205 "To believe a thing impossible": Ashton Applewhite and Tripp Evans, *And I Quote: The Definitive Collection of Quotes, Sayings, and Jokes for the Contemporary Speechmaker* (New York: St. Martin's, 1992), 28.

205 "The positive thinker sees the invisible": Winston Churchill, *My Early Life: 1874–1904* (New York: Scribner, 1996).

206 half the world's population: Kristen Bellstrom, "Why 2015 Was a Terrible Year to Be a Fortune 500 CEO," *Fortune*, December 23, 2015, fortune.com/2015 /12/23/2015-women-fortune-500-ceos/.

206 Research has shown that: "To Close the Gender Gap, What Needs to Change— Women or the System?" knowledge@Wharton, March 27, 2013, knowledge .wharton.upenn.edu/article/to-close-the-gender-gap-what-needs-to-change -women-or-the-system/.

206 In the last fifteen years: Candida G. Brush and Patricia G. Greene, "Women Entrepreneurs 2014: Bridging the Gender Gap in Venture Capital," www .babson.edu/newsevents/babson-news/Pages/140930-venture-capital-funding -women-entrepreneurs-study.aspx.

207 venture capital networks are dominated by male investors: Jason Greenberg and Ethan Mollick, "Activist Choice Homophily and the Crowdfunding of Female Founders," *Administrative Science Quarterly*, October 1, 2016, papers .ssrn.com/sol3/papers.cfm?abstract_id=2462254.

207 Some institutions are taking notice: CNN Money, "Goldman Sachs: Investing in Female Entrepreneurs Is Smart Economics," June 15, 2016, money.cnn .com/video/news/2016/06/15/goldman-sachs-10000 women.cnnmoney/.

208 The "overwhelm was never just": Brigid Schulte, *Overwhelmed: Work, Love, and Play When No One Has the Time* (New York: Farrar, Straus & Giroux, 2014), 95–96.

208 "'Fixing the women's problem'": Quoted in Slaughter, *Unfinished Business*, 59; from Debora L. Spar, *Wonder Women: Sex, Power, and the Quest for Perfection* (New York: Farrar, Straus and Giroux, 2013), 201.

208 Part of "fixing the organization": Adam Grant and Sheryl Sandberg, "Madam C.E.O., Get Me a Coffee," *New York Times*, February 6, 2015, www.nytimes .com/2015/02/08/opinion/sunday/sheryl-sandberg-and-adam-grant-on-women -doing-office-housework.html.

209 Kunal Modi, former copresident: Slaughter, *Unfinished Business*, 132.

209 "Raising children and running a household": Ibid.

210 "The shift in gender roles": McLaughlin, "The Rise of Primary Breadwinner Women."

211 I Am a Woman Who: Ivanka Trump, "The Trump Plan Will Help Working Mothers," *Wall Street Journal*, September 13, 2016, www.wsj.com/articles/the -trump-plan-will-help-working-mothers-1473803187.